Books by Dominique D'Ermo

THE CHEF'S DESSERT COOKBOOK	1975
THE MODERN PASTRY CHEF'S GUIDE TO PROFESSIONAL BAKING	1962

THE CHEF'S DESSERT COOKBOOK

Dominique D'Ermo

THE CHEF'S DESSERT COOKBOOK

New York
ATHENEUM
1976

Library of Congress catalog card number 75–13679
ISBN 0–689–10691–2
Published simultaneously in Canada by McClelland and Stewart Ltd.
Manufactured in the United States of America by
H. Wolff, New York
Designed by Kathleen Carey
First Edition

To Ed and Myrna Snider,

WITH MANY THANKS

Foreword

The judgment of any meal is affected greatly by the lingering impression left by the dessert course.

In this book many outstanding creations of the French classic cuisine are presented along with a wide range of popular American-born recipes, some used by professional chefs and some originated by intrepid "amateurs" who have parted with their secret recipes—only in exchange for others equally valuable.

Every ingredient listed in this book is available in any food store in the United States. All recipes have been tested for accuracy and performance. Nevertheless, practice and perseverance are necessary for complete mastery of the chemistry of baking.

To my readers I wish success, knowing that the creative diversion and compliments received for a job well done will be a well-deserved reward.

Acknowledgments

The preparation of this book has been facilitated by the achievements of many people—including the customers and friends of Dominique's restaurant who divulged some of their secret recipes.

My appreciation and thanks to Bernard Baudrand, Head Chef at Dominique's, for his valuable suggestions and to Judith Kern, editor at Atheneum, for her patience and understanding.

Contents

THE CHEF'S DESSERT COOKBOOK

Preface

KITCHEN UTENSILS FOR BAKING

Many of the following items are a "must," others *nice* to have on hand; choose according to your needs and budget.

A word of advice—augment your equipment gradually as your experience and "savoir faire" increase. Remember that your ancestors possessed far fewer utensils and yet produced delectable and fascinating desserts.

ESSENTIAL UTENSILS FOR BAKING:

Baking sheet pans 6 x 6, 8 x 8 and 10 x 12
Cake pans (9" round)
Can opener
Cast iron or copper skillet
Cookie cutter
Corkscrew
Custard or pudding cups
Doughnut cutter
Egg beater
Flour sifter
Forks
Grater and fruit squeezer
Knives

Mixing spoons (wood and metal; one large and one small of each)
Muffin pans
One set of mixing bowls
Oven thermometer (if stove is not equipped with one)
Pastry bag with assorted tubes
Pastry blender
Pastry brush
Pie plates (9″ round)
Rolling pin
Rubber scraper
Spatula
Standard measuring cups and spoons
Strainer
Wire whip
Wood cutting board

OTHER UTENSILS "NICE" TO HAVE

Apple corer
Assorted sets of fancy cutters
Cake tester
Candy or sugar thermometer
Colander
Cookie press
Deep-fat-frying thermometer
Earthenware dishes and soufflé molds
Electric blender
Electric ice cream freezer
Electric mixer
Electric timer
Frying pans (large and small)
Ice cube crusher
Nut cracker
Scissors
Waffle iron

GLOSSARY OF BAKING TERMS

BAKE To cook in indirect heat, usually in an oven.

BATTER A mixture of ingredients such as butter, shortening and any other elements called for in the recipe.

BEAT To blend ingredients in a rapid circular motion in order to introduce air into them. A wire whip, rotary beater or electric mixer are used.

BEAT UNTIL LIGHT AND FLUFFY If beating whole eggs, beat until eggs are thick or the consistency of whipped cream. If beating the yolks of the eggs alone, beat until the yolks are thick and pale in color.

BEAT UNTIL STIFF BUT NOT DRY To beat egg whites, sometimes adding sugar gradually until the eggs hold their shape when the batter is lifted from the bowl. (For detailed instructions on how to beat egg whites properly, see page 14)

BLANCHED A process of scalding nuts or fruits by dipping in hot water so that the skin may be removed easily.

BLEND THOROUGHLY To mix and combine several ingredients until well integrated.

BOIL To heat any liquid to the boiling point.

BOILING POINT The degree of temperature at which a liquid bubbles. For water, 212 degrees F. or 100 degrees C. (at sea level).

BRUSH To spread evenly, usually with a brush.

CARAMELIZE To heat sugar slowly until it is melted and brown in color.

CHILL To cool a mixture until cold but not frozen.

CHILL UNTIL SET To cool a mixture until it jells.

CHILL UNTIL STARTING TO SET OR UNTIL ALMOST SET To cool a mixture until it mounds slightly when dropped from a spoon. If the mixture has passed this stage and become too firm, place the bowl in warm water for one minute or so and stir rapidly to loosen the ingredients.

CHOP To cut into fine pieces or to shred with the help of a knife or chopper.

CLARIFIED BUTTER Butter melted over slow heat or over hot water without stirring. Do not allow butter to sizzle. Sediments will remain at the bottom. Pour carefully, leaving all solid matter at the bottom of the pan.

COAT To spread the entire surface of a food with a layer of cream, flour, sugar, etc.

COAT SPOON The point at which a cooking mixture forms a thin film on the spoon. Dip the spoon into the mixture and remove. Let the liquid run off it. The spoon should remain entirely covered with a thin layer of the mixture. If the spoon comes out clean, the mixture is not ready and should remain over the heat for an additional period of time.

COMBINE To mix ingredients thoroughly.

CORE To remove the core from a fruit such as an apple, pear, etc.

CREAM To soften ingredients.

CREAM TOGETHER To work and blend ingredients together until soft. In most cases this applies to butter, shortening and sugar.

CREAM UNTIL LIGHT To work or beat ingredients until soft, allowing enough air into the elements to form a light mixture.

CUT-IN To mix shortening with dry ingredients using a pastry blender or the tips of your fingers.

DICE To cut into small cubes, usually less than ½ inch square.

DISSOLVE To separate dry ingredients into particles for complete absorption in a liquid.

DOT To place small bits of butter, fat or cheese over the top of food.

DREDGE To sprinkle thoroughly with a dry substance such as flour, sugar, etc.

DUST To sprinkle lightly with flour, sugar, etc.

EGG WASH Mixture of whole eggs, milk, yolks, etc. depending upon the color intensity desired for a crust or outer layer. The most frequently used egg wash is made up of a combination of whole eggs lightly beaten with a fork or small whip, with enough milk added for a mixture that may be brushed on. If a stronger wash is needed, use only yolks instead of whole eggs. Milk egg wash is a very light wash made up of ⅔ whole eggs and ⅓ milk.

FLOURED Dusted or sprinkled with a thin coat of flour.

FOLD IN To add ingredients gently without loss of air. Usually accomplished with a spatula, large spoon, rubber scraper, etc. To fold beaten egg whites into a batter, pile all the beaten egg whites on top of the batter at once and proceed carefully and gently to blend the ingredients together by cutting down to the bottom of the mixture and then upward until a perfect blending is reached.

FRY To cook in hot, deep fat.

GARNISH To decorate (for eye appeal) with whipped cream, butter cream, candies, fruits, etc.

GLAZE To obtain a glossy finish by using a thin coating of sugar icing, fruit syrup, etc.

GRATE To tear food such as fruit peel, nuts, etc. into small shreds.

GRIND To crush food into small particles.

HALVE To separate into two equal parts.

HOT WATER BATH The double-boiler principle on a large scale; a deep pan filled with water and placed over heat until the water simmers or reaches an approximate temperature of 160 degrees F. Widely used to warm large or several small pots to prevent direct contact with heat.

IGNITE To place a long lighted match on warm alcohol to burn it. (See Flambé desserts, page 205)

KNEAD To work to a smooth consistency using the heel of your palm.

MACERATE To soften ingredients by placing them in liquid, syrup or alcohol. (Same as marinate.)

MASK To cover entirely with icing, frosting, sauce, etc.

MELT To change from a solid to a liquid state through heating.

MERINGUE Egg whites beaten with sugar to a stiff consistency.

PEEL To remove or strip off the skin or rind.

PINCH Approximately ⅛ teaspoon or the amount of the ingredient that can be held between the thumb and forefinger.

PREHEAT To heat equipment to a desired temperature before baking or cooking. This usually requires turning on the oven 15 to 20 minutes beforehand.

POACH To cook gently in syrup or liquid, keeping the temperature just below the boiling point, to maintain the original shape and texture of the food.

PURÉE To pass ingredients through a fine sieve.

ROLL OUT To spread onto a surface with a rolling pin.

SCALD To heat a liquid just to the boiling point or until bubbles appear around edges of the pan. DO NOT BOIL.

SET To obtain stiffness from a soft or liquid state.

SIFT To pass dry ingredients through a sifter.

SIMMER To boil gently; the surface of the water rolls. Just below the boiling point.

SOAK To place ingredients into liquid until absorbed.

SPRINKLE To dust dry ingredients onto the surface of a food.

STIR To mix gently using a circular motion.

WHIP To beat to a froth with an egg beater, fork, whisk or electric beater.

SPICES

When buying spices, purchase premium quality brands. Buy them only as needed. Always keep them well covered because they lose their flavor easily. Long exposure to moisture and heat should be avoided. Spices should be measured accurately as their pleasant flavors can become very distasteful if used to excess.

ALLSPICE Native to the West Indies. The flavor compares with a blend of cinnamon, nutmeg and cloves. Used in cakes, pies and cookies.

ANISE A tiny oval seed of the parsley family—has a licorice taste. Native to Spain, the Middle East and Mexico. Used in pastries such as anise cookies, *springerle,* etc.

CARAWAY Tiny oval seeds widely distributed throughout the world. Used in bread, cheese spreads, etc.

CINNAMON The oldest spice of all! The bark of a tree that grows in Indonesia, India and China. It comes in pieces or is ground. Widely used in desserts, pastries, pudding, cookies, etc.

CLOVES Dried flower buds of a tropical tree of the myrtle family. Used in cookies, puddings, etc.

GINGER The dried root of a tropical plant. Native to India. Used in cakes, pies, puddings, etc.

MACE The husks of the nutmeg, ground to a fine powder.

NUTMEG The aromatic seed of a tree originally from East Asia. Its husks are called MACE. Widely used in pies and cakes. Also used in cookies.

POPPY SEEDS Tiny round blue-black seeds of the poppy plant. Used in breads and rolls and sometimes in cookies.

SESAME SEEDS Small white seeds derived from the pods of a plant. They grow in the Middle East and South America. Used for bread and cookies.

LEAVENING AGENTS, FLOURS AND YEAST

LEAVENING AGENTS

BAKING POWDER Three types of baking powder are available:

1. *Double-Acting Baking Powder:* Produces a slow reaction, releasing approximately ⅓ of its carbon dioxide at room temperature, the rest on heating.
2. *Phosphate Baking Powder:* Reacts very slowly. Heat is required to release its power.
3. *Tartrate Baking Powder:* Reacts very quickly as soon as liquid is added.

Unless otherwise specified, recipes in this book may satisfactorily be prepared with any of the preceding baking powders. Remember, all baking powders must be accurately measured.

BAKING SODA Used mostly in cakes containing cocoa or chocolate. Rising will start during the heating process. *Measure accurately.*

FLOURS

In the recipes throughout this book, I have specified the type of flour to be used. The following descriptions should assist you in purchasing the proper flour.

ALL-PURPOSE FLOUR Also called family flour—A blend of hard and soft wheat flours. All-purpose flour can be used successfully in all types of home baking. *Always sift flour* before adding to any ingredients.

BREAD FLOUR Flour with a hard gluten content, made from hard wheat. Generally used for yeast dough. *Always sift flour* before adding to any ingredients.

CAKE FLOUR Made from selected soft wheat. A very finely milled flour which causes cakes to become fragile in appearance and smooth in texture. *Always sift flour* before adding to any ingredients.

CORN MEAL Coarsely ground kernels of corn, available in white or yellow.

PASTRY FLOUR Made of soft wheat, not as finely milled as cake flour. *Always sift flour* before adding to any ingredients.

BUCKWHEAT FLOUR Milled from buckwheat kernels. *Do not sift.*

RICE FLOUR Milled from raw rice. *Always sift flour* before adding to any other ingredients.

RYE FLOUR Milled from rye seeds. *Do not sift.*

SELF-RISING FLOUR Milled from winter or soft wheat, depending upon its origin. Has salt and leavening added. Follow recipes or instructions attached to the package.

WHOLE WHEAT FLOUR As the name indicates, such flour contains all the ingredients of the cleaned, whole wheat grain. *Do not sift.*

YEAST

The two kinds of yeast available are as follows:

DRY YEAST This type of yeast can be kept for months without any refrigeration. The label on the package carries a date indicating length of time it can be kept.

One package of dry yeast will form the same leavening reaction as one package of compressed or fresh yeast.

COMPRESSED OR FRESH YEAST Packaged in quantities of ⅔ ounce or ⅗ ounce. Will keep in good condition for about 2 weeks under refrigeration. The freshness of the yeast can be determined quickly by the coloring. If grayish, with a tendency toward browning, the yeast is no longer of any use.

Soften and *dissolve* yeast in liquid as explained in the individual recipe.

MILK AND CREAM

PASTEURIZED MILK Milk that has been heated to a temperature of 131–158 degrees F. for a period of at least 30 minutes and immediately cooled to 50 degrees F. or less. The purpose of this process is to destroy undesirable bacteria.

EVAPORATED MILK Milk from which half the water has been removed through a process of heating and then canned.

CONDENSED MILK Milk concentrated by evaporation, then sweetened.

BUTTERMILK The liquid remaining after the fat has been removed from sweet or sour milk or cream.

HEAVY CREAM Cream containing not less than 35% butterfat. (For detailed instructions on how to whip cream properly, see page 11.)

LIGHT CREAM Cream containing less than 30% butterfat.

SOUR CREAM Cream which is soured by an addition of lemon juice, vinegar or by the action of lactic acid on bacteria.

SOUR MILK Milk that has been soured by the same process as sour cream. One tablespoon of vinegar will sour one cup of milk.

HOW TO WHIP CREAM

1. Heavy cream contains at least 35% to 42% butterfat and if properly beaten should more than double in quantity.
2. Two tablespoons of sugar to each cup of heavy cream should be adequate to sweeten. Too much sugar will alter the taste and soften the cream.
3. Whipped cream must always be kept refrigerated.
4. Heavy cream that is at least 24 hours old will whip more quickly and retain its firm shape for a longer period of time.

5. Chill but *do not freeze* heavy cream before whipping.
6. To beat cream properly, place *chilled* cream in a deep *chilled* bowl and whip with a *chilled* wire whip, rotary beater or electric mixer. (If an electric mixer is used, place the bowl and beaters in the refrigerator for approximately 30 minutes prior to beating. Use medium speed.) Be extremely careful to avoid overbeating; the instant the cream maintains its shape it is ready. Even a few additional turns may result in a buttery and curdled cream. Begin by beating slowly and gradually increase speed until cream reaches the consistency of a thick shaving cream.
7. During the hot summer months, I recommend beating cream over crushed ice or cold water. Cream beaten in a warm place, or an overbeaten cream, will have a tendency to curdle because the fat will melt and separate from the milk.
8. Cream can be whipped in advance and stored in the refrigerator, but after a period of time it has a tendency to soften; a slight rewhipping prior to use will restore it to its stiff consistency.

Note: Various flavorings, such as vanilla or coffee extracts, etc., may be added to the whipped cream, but the most recommended and exquisite flavoring is vanilla sugar. See the following recipe:

VANILLA SUGAR

Cut a vanilla bean into 3 long pieces; mix well with 1 pound of fine granulated sugar. Store the vanilla and sugar in a tightly sealed jar. In a few days the delicate flavor of the vanilla will permeate the sugar. Replace the old vanilla bean with a fresh one about once every 6 weeks.

TO WHIP CREAM WITH AN ELECTRIC BLENDER

Pour no more than 1 cup heavy cream into a chilled blender and close cover. Turn to medium speed and beat for 30 seconds, flicking the motor off and on every 5 seconds or so. Remove the cover and check the consistency of the cream. It should appear to hold its shape. Add flavoring and sugar. Flick motor on and off until the whipped cream is thick. *Do not overbeat.* A few additional turns may result in a buttery and curdled cream.

SUGAR AND OTHER SWEETENING AGENTS

Brown sugar Its color is derived from the molasses and other substances it contains. The higher the percentage of molasses and other substances, the darker the color will be.

Light brown sugar Contains less molasses than brown sugar.

To avoid lumps, keep brown sugar and light brown sugar in airtight containers.

Granulated sugar and brown sugar Refined into tiny crystals from either sugar cane or sugar beets.

Fine granulated sugar Smaller crystals than granulated sugar. Will dissolve faster than regular granulated sugar.

Powdered sugar Finer crystals than any granulated sugar. *Always sift* before adding to other ingredients.

XXXX sugar or confectioners sugar Powdered sugar which has been reduced to the same consistency as flour. To avoid lumps, keep confectioners sugar in an airtight container. *Always sift* before adding to other ingredients.

Honey A sweetening agent of delicate flavor obtained from natural sources. Its use results in softer and chewier cakes or cookies.

Molasses A thick brownish liquid derived from the refining of granulated sugar. The lighter the color, the sweeter the molasses.

Glucose A mixture of thick consistency composed of dextrose and gum made from starch. Used as a moisture retainer and widely employed in the making of candy and icing.

Corn syrup A thick syrup derived from starch. Its uses are varied.

THE COOKING OF SUGAR

1. The desired proportion is approximately ½ cup water to 1 cup sugar.
2. Always use very clean utensils; copper or heavy cast metal pans are highly recommended. Pans should be deep enough to allow room for boiling.
3. Start boiling the sugar slowly; stir occasionally with a wooden spoon. When the sugar is well dissolved, increase the heat to maximum strength and with a flat brush dipped in water from time to

time brush the sides of the pan. This will prevent the sugar from graining. Remove the scum that forms when the sugar boils with a flat skimmer. When the sugar reaches the desired temperature, remove immediately from the heat and place the hot pan in cold water if necessary to prevent any further cooking.

STAGES IN THE BOILING OF SUGAR

There are many definitions used for the various stages in the boiling of sugar. For example: soft ball, small crack, hard crack, etc., and they all tend to denote a gradual and steady evaporation of water during the boiling process. A candy thermometer should always be available and placed in the sugar to observe the exact stage or temperature of the syrup.

Another way to determine the proper stage in the boiling of sugar is to dip your finger first in ice water, then into the hot syrup and back quickly into the ice water. The consistency of the sugar that remains on your finger will help you to determine the temperature of the sugar at that particular moment. This, of course, requires a little experience.

European pastry chefs very seldom use a thermometer and seem to prefer taking the risk of burning their fingers. I myself recommend the use of a thermometer for greater accuracy and, shall we say, less risk!

Another method is to spoon out a little hot syrup, drop it into cold water and observe the result. The characteristics of the sugar at a given temperature or stage will correspond to the temperature range indicated on a candy thermometer.

THREAD 230 degrees F.–236 degrees F. Syrup will spin a thread when dropped from a spoon.

SOFT BALL 235 degrees F.–240 degrees F. Syrup will form a soft ball when dropped into cold water but will lose its shape when removed from water.

HARD BALL 250 degrees F.–265 degrees F. Syrup will form a hard ball when dropped into cold water and will remain the same consistency when removed from the water.

SOFT CRACK 270 degrees F.–290 degrees F. Syrup will harden quickly in cold water and break when crushed between your fingers.

HARD CRACK 295 degrees F.–312 degrees F. Syrup will harden quickly in cold water and will not stick to your teeth when chewed.

CARAMEL 320 degrees F.–348 degrees F. Sugar will begin to turn a golden color and quickly become black and useless.

Caramel is also prepared by stirring dry sugar (without any water) over direct slow heat. Sugar will start melting at 320 degrees F. At about 340 degrees F. the caramel color and flavor will appear and the sugar should be removed from the heat immediately. Bear in mind that the sugar will continue to brown in the hot pan even after it is removed from the heat, so take precautions.

HOW TO BEAT EGG WHITES

1. Utensils used for beating egg whites must be thoroughly cleaned and free from any particles of grease.
2. The eggs must be separated carefully, making sure that no yolk-particles remain in the whites.
3. In order to produce a greater volume, egg whites should be kept at room temperature for at least one hour prior to beating.
4. First stage or *soft peak:* when air is added to the egg whites through the beating process, the whites will expand and become fluffy and creamy. If the recipe calls for sugar, this is the point at which it should be added *gradually*.
5. Second stage or *medium peak:* the mixture will form rounded glossy peaks when the batter is lifted from the bowl. Egg whites at this stage hold their shape and are *stiff but not dry*. This is the stage I suggest you use every time egg whites have to be folded into a soft batter (chiffon pies, mousses, soufflés, puddings, chiffon cakes, etc.).
6. Third stage or *stiff peak:* any continued beating after the second stage will result in *stiffer* and *larger* peaks. This is the stage generally used for the making of meringue, pie topping, frosting, etc.
7. Any further additions of sugar or other products into the beaten egg whites should be done gently and carefully or by folding* ingredients to be added with a flat skimmer or large spatula to avoid breaking the fragile air cells which have been beaten into the whites.
8. Continued beating in excess of the three stages described above will merely result in dry and useless egg whites.

9. An electric mixer, rotary beater or wire whip are the necessary tools for beating egg whites successfully.

* *Note:* To fold beaten egg whites into a batter: Pile all whites *on top* of the batter *at once* and proceed to blend gently. Cut down to the bottom of the mixture and then return in an upward motion until a perfect blending is achieved. *Do not overmix.*

ABOUT NUTS

HOW TO SALT NUTS
(*i.e. almonds, walnuts, pecans, hazelnuts, etc.*)

Roast the nuts to a golden brown in a moderate oven at 400 degrees F. Cool. Rub the nuts thoroughly with slightly beaten egg white (1 egg white for every 2 pounds of nuts). Dust with salt, shake well and return to a 300-degree F. oven for approximately 10 minutes or until dry. Store in a tightly closed jar.

Note: Melted butter can be substituted for egg white.

HOW TO REMOVE THE SKIN FROM ALMONDS
(*Blanching*)

Cover the nuts with boiling water and let soak for about 5 minutes or until the skin loosens. Drain and remove the skin with your fingers.

HOW TO REMOVE THE SKIN FROM HAZELNUTS

Place the hazelnuts in a 425-degree F. oven for about 10 minutes. Remove from the heat and rub nuts over a rough mesh sifter or strainer.

HOW TO MEASURE

Measuring correctly is important. All the recipes in this book have been tested with *standard measuring cups and spoons, and all our measurements are level.*

FLOUR If a recipe calls for *sifted* flour, sift it onto a piece of paper and spoon the sifted flour into a measuring cup. Do not pack the flour. Level the excess with a straight-edged knife. Do not shake the cup to level it off and do not sift flour directly into the measuring cup. If the recipe *does not* call for sifted flour, simply spoon the flour from the bag into the measuring cup. Do not shake the cup to level it off. Follow instructions outlined in the recipe. You may have to sift the flour *after* it is measured. All recipes have been carefully tested; however, a little more or less flour may be necessary, depending upon the quality of flour available.

BAKING POWDER, SALT, SPICES, ETC. I stress the accurate use of these ingredients because an incorrect amount, even to a slight degree, can mean failure. One pinch is as much as can be taken between the tip of the finger and the thumb. One dash is less than ⅛ teaspoon. Other measurements are level.

EGGS Eggs vary in size. All recipes were tested with large size eggs. To divide one egg in half, beat the egg, measure it, then divide.

GRANULATED SUGAR AND CONFECTIONERS SUGAR If lumpy, sift before spooning into measuring cup; level off with a straight-edged knife.

BROWN SUGAR If lumpy, roll with a rolling pin and sift. Spoon into the measuring cup. Pack the sugar with the back of a spoon or spatula just enough to hold together when unmolded from the cup.

GRANULATED BROWN SUGAR Granulated brown sugar will work only in recipes calling for it specifically.

LIQUIDS For accurate measurements, pour the liquid into a cup and place the cup on a flat surface. Hold at eye level to read. Grease the inside of the cup when measuring molasses, honey, syrup, etc. to keep ingredients from sticking to the sides.

AN ACCURATE METHOD OF MEASURING BUTTER OR SHORTENING

The water displacement method is the simplest and most accurate method for measuring butter and bulk shortening.

First, pour the proper amount of cold water (according to the following table) into the measuring cup. *Second,* add the butter or shortening until the water reaches the one-cup level.

BERRIES: 1 pint of berries equals approximately 1¾ cups.

BAKING POWDER: 1 ounce of baking powder equals approximately 3½ tablespoons.

BREAD CRUMBS: 3½ ounces of bread crumbs equal approximately 1 cup.

BUTTER: 1 pound of butter equals 2 cups. ¼ pound equals 8 tablespoons or ½ cup.

CHEESE: ½ pound American Cheddar cheese equals 2 cups of grated cheese. ½ pound cottage cheese equals 1 cup. ½ pound cream cheese equals 1 cup.

CHOCOLATE: 1 ounce equals 1 square.

CINNAMON: 1 ounce equals 4 tablespoons.

CORN MEAL: 1 pound equals approximately 3 cups.

CORNSTARCH: 4½ ounces equal 1 cup.

CREAM: ½ pint equals 1 cup unwhipped; ½ pint equals 2 cups whipped.

EGGS: 1 U.S. large grade egg equals approximately 2 ounces.
1 U.S. large egg-white equals approximately 1 ounce or 2 tablespoons.
1 U.S. large egg-yolk equals approximately ½ ounce or 1 tablespoon.
5 whole eggs equal 1 cup.
8 to 10 egg whites equal 1 cup.
12 to 14 egg yolks equal 1 cup.

FLOUR: *All-purpose flour or family flour:*
1 cup of all-purpose flour *sifted* equals 3⅞ ounces.
1 cup of all-purpose flour *unsifted* equals 4¼ ounces.
Bread flour:
1 cup of *sifted* bread flour equals 4 ounces.
1 cup of *unsifted* bread flour equals 4½ ounces.
Cake flour:
1 cup of *sifted* cake flour equals 3⅜ ounces.
1 cup of *unsifted* cake flour equals 3⅞ ounces.

HONEY: 1 cup equals approximately 12 ounces.

LEMON JUICE: 1 lemon produces approximately 2½ tablespoons.

LEMON RIND, GRATED: 1 lemon equals 2 teaspoons.

OIL: 1 cup equals approximately 7¾ ounces.

RAISINS: 1 pound equals approximately 3 cups.

RICE: 1 pound equals 2 cups of raw rice and 3 cups of cooked rice.

SHORTENING: 1 cup equals 7 ounces.

For ¾ cup butter or shortening, use ¼ cup cold water
For ⅔ cup butter or shortening, use ⅓ cup cold water
For ½ cup butter or shortening, use ½ cup cold water
For ⅓ cup butter or shortening, use ⅔ cup cold water
For ¼ cup butter or shortening, use ¾ cup cold water

Also remember that 1 pound of butter equals 2 cups stick is equal to ⅛ pound or ¼ cup. One stick of butter ¼ pound or ½ cup. Two sticks of butter are equal to ½ 1 cup. Three sticks of butter are equal to ¾ pound or 1½ cu

To measure butter or shortening in measuring spoons, butter or shortening firmly into the measuring spoons and a straight-edged knife.

TABLE OF EQUIVALENT MEASU

1 pinch equals as much as can be taken between the of a finger and the thumb
⅓ of 1 tablespoon equals 1 teaspoon
3 teaspoons equal 1 tablespoon
2 tablespoons equal ⅛ cup
4 tablespoons equal ¼ cup
8 tablespoons equal ½ cup
12 tablespoons equal ¾ cup
14 tablespoons equal ⅞ cup
16 tablespoons equal 1 cup
1 cup equals ½ pint (8 oz.)
2 cups equal 1 pint (16 oz.)
4 cups equal 1 quart (32 oz.)
4 quarts (liquid) equal 1 gallon
8 quarts (solid) equal 1 peck
4 pecks equal 1 bushel
16 ounces equal 1 pound

ALMONDS: 4 ounces of shelled, chopped or powdered almon approximately ¾ cup.
ALMOND PASTE: 1 pound almond paste equals 1¾ cups.
APPLES: 1 pound of sliced apples equals approximately 3 cups.

SUGAR: *Brown*—1 cup well-packed sugar equals 8 ounces.
Granulated—1 cup equals 7 ounces.
Confectioners—1 cup equals 4¾ ounces, sifted.

CONVERSION OF FAHRENHEIT INTO CENTIGRADE

To convert Fahrenheit into Centigrade, subtract 32, multiply by 5, and divide by 9.

EXAMPLE: 212° (Fahrenheit) less 32 equals 180°;
180 × 5 equals 900°;
900 divided by 9 equals 100°, or the
temperature of boiling water on a Centigrade thermometer.

To convert Centigrade into Fahrenheit, multiply by 9, divide by 5, and add 32.

EXAMPLE: 100° (Centigrade) × 9 equals 900°;
900 divided by 5 equals 180°;
180° plus 32 equals 212° or the exact
temperature of boiling water on a Fahrenheit thermometer.

Popular Cakes

HINTS ABOUT CAKE BAKING

1. Read recipe twice.
2. Assemble all necessary ingredients and utensils.
3. All ingredients should be at room temperature unless othrewise specified.
4. Preheat oven at least 15 minutes prior to use, allowing temperature to reach the required degree.
5. *Sifted flour* is flour that must be measured after it is sifted. Where a recipe calls for *flour* only (omitting the word sifted), measure the required amount of flour before sifting. Sift flour as many times as prescribed in the recipe.
6. Cake pans should be prepared as explained in the recipes prior to any mixing. To *grease* pans use approximately 1 teaspoon shortening for a 9-inch pan. To *flour* a cake pan, dust flour in the bottom of each greased pan and shake until the flour is well distributed. To *line pan with paper,* lay the pan over parchment or brown unglazed paper and trace around the edge with a pencil. Cut approximately ¼ inch outside the pencil mark. Grease on both sides and fit in the bottom of greased pan.

7. Follow *mixing* directions carefully. If recipe calls for beaten egg whites, pay special attention to instructions for beating egg whites. See page 14.
8. Cake has finished *baking* when it shrinks from the sides of the pan or when the point of a knife or cake tester inserted through the center comes out clean. To unmold, place cake in pan right side up on cake rack and cool for 10 minutes before reversing it. Cool thoroughly before removing from pan and frosting.
9. To *fill and frost* cakes, first brush off loose crumbs. Split cake as directed, using a sharp knife. Sandwich layers together with filling. Use a flexible spatula to spread the frosting quickly and evenly.
10. To *cut* cakes always use a sharp knife. Wipe knife with a towel after each cutting.

BUTTER CAKES

WHITE CAKE
(with unbeaten egg whites)

3½ *cups sifted cake flour*
3 *teaspoons baking powder*
½ *teaspoon salt*
1 *cup butter*
2 *cups granulated sugar*
6 *egg whites, unbeaten*
1 *cup milk*
½ *teaspoon almond extract*

Set oven at 375 degrees F.
Two greased and floured 9-inch round cake pans (pans may be lined with greased wax paper for easier removal)

Sift twice together: flour, baking powder and salt. Cream butter and sugar until fluffy. Gradually add egg whites to butter and sugar, 2 at a time, beating well after each addition. Alternately stir in the milk and the sifted ingredients. *Blend well.* Add almond extract. Pour into prepared cake pans. Bake at 375 degrees F. for approximately 30 minutes or until done. Cool.
YIELD: 8 SERVINGS

SUGGESTED FROSTING

½ cup soft butter
4 cups confectioners sugar
½ cup light cream
4 drops vanilla or almond extract

Beat butter and confectioners sugar until smooth. Gradually stir in light cream and extract. Beat until fluffy and smooth.
YIELD: ENOUGH FROSTING FOR TWO 9-INCH LAYERS

WHITE CAKE
(with beaten egg whites)

1 cup butter
1½ cups granulated sugar
½ teaspoon almond extract
2¾ cups sifted cake flour
4 teaspoons double-acting baking powder
1 cup cold milk
5 egg whites
½ cup sugar

Set oven at 350 degrees F.
Two 9-inch round cake pans lined with greased paper

Cream butter and 1½ cups sugar till light and fluffy. Add almond extract. Sift flour and baking powder together twice. Add half the flour alternately with half the milk to the butter and sugar; then add the remaining flour and remaining milk. Blend all ingredients well. Scrape sides and bottom of the bowl to insure proper mixing. Beat egg whites stiff but not dry, adding ½ cup sugar gradually while beating. Immediately fold into the prepared mixture. *Do not overmix.* Blend all ingredients thoroughly. Divide batter equally into prepared cake pans. Bake at 350 degrees F. for about 30 to 35 minutes or until done. Frost layers with icing of your choice.
YIELD: 8 SERVINGS

LIGHT SPONGE CAKE

5 *eggs, separated*
1 *cup superfine granulated sugar*
2 *teaspoons grated lemon rind*
4 *teaspoons lemon juice*
2 *tablespoons cold water*
1/6 *teaspoon cream of tartar*
1 *cup sifted cake flour*

Set oven at 350 degrees F.
Two 9-inch round cake pans or one 10-inch tube pan, greased and floured

Beat egg yolks with 1/2 cup sugar until fluffy and pale in color. Stir in cold water and lemon juice mixed with rind. Beat egg whites and cream of tartar together until soft peaks form. Add the remaining sugar gradually and continue beating until stiff. Gently stir sifted flour into the yolks. Then gently fold stiff egg whites into yolk mixture. Thoroughly blend all ingredients. Pour batter into prepared cake pans or tube pan. Bake for about 30 minutes at 350 degrees F. or until the point of a knife, when inserted through the center, comes out clean.
YIELD: 8 TO 10 SERVINGS

DEVIL'S FOOD LAYER CAKE

2/3 *cup butter*
2 1/3 *cups sifted cake flour*
2 *cups granulated sugar*
3/4 *teaspoon salt*
1 *teaspoon baking soda*
1 *teaspoon double-acting baking powder*
1 1/3 *cups milk*
3 *eggs*
3 *squares or 3 oz. melted unsweetened chocolate*
3 *drops red food coloring*

Set oven at 350 degrees F.
Two 9-inch round cake pans, greased, floured and greased again

Cream butter until smooth and fluffy. Sift cake flour; *measure,* sift again with sugar, salt, baking soda and baking powder. Add sifted ingredients, followed by approximately 1/2 cup milk, to the butter. Beat at moderate speed until a smooth and light batter is obtained. Stir in remaining milk, eggs, melted chocolate and red food coloring.

Beat well to blend all ingredients thoroughly. Pour into prepared baking pans. Bake at 350 degrees F. for approximately 35 minutes or until done. Cool.

YIELD: 8 SERVINGS

Fill and frost layers with the following frosting.

CHOCOLATE FROSTING FOR DEVIL'S FOOD LAYER CAKE

3 oz. or 3 squares unsweetened chocolate
2 oz. or 2 squares sweet chocolate
¼ cup butter
4¼ cups sifted confectioners sugar
⅛ teaspoon salt
¾ cup light cream
1 teaspoon vanilla extract
½ teaspoon red food coloring

Melt chocolate and butter together over hot water. Stir well to dissolve properly. Combine sugar, salt, light cream, vanilla extract and coloring. Add chocolate mixture. Place over cold water or in the refrigerator, stirring from time to time to accelerate cooling. As soon as frosting reaches spreading consistency, use immediately.

YIELD: ENOUGH FROSTING FOR TWO 9-INCH LAYERS

CHOCOLATE CAKE
(with cocoa)

2 cups sifted cake flour
1¾ cups sugar
⅔ cup good quality unsweetened cocoa
1½ teaspoons baking soda
¾ teaspoon salt
½ teaspoon double-acting baking powder
¾ cup shortening or butter
1⅓ cups milk
3 eggs, beaten with a fork
½ teaspoon vanilla extract
4 drops red food coloring

Set oven at 350 degrees F.
Two greased and floured 9-inch round cake pans

In a large mixing bowl, sift together twice: flour, sugar, cocoa, baking soda, salt and baking powder. Add shortening and about 1 cup milk. Beat at medium speed with an electric mixer or rotary beater for at least three minutes, blending all ingredients well. Add beaten eggs, remaining milk, vanilla extract and red food coloring. Mix thoroughly and pour into prepared cake pans. Bake at 350 degrees F. for approximately 30 minutes or until done. Cool.
YIELD: 8 SERVINGS

AMERICANA CHOCOLATE CAKE

½ cup soft butter
1½ cups granulated sugar
2 large eggs
⅓ cup good quality sifted unsweetened cocoa
⅓ cup cold milk
2 cups sifted cake flour
1 teaspoon baking soda
½ teaspoon salt
4 drops red food coloring blended in
½ cup of buttermilk

Set oven at 325 degrees F.
Two 8-inch round cake pans, greased and lined with paper

Cream butter and sugar together until light. Add eggs, one at a time, beating well after each addition. Mix together sifted cocoa and cold milk until blended. Sift cake flour, baking soda and salt together. Stir flour into egg batter alternately with the buttermilk, cocoa mixture and food coloring, ⅓ at a time. *Do not overmix.* Blend all ingredients thoroughly. Pour into prepared cake pans. Bake at 325 degrees F. for approximately 35 to 40 minutes or until done. Cool.
YIELD: 6 SERVINGS

AMERICANA BUTTERCREAM CHOCOLATE CAKE

Fill and frost Americana chocolate cake with Chocolate Buttercream (page 284). Place in the refrigerator to harden for about 1 hour before attempting to cut with a sharp knife.

CHOCOLATE WHIPPED CREAM CAKE

Fill and frost layers of Americana Chocolate Cake with whipped cream flavored with coffee (page 277). Dust with grated sweet chocolate. Chill before serving.

PUMPKIN CAKE

½ cup butter
1 cup brown sugar
2 eggs
2½ cups sifted cake flour
2½ teaspoons baking powder
⅓ teaspoon baking soda
½ teaspoon salt
1 teaspoon cinnamon
⅓ teaspoon allspice
⅓ teaspoon powdered ginger
¾ cup buttermilk
¾ cup canned pumpkin
⅔ cup finely chopped pecans
1 cup whipped cream (optional)

Set oven at 350 degrees F.
Two greased 9-inch round cake pans

Cream butter and sugar together until light and fluffy. Add eggs, one at a time, blending well after each addition. Sift together twice: flour, baking powder, baking soda, salt, cinnamon, allspice and ginger. Add to the egg mixture followed by the buttermilk. Mix well. Add pumpkin and chopped pecans and blend thoroughly. Scrape sides and bottom of bowl to insure proper mixing. Divide batter equally into prepared cake pans and bake at 350 degrees F. for approximately 25 minutes or until a knife, when inserted through the center, comes out clean. Cool for 10 minutes. Then remove from pan and place in the refrigerator for 45 minutes or until cold. Frost with an icing of your choice or fill and frost with whipped cream before serving.
YIELD: 8 SERVINGS

RUM CAKE

6 eggs, separated
½ cup granulated sugar
1 tablespoon lemon juice
1 tablespoon grated lemon rind
1 teaspoon almond extract
1 cup cake flour
1 cup Vanilla Pastry Cream (page 289)
1 tablespoon rum
1½ cups whipped cream
2 tablespoons grated sweet chocolate

Set oven at 350 degrees F.
Two greased and floured 9-inch round cake pans

Beat egg yolks until thick. Stir in gradually: sugar, lemon juice, rind and almond extract. Beat until light and fluffy. Sift flour and fold gently into egg yolks. Beat egg whites until stiff but not dry. Gently fold into yolk mixture. Divide batter equally into prepared cake pans. Bake at 350 degrees F. for approximately 35 minutes or until the point of a knife, when inserted through the center, comes out clean. Cool. Fill with Vanilla Pastry Cream blended with rum. Spread top and sides of the cake with whipped cream. Dust with grated sweet chocolate and serve.
YIELD: 8 TO 10 SERVINGS

COCONUT LAYER CAKE

Two baked and cooled 9-inch layers of White Cake or Light Sponge Cake (pages 22, 23)

FILLING

1 cup Vanilla Pastry Cream (page 289)
1 tablespoon kirsch

MERINGUE FROSTING

1⅓ cups granulated sugar
⅔ cup water
4 egg whites
¼ teaspoon cream of tartar
½ teaspoon almond extract
1 cup shredded coconut

Fill two layers of sponge cake or white cake with the Vanilla Pastry Cream, blended with the kirsch. (Pastry cream and sponge cake can easily be prepared the day before.)

Boil sugar and water to 235 degrees F. on a candy thermometer. Meanwhile, beat egg whites and cream of tartar together until stiff. Continue boiling sugar until it reaches 240 degrees F., then pour into the beaten egg whites in a continuous stream, beating slowly. Add almond extract and continue beating until light and fluffy. Spread cake entirely with meringue. Cover with shredded coconut.

YIELD: 8 SERVINGS

ANGEL FOOD & CHIFFON CAKES

ANGEL FOOD CAKE

1¼ cups egg whites (about 9 or 10 whites) at room temperature
1 cup sifted cake flour
½ cup confectioners sugar
¼ teaspoon salt
¾ teaspoon cream of tartar
1 cup granulated sugar
1 teaspoon almond extract
chopped shredded coconut

Set oven at 375 degrees F.
One 10-inch ungreased tube cake pan

Allow egg whites to remain at room temperature for at least 1 hour.

Sift flour and confectioners sugar together at least 3 times.

Place egg whites in a large deep bowl. Add salt and beat with a rotary or electric beater until foamy. Add cream of tartar and continue beating until egg whites are stiff but not dry. Fold in granulated sugar, ⅓ cup at a time; blend gently. Add almond extract with the last addition of sugar.

Sift the sifted ingredients again over the beaten egg whites and very gently and carefully, using a rubber spatula, blend all ingredients well. Pour immediately into cake pan. Bake at 375 degrees F. for approximately 35 minutes or until done. Remove from oven and invert pan on a wire rack or over the neck of a bottle. Let cool for approximately 1 hour. Loosen sides with a flexible spatula. Unmold. Serve dusted with confectioners sugar or frost with Italian or Swiss

Meringue (pages 281, 283) and sprinkle with chopped shredded coconut.

YIELD: 8 TO 10 SERVINGS

CHOCOLATE ANGEL FOOD CAKE

Follow directions for Angel Food Cake but reduce cake flour to ¾ cup instead of 1 cup. Add 6 tablespoons good quality unsweetened cocoa to the flour and confectioners sugar. Reduce oven temperature to 350 degrees F. instead of 375 degrees F. Bake for 45 to 50 minutes. Frost with Mocha Rum Buttercream (page 190).

LEMON CHIFFON CAKE

8 *egg whites* (1 *cup*)
2⅓ *cups sifted cake flour*
1½ *cups superfine granulated sugar*
3 *teaspoons baking powder*
1 *teaspoon salt*
½ *cup salad oil*
5 *egg yolks*
¼ *cup cold water*
2 *teaspoons grated lemon peel*
⅓ *cup lemon juice*
⅓ *teaspoon cream of tartar*
1 *recipe for Lemon Cream Filling* (*page* 287)
¼ *cup confectioners sugar to dust cake after baking*

Set oven at 350 degrees F.
One 10-inch ungreased tube pan

Allow egg whites to remain at room temperature for approximately 30 minutes.

Sift together twice into a deep bowl: flour, sugar, baking powder and salt. Make a hole in the center and gradually add salad oil, egg yolks, water, lemon peel and lemon juice; then stir well to obtain a smooth batter.

Beat egg whites with cream of tartar until stiff but not dry. Fold gently into prepared yolk mixture, blending all ingredients well. *Do not overmix.* Pour into tube pan. Bake at 350 degrees F. for about 50 minutes or until done. Invert pan on rack or over the neck of a bottle and let cool for at least 1 hour before unmolding. When cool, split evenly into four layers and fill each layer with Lemon Cream. Dust with confectioners sugar and serve.

YIELD: 10 TO 12 SERVINGS

CHIFFON SPONGE CAKE

4 eggs, separated
1 cup superfine granulated sugar
1½ cups hot water
grated rind of 1 lemon
1½ cups sifted cake flour
1 pinch salt
¼ teaspoon double-acting baking powder
½ cup granulated sugar

Set oven at 325 degrees F.
One 9-inch tube pan, greased and floured

Beat egg yolks with ½ cup superfine sugar until thick and pale in color. Gradually stir in the hot water and lemon rind. Sift cake flour together with salt and baking powder. Fold into the yolk batter. Beat egg whites until stiff but not dry, with ½ cup of sugar, gradually adding remaining ½ cup sugar while beating. Fold egg-white mixture carefully into yolk mixture using a flat skimmer or wooden spoon. Pour batter into prepared pan and bake at 325 degrees F. for approximately 50 minutes or until a knife, when inserted through the center, comes out clean. Remove from pan and cool.
YIELD: 8 SERVINGS

JELLY ROLLS

AMERICANA JELLY ROLLS

4 eggs, at room temperature
¾ cup sifted cake flour
¾ teaspoon double-acting baking powder
¼ teaspoon salt
⅔ cup granulated sugar
1 tablespoon melted butter
grated rind of 1 lemon
fine granulated sugar, to dust cake
1 cup currant jelly
confectioners sugar, to dust cake

Set oven at 400 degrees F.
One 15 x 10 x 1-inch baking sheet, lined with greased wax paper

Place eggs in a deep bowl. Beat just enough to blend egg yolks and whites well together. Sift together twice: flour, baking powder and salt. Beat eggs rapidly with an electric mixer, adding sugar gradually while beating. Continue beating until thick or until egg mixture has tripled in volume. Gently fold sifted ingredients into beaten eggs; add melted butter (cooled to lukewarm) and lemon rind. Pour and spread batter into prepared sheet pan. Bake at 400 degrees F. for approximately 12 minutes, or until golden brown, *no darker*. Remove from heat. Loosen edge of cake with the point of a knife and invert cake onto a cloth dusted with fine granulated sugar. Cool for about 5 minutes. Spread jelly evenly over cake but not too close to the edges. Roll up cake, *not too tight*. Cool. Dust with confectioners sugar, slice crosswise with a sharp knife into pieces approximately ½ inch thick.

YIELD: 6 SERVINGS

JELLY ROLL

3 *eggs, separated*
½ *cup granulated sugar*
1 *tablespoon lukewarm water*
½ *teaspoon vanilla extract*
½ *cup sifted cake flour*
1 *cup jelly, flavor of your choice*

Set oven at 400 degrees F.
One 15 x 10 x 1-inch baking sheet, lined with greased paper

Combine egg yolks, ¼ cup sugar and water in a deep bowl. Beat with a wire whip or electric mixer for approximately 8 minutes. Stir in vanilla.

Beat egg whites until soft peaks form; gradually add the remaining ¼ cup sugar and continue beating until stiff. Stir yolk mixture into beaten egg whites. Blend well. Sift flour over the eggs and fold in gently. Spread batter on baking sheet.

Bake at 400 degrees F. for about 12 minutes or until golden brown. Remove from oven and cool for approximately 3 minutes. Spread jelly evenly over cake and roll tight. Cool. Finish as Americana Jelly Roll.

YIELD: 6 SERVINGS

CHERRY CHOCOLATE WHIPPED CREAM ROLL

5 eggs, separated
1 cup plus 1 tablespoon granulated sugar
3 tablespoons cocoa
1 tablespoon cake flour
2 cups whipped cream
1 cup drained pitted black cherries cut in half
confectioners sugar

Set oven at 350 degrees F.
One 10 x 12 x 1-inch baking sheet, greased and floured

Beat egg yolks with ½ cup sugar until light and fluffy. In a separate bowl, beat egg whites until stiff but not dry, adding ½ cup sugar gradually while beating. Sift cocoa together with flour and stir into egg whites, one tablespoon at a time. Fold beaten egg-white mixture into the beaten egg yolks. Blend all ingredients gently and spread evenly on the prepared baking sheet. Bake at 350 degrees F. for approximately 15 minutes or until done. Remove from pan and reverse on a large sheet of paper sprinkled evenly with 1 tablespoon granulated sugar. Cool thoroughly. Spread with whipped cream entirely over the surface of the cooled chocolate cake sheet; sprinkle with well-drained, halved black cherries and roll tightly like a jelly roll. Dust with confectioners sugar and serve cold.
YIELD: 6 SERVINGS

Note: This cake can also be served with chocolate or any other sauce of your choice (see sauces in *Frostings, Sauces, Candies,* below).

FRUIT CAKES, POUND CAKES AND LOAF CAKES

HINTS ABOUT FRUIT CAKES

1. Fruit cakes can be baked weeks in advance; a tremendous advantage!
2. Always use fresh nuts and moist candied fruits; beware of dry fruits and rancid nuts.
3. In lining greased pans, use only parchment or brown unglazed paper. Never use wax paper.

4. All ingredients for mixing should be at room temperature unless otherwise specified.
5. Mix and bake specifically as directed. Cool cakes thoroughly before attempting to remove from pans.
6. Store cakes enclosed in aluminum foil. Once cake has been cut keep leftover portion wrapped in waxed paper, then in aluminum foil.

Fruit cakes are always convenient to have on hand for unexpected guests, forgotten gifts, etc. and they are so much fun to prepare!

GOLDEN FRUIT CAKE

A flavor and fruit combination second to none!

¾ cup whole candied red cherries
¼ cup diced candied lemon peel
¼ cup diced green candied pineapple
¼ cup diced green candied cherries
¾ cup dark seedless raisins
¾ cup currant raisins
½ cup chopped pitted dates
¼ cup good brandy
grated rind of 1 lemon
½ cup chopped pecans

Combine all the above ingredients and let them soak in a cool place overnight.

¼ cup yellow corn meal
1½ cups all-purpose flour
½ teaspoon baking powder
¼ teaspoon ground cinnamon
1 pinch nutmeg (optional)
½ cup butter
1 cup granulated sugar
2 eggs (approximately ½ cup)

Set oven at 400 degrees F.
One 9 x 5 x 3-inch loaf pan or one 9-inch tube pan lined with heavy paper. One larger pan deep enough to hold 2 inches of water.

Thoroughly drain soaked fruits and nuts for at least one hour. Spread fruits and nuts on a large piece of foil and dust with corn meal and ¼ cup flour. Blend well. Sift remaining 1¼ cups of flour with the baking powder, cinnamon and nutmeg and place in the refrigerator to chill. Meanwhile, cream butter and sugar well. Add eggs one at a time, creaming well after each addition. Scrape sides and bottom of the bowl to insure a lump-free batter. When all the eggs have been added, remove chilled flour from the refrigerator and fold into egg mixture. Stir in prepared fruits and nuts. Blend thoroughly. Pour into the prepared loaf or tube pan. Set pan in a shallow pan containing approximately 2 inches of water. Bake at 400 degrees F. for about 10 minutes or until a thin crust forms over the batter. Turn down the oven to 300 degrees and open the door until temperature is reduced. Then close the door and finish baking for approximately 1 hour and 30 minutes or until a knife, when inserted through the center, comes out clean. Remove from water bath and cool in the pan for at least 1 hour. Then remove from pan and peel off paper. Wrap in foil and store in the refrigerator until ready for use. The quality of the cake will improve with age. It can be kept for months in an airtight container.

YIELD: 24 SLICES

DARK FRUIT CAKE

Use brown sugar instead of granulated sugar.

RAISIN CAKE

2 *cups dark raisins*
2 *cups cold water*
2 *teaspoons baking soda*
1 *tablespoon lemon juice*
¼ *cup yellow corn meal*
1 *cup plus* 1 *tablespoon butter*
2 *cups granulated sugar*
4 *eggs*
4 *cups sifted cake flour*
2 *teaspoons baking powder*
1 *cup juice from the soaked raisins*
grated rind of 1 *lemon*
a few drops of vanilla extract

Set oven at 375 degrees F.
One 9 x 9 x 2-inch baking pan lined with paper

Soak the raisins in the water with the baking soda and lemon juice overnight. Next morning, drain the raisins and set aside one cup of the juice. Place the raisins in the refrigerator to chill; when cool, dust them with corn meal and mix them well.

Cream the butter and sugar together; add the eggs, 2 at a time, creaming well after each addition. Sift the flour and baking powder together. Add the flour alternately with the raisin juice to the butter and eggs. Mix until smooth. Add the lemon rind and vanilla extract. Fold in the prepared raisins. Place batter in prepared pan and bake at 375 degrees F. for approximately 40 minutes or until a knife, when inserted through the center, comes out clean.
YIELD: 8 SERVINGS

WHITE FRUIT CAKE

¾ cup chopped red candied cherries
½ cup dark seedless raisins
⅔ cup chopped green candied pineapple
⅓ cup diced candied lemon peel
⅓ cup chopped unsalted nuts
1 teaspoon grated lemon peel
⅓ cup good brandy

Combine all the above ingredients and let them soak in a cool place overnight.

⅓ cup yellow corn meal
2 cups sifted all-purpose flour
⅓ teaspoon baking soda
¾ cup soft butter
1¼ cups granulated sugar
6 egg whites

Set oven at 325 degrees F.
One 9 x 5 x 3-inch loaf pan, or one 9-inch tube pan, lined with heavy paper

Thoroughly drain the soaked fruits and nuts for at least 1 hour. Spread the fruits and nuts on a large piece of foil and dust with the corn meal and ½ cup flour. Blend well. Sift the remaining flour together with the baking soda. Cream the butter and ¼ cup sugar together until light. Stir in the flour and prepared fruits. Beat the egg whites stiff, adding the remaining cup of sugar gradually while beating. Fold into the fruit mixture. Blend well. Pour batter into the prepared loaf or tube pan. Bake at 325 degrees F. for approximately 1 hour and 30 minutes or until the point of a knife, when inserted through the center, comes out clean. Cool in the pan for at least 1 hour. Remove and peel off paper. Store well-wrapped in foil or in tight container.
YIELD: 6 TO 8 SERVINGS

PINEAPPLE UPSIDE DOWN CAKE

PREPARATION OF PAN:

1/3 cup butter
2/3 cup brown sugar
6 round canned pineapple slices, drained
6 maraschino cherries

Melt butter and brown sugar in an 8-inch-square pan. Arrange drained pineapple slices and cherries alternately in the pan; put aside while preparing the following mixture:

BATTER FOR PINEAPPLE UPSIDE DOWN CAKE

1/4 cup vegetable shortening
1/2 cup granulated sugar
1 egg
1 cup sifted cake flour
1 1/2 teaspoons double-acting baking powder
1 teaspoon grated lemon rind
1/3 cup milk
1/2 teaspoon almond extract

Set oven at 350 degrees F.

Beat shortening, sugar and egg together in a deep bowl. Sift flour and baking powder together onto a large piece of paper and sprinkle with grated lemon rind. Add to egg mixture sifted ingredients alternately with the milk and almond extract. Blend all ingredients thoroughly. Pour into the prepared pan. Bake at 350 degrees F. for about 35 minutes or until done. Remove from the pan while still warm by pressing pan into a large serving tray. If you wish, you may glaze the pineapple with Apricot Glaze (page 80).

YIELD: 6 SERVINGS

GRATED APPLE CAKE

An old favorite—always welcome!

½ cup soft butter
⅔ cup granulated sugar
½ cup dark brown sugar
2 eggs
2 teaspoons lemon juice
1 teaspoon grated lemon rind
1 teaspoon baking soda
2½ cups sifted all-purpose flour
1 teaspoon baking powder
2½ cups finely chopped or grated apples
⅔ cup chopped nuts (pecans, walnuts or others)
3 tablespoons granulated sugar
1 teaspoon cinnamon powder

Set oven at 350 degrees F.
One 13 x 9 x 2-inch greased baking pan

Cream together well: butter, granulated sugar and brown sugar. Add eggs, one at a time, mixing well after each addition. Add lemon juice and grated lemon rind. Sift together twice: flour, baking powder and soda, and add to the egg mixture. Gradually add apples. Blend all ingredients well. Pour into prepared pan. Dust with chopped nuts and granulated sugar well mixed with ground cinnamon.

Bake at 350 degrees F. for approximately 1 hour or until the point of a knife, when inserted through the center, comes out clean.
YIELD: 6 SERVINGS

AMERICANA OLD FASHIONED STRAWBERRY SHORTCAKE

1 cup sifted cake flour
½ cup sifted all-purpose flour
2 teaspoons double-acting baking powder
1 pinch salt
⅓ cup soft butter
2½ tablespoons confectioners sugar
grated rind of 1 orange
⅓ cup cold milk, approximately
1 pint fresh sliced strawberries sprinkled with 2 tablespoons of sugar
1½ cups whipped cream

Set oven to 450 degrees F.
One 10 x 12 x 1-inch baking sheet, greased

Sift both flours, baking powder and salt together twice into a deep bowl. Make a hole or well in the center. Place soft butter, confectioners sugar and grated orange rind in the well and proceed as in the making of Pastry Dough (page 54) by cutting the butter into the flour until a crumbled mixture has formed. Then add cold milk gradually until a dough of rolling but soft consistency is obtained. Place in the refrigerator to chill for at least 30 minutes. When chilled, roll out about ½-inch thick on a floured board. Prick the dough and cut into 2-inch circles with a plain round cutter. Place circles on the prepared baking sheet leaving enough space between each cake to permit the heat to circulate. Bake at 450 degrees F. for approximately 12 minutes or until done.

Cool. Split each cake in two; place the bottom halves on a serving dish or platter and cover each one with the sugared strawberries. Place the top halves of the cakes over the strawberries and garnish with whipped cream.

YIELD: 6 SERVINGS

AMERICANA BANANA CAKE

⅔ *cup butter*
1½ *cups granulated sugar*
3 *eggs*
2½ *cups sifted cake flour*
1 *teaspoon double-acting baking powder*
¾ *teaspoon baking soda*
½ *teaspoon salt*
½ *cup buttermilk*
1⅓ *cups mashed, ripe bananas*
½ *cup finely chopped pecans*
1 *cup Vanilla Pastry Cream (page 289)*
2 *tablespoons diced maraschino cherries*
4 *large ripe bananas, sliced thin*
⅓ *cup Clear Apricot Glaze (page 80)*

Set oven at 350 degrees F.
Two greased and floured 9-inch round cake pans

Cream butter and sugar until light and fluffy. Add eggs, one at a time, beating well after each addition. Sift together twice: flour, baking powder, baking soda and salt. Blend together buttermilk and mashed bananas. Add banana mixture, then sifted ingredients, to the egg mixture. Beat rapidly to obtain a smooth batter. Stir in the finely chopped pecans. Divide evenly into two prepared pans. Bake at 350 degrees F. for approximately 35 minutes or until a knife, when inserted through the center, comes out clean. Cool.

Fill with Vanilla Pastry Cream blended with maraschino cherries. Cover the top entirely with sliced bananas arranged in circles, one slice overlapping another. Coat with hot Apricot Glaze. Keep in the refrigerator until ready to serve.

YIELD: 8 SERVINGS

BANANA LOAF CAKE

2 cups sifted all-purpose flour
2 teaspoons double-acting baking powder
¼ teaspoon baking soda
⅓ teaspoon salt
1 teaspoon grated lemon rind
⅓ cup butter at room temperature
⅔ cup granulated sugar
2 eggs
1 egg yolk
1 cup mashed very ripe banana
1 cup seedless raisins
½ cup chopped pecans

Set oven at 350 degrees F.
One 9 x 5 x 3-inch loaf pan, greased and lined, bottom and sides, with greased paper

Sift together flour, baking powder, baking soda and salt and sprinkle with grated lemon rind. Cream together butter and sugar until light and fluffy. Add eggs and extra yolk one at a time, beating well after each addition. Add sifted ingredients to bananas, raisins and nuts. Then blend all ingredients well into a smooth batter. Pour mixture into prepared pan. Bake at 350 degrees F. for approximately 1 hour or until the point of a knife, when inserted through the center, comes out clean.

YIELD: 6 SERVINGS

AMERICANA HONEY LOAF CAKE

2 eggs
⅔ cup light brown sugar
3 tablespoons brewed coffee
1 cup honey
1½ tablespoons vegetable oil
2 cups sifted cake flour
1 teaspoon baking powder
⅓ teaspoon baking soda
2 teaspoons grated orange rind
¾ cup chopped pecans
¾ cup chopped diced glazed fruits
⅓ cup seedless raisins
1 tablespoon rum

Set oven at 325 degrees F.
One 9 x 5 x 3-inch loaf pan, greased and lined with paper

Beat eggs and sugar until light and fluffy. Stir in coffee, honey and vegetable oil. Sift flour together with baking powder and soda and fold into egg mixture. Blend all ingredients well. Add orange rind, pecans, diced fruits, raisins and rum. Pour into prepared pan and bake at 325 degrees F. for approximately 1 hour or until the point of a knife, when inserted through the center, comes out clean.
YIELD: 6 SERVINGS

JEWISH HONEY CAKE

¼ cup vegetable oil
¾ cup granulated sugar
3 eggs
1 cup honey
1 cup water
3 drops almond extract
3 cups cake flour
2 teaspoons double-acting baking powder
¾ teaspoon baking soda
¾ teaspoon ground cinnamon
½ teaspoon ground nutmeg
½ cup chopped pecans
⅓ cup seedless raisins
1 teaspoon grated orange rind

Set oven at 325 degrees F.
One 10-inch tube pan, greased and floured

Beat oil and sugar well. Add eggs and continue beating until light and thick. Stir in honey, water and almond extract. Sift flour and baking powder together. Sift once more with baking soda, cinnamon and nutmeg. Blend into egg mixture alternately with pecans, raisins and orange rind. Mix thoroughly and pour into prepared pan. Bake at 325 degrees F. for approximately 1 hour or until the point of a knife, when inserted through the center, comes out clean. Remove carefully and cool.

YIELD: 10 SERVINGS

AMERICANA CHOCOLATE MARBLE CAKE

2 cups sifted cake flour
1¼ cups granulated sugar
2¾ teaspoons baking powder
¾ teaspoon salt
⅓ cup butter at room temperature
1 cup cold milk
1 teaspoon grated lemon rind
1 teaspoon almond extract
4 egg yolks, beaten with a fork
1½ ounces or 1½ squares sweet chocolate
2 tablespoons hot water

Set oven at 350 degrees F.
One 9 x 5 x 3-inch loaf pan greased and lined with greased paper *or*
One 10 x 4-inch tube pan greased and lined with greased paper

Combine cake flour, sugar, 2½ teaspoons baking powder and salt and sift together into a deep bowl. Add soft butter, milk, lemon rind and almond extract. Beat well to blend all ingredients. Add beaten yolks, one at a time, mixing well after each addition, scraping sides and bottom of the bowl. Melt chocolate in a small cup over hot water. Stir in water and the remaining baking powder. Cool. Remove approximately ¼ of the cake batter and place in a small, round-bottomed bowl. Add the chocolate mixture and stir just enough to blend well. Pour both batters alternately, by the spoonful, into the prepared pan. With the back of a spoon dipped into the filled pan, mix the batter gently to create a marble effect. Bake at 350 degrees F. for approximately 35 to 40 minutes or until done. Cool for 15 to 20 minutes before removing from pan. Peel off the paper.

YIELD: 6 TO 8 SERVINGS

POUND CAKE

Light as a feather—so tasty, and it improves with age!

1 cup butter
1½ cups sifted cake flour
¾ teaspoon baking powder
grated rind of 1 lemon
1 tablespoon lemon juice
4 eggs, separated
1¼ cups confectioners sugar

Set oven to 350 degrees F.
One 9 x 5 x 3-inch loaf pan, greased and lined with greased paper

Cream butter. Sift flour together with baking powder and add to butter. Stir in lemon rind and juice. Beat egg yolks and confectioners sugar together until fluffy. Add gradually to the flour mixture. Blend all ingredients well. Beat egg whites until stiff and fold into batter. Pour into prepared pan and bake at 350 degrees F. for approximately 45 minutes or until the point of a knife, when inserted through the center, comes out clean.
YIELD: 6 to 8 SERVINGS

Note: If you wish, store in the refrigerator wrapped in foil.

ALMOND SOUR CREAM POUND CAKE

⅓ cup almond paste
3 cups plus 2 tablespoons granulated sugar
6 eggs, separated
½ pound butter
grated rind of 1 orange
3 cups cake flour, sifted twice with
1 pinch baking soda
1 cup thick sour cream

Set oven at 300 degrees F.
One 10-inch tube pan, greased and floured

Combine almond paste and 3 cups of sugar in a deep bowl and rub together thoroughly with your fingers. Add one egg yolk and cream the mixture for approximately 1 minute. Then add butter and blend all ingredients well. Add remaining egg yolks, one at a time, mixing well and scraping sides and bottom of the bowl after each addition. Add orange rind and cake flour sifted with soda alternately with the sour cream. Blend well to obtain a batter free of lumps. Beat egg whites until stiff, adding remaining sugar gradually while beating. Gently fold egg whites into batter. Pour into prepared pan. Bake at 300 degrees F. for approximately 1 hour and 30 minutes or until the point of a knife, when inserted through the center, comes out clean. YIELD: 8 SERVINGS

Note: Any other shape pan can also be used. This is a very light-textured pound cake which will keep for about a week in the refrigerator if well wrapped in foil.

CHEESE CAKES

AMERICANA CHEESE CAKE

The great favorite of millions at the Americana Hotel in Miami Beach, Florida. They proudly proclaim it a splendid dessert, delicious to eat and delightful to look at!

1½ *cups graham cracker crumbs or*
18 *single graham cracker squares, crushed*
2 *tablespoons melted butter*
2 *tablespoons granulated sugar*

Set oven at 350 degrees F.
One 10-inch spring-form pan, 3 inches deep, greased

Blend graham crackers, melted butter and granulated sugar and press firmly into the bottom of the spring-form pan. Bake at 350 degrees F. for approximately 6 minutes, remove and cool. Raise oven to 425 degrees F.

3 *pounds cream cheese at room temperature*
2¾ *cups granulated sugar*
3 *tablespoons cornstarch*
½ *teaspoon salt*
6 *eggs plus* 6 *egg yolks*
¾ *cup light cream*
grated rind of 1 *lemon*
juice of 1 *lemon*
¼ *teaspoon vanilla extract*

In a large deep bowl, cream the cheese until smooth. Add sugar, cornstarch and salt. Mix until smooth. Gradually add eggs and extra yolks, two at a time, mixing well and scraping sides and bottom of the bowl after each addition. Stir in the remaining ingredients and blend to a smooth batter. Pour filling into prepared pan and place this in a larger pan filled with cold water to the depth of 1 inch. Bake at 425 degrees F. for about 15 minutes. Remove from the oven and let cool while reducing oven temperature to 325 degrees F. Then return cake and pan with cold water to the cooled oven and finish baking for 1 hour and 30 minutes or until the point of a knife, when inserted through the center, comes out clean. Cool in the pan for about 2 hours before removing sides of pan. Then chill.

YIELD: 12 TO 14 SERVINGS

Note: Cheese cake will keep for days if stored in a cool place. For a smaller cheese cake, use ½ of the preceding recipe; it will fill a 7-inch spring-form pan. Bake as directed above but only 1 hour at 325 degrees F. until firm.

AMERICANA STRAWBERRY CHEESE CAKE
(with fresh strawberries)

A super-delicious cheese cake, extravagant in appearance and especially delectable to eat.

1 *Americana Cheese Cake Crust (page 43)*
½ *recipe for Americana Cheese Cake (page 43)*
1½ *pints fresh ripe strawberries*
½ *cup currant jelly*
a few drops of red food coloring

One 10-inch spring form pan 2 inches deep

Follow the directions on page 43 for the Americana Cheese Cake Crust. Make ½ the recipe for Americana Cheese Cake, following mixing and baking directions on page 43. Total baking time will be about 1 hour and 10 minutes. Cool in the pan for approximately 2 hours, then remove sides.

Hull and clean the strawberries and arrange them on top of the cooled cheese cake in an upright position, stem side down. Place them in an orderly fashion and as close to each other as possible.

Boil the currant jelly gently. Remove from heat; stir in a few drops of red food coloring and let stand approximately 5 minutes. Brush fruits with the warm glaze. Then chill.

YIELD: 10 TO 12 SERVINGS

An alternate topping for this cake can be made with frozen strawberries, as described below:

1 10-oz. *package of frozen strawberries, thawed and drained*
⅔ *cup juice from the drained strawberries*
2 *tablespoons cornstarch*
few drops of red food coloring

Thaw strawberries. Drain and save ⅔ cup of the juice. Place the cornstarch in a deep saucepan; gradually add strawberry juice and stir. Bring to a boil and continue stirring for one minute or until thickened. Remove from heat; add thawed strawberries and red food coloring. Spoon topping over the cheese cake, and brush entirely with warm currant jelly glaze. Chill before serving.

BLUEBERRY CHEESE CAKE

Follow the recipe for Americana Strawberry Cheese Cake (page 44) using fresh blueberries instead of strawberries.

PINEAPPLE CHEESE CAKE

Follow the recipe for Americana Strawberry Cheese Cake (page 44) using pineapple chunks or slices instead of fresh strawberries. Brush the fruit with the following apricot glaze:

½ *cup clear apricot jam*
1 *tablespoon water*
maraschino cherries, to decorate

Combine jam and water in a saucepan and bring to a boil. Remove from heat and brush over fruit. Decorate with maraschino cherries.

Pineapple Cheese Cake can also be finished successfully with the following combination of pineapple and apricot glaze instead of the pineapple chunks or slices:

1 tablespoon cornstarch
2 tablespoons granulated sugar
1 cup crushed pineapple with juice
1 teaspoon lemon juice
few drops yellow food coloring

Combine the first four ingredients together in a saucepan. Bring to a boil, stirring for 1 minute until thickened. Add food coloring and stir well. Spoon hot glaze over the top of the cheese cake. Cool and brush again with hot apricot glaze (page 45). Chill before serving.
YIELD: 10 SERVINGS

SOUR CREAM CHEESE CAKE

Light as a feather and fabulous to eat!

1 Americana Graham Cracker crust (page 43)
1 pound cream cheese
3 eggs, separated
⅔ cup plus 2 tablespoons granulated sugar
2 tablespoons cornstarch
⅔ cup sour cream
1 teaspoon lemon juice

Set oven at 325 degrees F.
One 8-inch spring-form pan, 3 inches high, greased

Line the bottom of the spring-form pan with the Americana Graham Cracker crust. Combine egg yolks and cream cheese and beat until smooth. Add ⅔ cup sugar, cornstarch, sour cream and lemon juice. Blend all ingredients well and beat to a very smooth lump-free batter. Beat egg whites stiff but not dry, gradually adding sugar while beating. Fold egg whites gently into cheese batter. Pour into prepared pan, and place this in a larger pan filled with cold water to the depth of 1 inch. Bake for one hour at 325 degrees F., or until the point of a knife, when inserted through the center, comes out clean. Cool for 4 hours. Remove sides and serve plain or with any of the fruit toppings as explained (page 45).
YIELD: 8 TO 10 SERVINGS

REFRIGERATOR CREAM CHEESE CAKE

A tasty dessert that requires absolutely no baking.

1½ *cups graham cracker crumbs or*
18 *single graham cracker squares, crushed*
6 *tablespoons melted butter*
4 *tablespoons granulated sugar*
½ *teaspoon cinnamon*

One 10-inch spring-form pan, 3 inches high, greased

Combine all ingredients in order listed and spread evenly in the bottom of the prepared pan. Chill in refrigerator while preparing the cheese filling.

3 *(8-oz.) pkgs. cream cheese, softened*
3 *envelopes or* 3 *tablespoons unflavored gelatin*
½ *cup hot water*
1⅓ *cups heavy cream*
3 *eggs, separated*
½ *cup of milk*
1⅓ *cups granulated sugar*
¾ *teaspoon salt*
3 *tablespoons lemon juice*
1 *tablespoon grated lemon rind*

Cream the cheese in a deep bowl until smooth and free of lumps. Sprinkle gelatin over hot water to dissolve. Beat heavy cream until stiff and let stand in the refrigerator.

Beat egg yolks with a fork and combine in a bowl with milk, 1 cup sugar and salt. Place over hot water and stir well; when finger dipped into the mixture will not tolerate the heat any longer, remove from heat and stir in dissolved gelatin, lemon juice and grated lemon rind. Mix well to dissolve, then pour into the cream cheese. Blend all ingredients thoroughly. Place in the refrigerator or over cold water and stir from time to time to accelerate cooling. When the mixture starts to set and mounds slightly when dropped from a spoon, fold in the whipped cream. Beat the egg whites stiff but not dry, adding remaining ⅓ cup of sugar gradually while beating, and quickly fold into the cheese mixture. Pour into the prepared pan. Chill for about 4 hours until firm. Remove sides of pan to serve.

YIELD: 10 TO 12 SERVINGS

REFRIGERATOR COTTAGE CHEESE CAKE

Line a greased 8-inch spring-form pan with graham cracker mixture as for Refrigerator Cream Cheese Cake (page 47) and chill in the refrigerator while preparing the following filling:

2⅓ cups cottage cheese
1 teaspoon grated lemon rind
2 tablespoons lemon juice
½ teaspoon salt
2 envelopes or 2 tablespoons unflavored gelatin
½ cup plus 3 tablespoons granulated sugar
½ cup milk
2 eggs, separated
1 cup heavy cream

Pass the cottage cheese through a fine sieve. Place in a deep bowl and stir in lemon juice, lemon rind and salt. Place gelatin, ½ cup sugar and milk in a saucepan over hot water and stir well. When a finger dipped into the mixture will not tolerate the heat any longer, remove from heat and let stand to cool a little. Stir egg yolks into the cottage cheese and blend well. Add gelatin mixture and beat vigorously until smooth and creamy. Place in the refrigerator or over cold water, stirring from time to time to accelerate cooling. When the mixture starts to set and mounds slightly when dropped from a spoon, beat the heavy cream until stiff. Beat the egg whites until stiff but not dry, adding the remaining 3 tablespoons of sugar gradually while beating; fold alternately with the whipped cream into the cheese mixture. Pour into prepared pan and chill for approximately 4 hours or until firm. Remove sides of pan to serve.
YIELD: 10 TO 12 SERVINGS

REFRIGERATOR CHEESE CAKE WITH FRUIT

To make Refrigerator Cheese Cake with Fruit, simply combine ¾ cup of any fresh or well-drained canned fruits (strawberries, blueberries, Bing cherries, sliced peaches, diced pineapple, etc.) with the filling for either of the above refrigerator cheese cakes immediately after folding in the egg whites and whipped cream.

QUICK CHEESE CAKE

¾ cup graham cracker crumbs
1 tablespoon sugar
1 teaspoon melted butter

Set oven at 350 degrees F.
One 9-inch spring-form pan, greased

Combine cracker crumbs, sugar and melted butter; press firmly into the bottom of the prepared pan. Put in a cool place while preparing the following:

1½ cups or 12 oz. cottage cheese
12 oz. cream cheese
2 tablespoons cornstarch
1 cup granulated sugar
juice of 1 lemon
5 eggs plus 1 egg yolk
½ teaspoon grated lemon rind
¾ cup sour cream

Pass the cottage cheese through a fine sieve; blend with cream cheese, cornstarch, sugar and lemon juice in a deep bowl. Add the eggs and extra yolk, one at a time, stirring well after each addition. Scrape the sides and bottom of the bowl to insure a lump-free batter. Add the lemon rind and sour cream and blend thoroughly. Pour the cheese mixture into the prepared pan and bake at 350 degrees F. for about 1 hour or until the point of a knife, when inserted through the center, comes out clean. Cool overnight before removing sides of pan.

YIELD: APPROXIMATELY 10 SERVINGS

CHEDDAR BEER CHEESE CAKE

Ultra-delicious—and so different!

1 cup graham cracker crumbs, blended with
1½ tablespoons melted butter and
1½ tablespoons granulated sugar

Set oven at 425 degrees F.
One 8-inch spring-form pan, greased

Press the graham cracker mixture approximately ¼-inch thick firmly into the bottom of the prepared pan and dust the sides of the pan with the remaining graham cracker mixture. Put the pan aside in a cool place while preparing the following mixture:

4 8-oz. pkgs. cream cheese at room temperature
1 teaspoon cornstarch
1 cup finely grated Cheddar cheese at room temperature
1½ cups granulated sugar
½ teaspoon grated lemon rind
½ teaspoon grated orange rind
4 eggs plus 2 egg yolks
¼ cup ale beer
¼ cup heavy cream

Beat cream cheese, cornstarch and Cheddar cheese until smooth. Combine the sugar and grated rinds and add gradually to the cheese mixture. Add the eggs and extra yolks one at a time, beating well after each addition to prevent lumps. Stir in the beer and heavy cream. Pour the cheese mixture into the prepared pan and bake at 425 degrees F. for 15 minutes, until the top is lightly browned. Remove cheese cake from oven. Open the oven door and reduce heat to 225 degrees F. then return the cake to the oven, close the door and finish baking for about 1 hour and 5 minutes or until the point of a knife, inserted through the center, comes out clean. Cool thoroughly before removing sides of pan or chill in the refrigerator and serve cold. Cut with a sharp knife dipped in water.
YIELD: 6 SERVINGS

CHEESE PIE

½ the recipe for Tart Dough (page 78)

Set oven at 450 degrees F.
One 10-inch pie plate

Roll out tart dough approximately ⅛-inch thick, press it into the pie plate and chill.

3 8-oz. pkgs. cream cheese
½ cup sugar
1½ tablespoons sifted cake flour
1 teaspoon grated lemon peel
1 teaspoon lemon juice
3 eggs plus 2 egg yolks
¼ cup heavy cream

Cream the cheese until smooth. Add the sugar, sifted flour, lemon peel and lemon juice. Blend well. Add the eggs and extra yolks one at a time, scraping the sides and bottom of the bowl to obtain a lump-free batter. Stir in the cream. Pour into the prepared pie plate and bake at 450 degrees F. for 10 minutes or until the cheese mixture begins to brown. Remove from oven and allow to cool. Reduce the heat to 375 degrees F. and finish baking for 35 minutes or until firm. Cool thoroughly before serving.

This type of cheese cake is even more delicious when made the night before and will store in the refrigerator for days.

YIELD: 8 SERVINGS

BLUEBERRY OR STRAWBERRY CHEESE PIE

Cover the top of a cheese pie entirely with fresh fruit. Melt ½ cup currant jelly over slow heat. Add 2 drops red food coloring. Allow to cool for about 10 minutes. Then brush the fruit with the warm jelly. Chill before serving.

GRAHAM CRACKER CRUST
(for baked crust)

1½ *cups crushed graham crackers (approximately* 20 *crackers)*
¼ *cup granulated sugar*
¼ *cup soft butter*

Set oven at 350 degrees F.
One 9-inch pie plate, well greased

Combine crushed graham crackers with sugar and butter. Blend all ingredients thoroughly. Press firmly into prepared pie plate. Bake at 350 degrees F. for about 10 minutes or until crust is golden brown. Cool before filling.

GRAHAM CRACKER CRUST
(for unbaked crust)

1¼ cups crushed graham crackers (approximately 18 crackers)
¼ teaspoon ground cinnamon
⅛ teaspoon ground nutmeg
¼ cup brown sugar
¼ cup melted butter

One 9-inch pie plate or cake pan, well greased

Combine all ingredients. Press firmly with back of a spoon or a flat spatula into the bottom and sides of prepared pie plate or cake pan, as called for in the recipe. Chill in the refrigerator while preparing filling.

STRAWBERRY CHEESE CHIFFON PIE

Light, fluffy and so marvelous to eat!

one 9-inch baked Graham Cracker Pie Shell (see page 51)
1 8-oz. pkg. cream cheese
2 egg yolks
1 pkg. or 1 tablespoon unflavored gelatin
2 tablespoons hot water
4 egg whites
½ cup granulated sugar
1 cup fresh sliced strawberries
1 cup heavy cream
6 whole strawberries (optional)

Cream the cheese until smooth and without lumps. Add the egg yolks and blend well. Dissolve the gelatin in hot water, and stir it into the cheese mixture. Beat the egg whites until stiff, gradually adding ½ cup of the sugar less one tablespoon while beating. Fold the beaten egg whites into the cheese mixture. Cover the bottom of the cooled baked pie shell with sliced strawberries. Pour the cheese mixture over it, just enough to cover the fruit. Drop in more strawberries and add the remaining filling. Place in the refrigerator for at least 2 hours or until firm. Whip the cream with the remaining sugar and spread over the top of the filling. Decorate with whole fresh strawberries, if desired.

YIELD: 8 SERVINGS

Variations: Fresh blueberries, diced canned pineapple, fresh pitted or drained canned black or red cherries can also be used in place of the strawberries.

Pies, Tarts & Tartlets

PLAIN PASTRY OR PIE DOUGH

PLAIN PASTRY OR PIE DOUGH

2 cups sifted all-purpose flour
¾ teaspoon salt
1 teaspoon superfine granulated sugar
⅔ cup shortening (half butter and half Crisco), blended together at room temperature
4 to 6 tablespoons ice water

Chill flour in the refrigerator for 5 minutes. Sift flour, salt and sugar together into a mixing bowl. Blend shortening and butter; cut it into the sifted flour with a pastry blender or with the tips of your fingers until the mixture is partially blended. Sprinkle the ice water, 2 tablespoons at a time, over the flour mixture while tossing with your fingertips. Add only enough water to obtain a dough that holds together under pressure of your finger. Divide dough in 2 equal parts and roll into balls. Wrap in wax paper or foil and chill in the refrigerator for at least 2 hours before rolling. (For further information concerning the preparation of pie dough see Hints for the Preparation of Fruit Pies, page 55.)

YIELD: ONE 9- OR 10-INCH PIE CRUST WITH TOP, OR 12 TARTLET SHELLS.

CHEESE PIE DOUGH

Prepare plain pastry dough above. Roll out to approximately ¼-inch thick. Sprinkle evenly with 2 tablespoons grated American cheese and finish rolling as explained in "Hints for the Preparation of Fruit Pies."

FRUIT PIES

HINTS FOR THE PREPARATION OF FRUIT PIES

Pies, as we all know, are an American favorite. The preparation of a proper crust is very important to a successful product.

Flour, in the making of plain pastry or pie dough, should be *chilled* in the refrigerator in advance. Butter and shortening should be blended together. The fat should be distributed into the flour as evenly as possible. All ingredients have been sufficiently mixed when the shortening is the size of small peas. During the baking process, the particles of fat will melt into crisp flakes. Lard, because of its softer consistency, is sometimes used instead of shortening or butter. Ice water should be added carefully; in most cases, the amount of water specified in the recipe will have to be decreased slightly.

Don't ever try to roll out *fresh* pie dough; your chances of succeeding will be very slim. Allow the dough to chill for at least 2 hours in the refrigerator before attempting to roll. Or, to make rolling even easier, prepare the pie dough a day in advance and allow it to remain in the refrigerator overnight.

Roll out the pastry on a lightly floured board to approximately ⅛-inch thick; then fold it in half and lift it quickly into a greased pie plate. *Do not pull the dough.* Trim overhanging edges with a sharp knife and place the pie plate in the refrigerator. Roll the dough for the top crust slightly thinner, making sure it is large enough to cover the entire pie (the circle should be approximately 13 inches in diameter for a 9-inch pie) and to extend about 1½ inches beyond the edge of the pie plate. Place this on a floured baking sheet and let chill.

Prepare the filling. Then remove the pie plate from the refrigerator and brush the bottom with melted butter. Pour the filling into the pie plate. Moisten the edges of the dough with cold water. Place the top crust over the filling and seal both crusts together. Using both hands, turn the pie plate gradually until all the edges are well secured. Trim the excess dough with a sharp knife. Prick the top crust with a fork to allow the steam to escape and brush entirely with clarified butter (page 5). Dust evenly with fine granulated sugar and bake according to directions.

Note: To grease the pie plate easily and effectively, mix ½ cup shortening with 1 tablespoon flour to produce a smooth paste. Spread the mixture evenly with a round brush over the entire surface of the pie plate. Keep a supply of this mixture on hand and use when needed.

LATTICE TOP PIES

A lattic top is generally used for fruit pies because it greatly enhances their appearance.

Roll out the dough for the top crust to approximately ⅛-inch thick and cut it into strips ½-inch wide. Lay out half the strips about 1 inch apart, all the way across the cooled filling. When pie is entirely and evenly covered, place the remaining strips diagonally across and seal the ends to the bottom crust. Make certain they are securely sealed. Brush with 1 egg yolk well beaten with 1 tablespoon cold water and bake according to directions.

APPLE PIE

America's greatest favorite! Delectable and so simple to make.

6 *cups sliced apples (approximately 7 medium apples)*
¾ *cup granulated sugar*
2 *tablespoons cornstarch*
1 *teaspoon cinnamon*
¼ *teaspoon nutmeg*
4 *tablespoons melted butter*
1 *teaspoon lemon juice*
1 *tablespoon superfine granulated sugar*
pastry for a two-crust pie (page 54*)*

Set oven at 400 degrees F.
One 9-inch pie plate, greased

Greening, McIntosh, Rome Beauty or Oldenburg are the best varieties of apple to use for a successful apple pie.

Peel, core and quarter the apples and slice approximately ¼ inch thick. Combine the apples, granulated sugar, cornstarch, cinnamon, nutmeg, 3 tablespoons of butter and the lemon juice in a bowl and mix thoroughly. Line greased pie plate with pie dough as explained on page 55. Mound the filling well above the top of the plate because the fresh apples will shrink about ⅓ of their volume while baking. Secure the top crust. Brush with the remaining tablespoon of melted butter and sprinkle evenly with superfine granulated sugar. Prick with a fork and bake at 400 degrees F. for approximately 50 minutes or until golden brown. Serve warm.

YIELD: 6 SERVINGS

Note: For *cheese apple pie,* roll out top crust as explained in cheese pie dough (page 55) and serve warm with a thin slice of American cheese on top.

DEEP DISH APPLE PIE

8 *cups sliced apples, cored and peeled*
grated rind and juice of 1 *lemon*
¾ *cup light brown sugar*
¼ *cup water or canned fruit juice*
1 *teaspoon ground cinnamon*
1 *pinch ground nutmeg*
3 *tablespoons melted butter*
¾ *cup raisins*
2 *tablespoons light cream*
pastry for 1 *pie crust (page 54)*

Set oven at 425 degrees F.
One 3-quart deep baking dish

Combine the first eight ingredients and place in the baking dish. Cover with pastry dough. Make a hole approximately 1 inch in diameter in the center of the pie crust to permit the steam to escape. Brush the crust with light cream and bake at 425 degrees F. for about 15 minutes, then reduce the temperature to 350 degrees F. and finish baking for another 40 minutes. Serve hot.

YIELD: 8 SERVINGS

DEEP DISH BLUEBERRY PIE

1 cup sugar
2 tablespoons cornstarch
1 pinch salt
4 cups fresh blueberries
1 tablespoon melted butter
juice of 1 lemon
pastry for 1 pie crust (page 54)
1 tablespoon melted butter
1 tablespoon granulated sugar

Set oven at 425 degrees F.
One 1½-quart deep baking dish or soufflé mold

Combine sugar and cornstarch. Add salt and blueberries. Cook ingredients over slow heat until the juice thickens. Add the melted butter and lemon juice. Place in the baking dish and cover with pastry dough. Brush with melted butter; sprinkle evenly with granulated sugar. Bake at 425 degrees F. for approximately 35 minutes. Serve warm.
YIELD: 4 TO 5 SERVINGS

DATE OR RAISIN SOUR CREAM PIE

1 cup chopped dates or seedless raisins
1 egg
¾ cup dark brown sugar
1 cup sour cream
1 teaspoon ground cinnamon
¾ teaspoon ground nutmeg
1 pinch salt
juice of 1 lemon
pastry for 1 two-crust pie (page 54)
1 egg
1 tablespoon milk
whipped cream

Set oven at 425 degrees F.
One 9-inch pie plate, greased

Combine all filling ingredients in a deep saucepan and let soak for approximately 20 minutes. Line a greased 9-inch pie plate with pastry dough, as explained on page 55. Spoon in filling. Make a lattice design with the remaining dough. Brush with 1 egg beaten with 1 tablespoon of milk. Bake at 425 degrees F. for about 12 to 15 minutes. Reduce heat to 375 degrees F. and finish baking for approximately 35 minutes or until golden brown. Chill and serve with whipped cream.
YIELD: 6 SERVINGS

HONEY RAISIN PIE

1⅔ cups seedless raisins
1 cup fresh orange juice
2 tablespoons lemon juice
1 cup water
½ cup honey
1 pinch salt
3 tablespoons cornstarch
grated rind of 1 lemon
pastry for 1 two-crust pie (page 54)
⅓ cup crushed graham crackers
1 tablespoon melted butter
1 tablespoon superfine granulated sugar
sour cream

Set oven at 425 degrees F.
One 9-inch pie plate, greased

Wash and sort the raisins carefully. Combine in deep saucepan: orange juice, lemon juice, ⅔ cup water, honey and salt. Bring to a boil. Meanwhile, combine the cornstarch in the remaining water to dissolve it. Then add it gradually to the hot mixture and stir rapidly until all ingredients return to a boil. Remove from heat. Add grated lemon rind and raisins. Line a pie plate with pastry dough as explained on page 55. Sprinkle the bottom with crushed graham crackers. Then pour in the filling. Dot here and there with small pieces of butter. Cover with the top crust. Brush with melted butter and sprinkle with superfine granulated sugar. Prick with a fork. Bake at 425 degrees F. for approximately 35 minutes. Serve warm, accompanied by sour cream.
YIELD: 6 SERVINGS

RED SOUR CHERRY PIE

2 cups canned red sour pitted cherries
2 tablespoons cornstarch
3 tablespoons granulated sugar
1 pinch salt
1 tablespoon lemon juice
1 cup juice from the canned cherries
1 tablespoon melted butter
2 drops red food coloring
pastry for 1 two-crust pie (page 54)
1 tablespoon melted butter
1 tablespoon superfine granulated sugar

Set oven at 425 degrees F.
One 9-inch pie plate, greased

Drain the cherries and reserve one cup of juice. Blend the cornstarch, sugar and salt together. Add the lemon juice and cherry juice gradually to the cornstarch mixture. Place over a slow fire and cook slowly until the mixture boils. Add the butter, cherries and red food coloring; remove from heat and allow ingredients to cool thoroughly. In the meantime, line a greased pie plate with pastry dough, as explained on page 55. Pour in the prepared and cooled filling and cover with the top crust. Brush with the melted butter and sprinkle with granulated superfine sugar. Prick with a fork. Bake at 425 degrees F. for approximately 15 minutes. Reduce the heat to 375 degrees F. and continue baking for about 35 minutes longer or until the crust is browned.

YIELD: 6 SERVINGS

BLUEBERRY PIE

pastry for 1 *two-crust pie (page* 54*)*
4 *cups fresh blueberries*
1 *cup granulated sugar*
1 *tablespoon cornstarch*
1 *pinch salt*
1 *tablespoon lemon juice*
1 *tablespoon melted butter*
1 *tablespoon superfine granulated sugar*

Set oven at 400 degrees F.
One 9-inch pie plate, greased

Wash and clean the berries. Line the prepared pie plate with pastry dough as explained on page 55 and refrigerate while preparing the filling. Drain the berries thoroughly; then mix all above filling ingredients together. Pour into the prepared pie shell. Cover with the top crust and seal the edges. Brush with melted butter and sprinkle with superfine granulated sugar. Prick with a fork. Bake at 400 degrees F. for approximately 40 minutes or until golden brown. Cool before serving.

YIELD: 6 SERVINGS

MANGO PIE

pastry for 1 *two-crust pie (page* 54)
4 *cups peeled mango slices* (not *too ripe*)
¾ *cup granulated sugar*
½ *teaspoon ground cinnamon*
¼ *teaspoon ground nutmeg*
2 *tablespoons cornstarch*
1½ *tablespoons lemon juice*
1 *tablespoon melted butter*

Set oven at 425 degrees F.
One 9-inch pie plate, greased

Line the prepared pie plate with pastry dough as explained on page 55. Arrange a layer of sliced mangos on the bottom of the plate and dust with sugar, spices and cornstarch. Cover with the remaining mangos. Sprinkle with lemon juice. Cover with the top crust and brush with melted butter. Prick with a fork. Bake at 425 degrees F. for approximately 15 minutes. Reduce heat to 350 degrees F. and continue baking for about 30 minutes or until golden brown.
YIELD: 6 SERVINGS

NEW ORLEANS FRY PIES

I. FILLING

2 *cups sliced apples or apricots, stewed until tender or*
fresh sliced peaches, cherries or blueberries
2 *tablespoons granulated sugar*
pinch of cinnamon

Combine the fruit with the sugar and cinnamon.

II. DOUGH

1 *cup all-purpose flour*
¼ *teaspoon double-acting baking powder*
1 *teaspoon granulated sugar*
½ *teaspoon salt*
2 *tablespoons melted butter*
1 *egg, beaten with a fork*
2 *tablespoons milk, approximately*
½ *cup confectioners sugar*

One 2-quart deep saucepan
2 quarts oil or shortening, heated to 365 degrees F.

Sift together twice: flour, baking powder, sugar and salt. Make a hole in the center of the flour and place melted butter and beaten egg in it. Blend all ingredients well, adding milk gradually until dough of a rolling consistency is obtained (a little more or less milk may be necessary, depending on the quality of the flour).

Form dough into a ball. Wrap in wax paper and place in the refrigerator to chill until firm or for approximately 30 minutes. Then roll it to about ⅛-inch thick on a floured board and cut into 3-inch squares. Place approximately 2 tablespoons of fruit filling in the center of each square. Moisten the edges with cold water, fold into a triangle and seal the edges tightly together by pressing with your fingers. Let stand in the refrigerator for 15 minutes. Fry in deep fat until golden brown. Serve hot, dusted with confectioners sugar.

YIELD: 4 INDIVIDUAL PIES

CHIFFON AND CREAM PIES; ONE-CRUST PIES

HOW TO PREPARE AND BAKE ONE-CRUST FLUTED PIE SHELLS
(*for Chiffon Pie, Cream Pie, Custard Pie, etc.*)

Prepare half of the recipe given for plain pastry or pie dough (page 54). Roll out to approximately ⅛-inch thick. Place in a greased pie plate. Trim the edge of the dough approximately ¾-inch beyond the edge of the pie plate. Make a rim with your fingers by pinching the dough all around the pie plate, securing the dough properly and evenly against the border of the pie plate. Press gently with your thumb and forefinger to make an attractive fluted design.

If a *partially baked* pie shell is needed (for Custard Pie, Pecan Pie, etc.) prick all over with a fork. Cover dough with a 14-inch circle of wax paper and fill to the top with uncooked beans or raw rice (this is done to keep the dough from rising during the baking process). Bake at 425 degrees F. for about 15 minutes. Take out of oven; remove paper and rice or beans and cool shell. Proceed as explained in recipe.

If a *fully baked* pie shell is needed (for Chiffon Pie, Cream Pie, Cheese Pie, etc.) proceed as explained above. Take out of oven; remove paper and rice or beans. Reduce heat to 400 degrees F.; return shell to oven and finish baking for approximately 15 minutes or until golden brown. *Always* bake pie shells thoroughly and *always* cool before adding desired filling. Proceed as explained in recipe.

CHIFFON AND CREAM PIES

PIE SHELLS FOR CHIFFON OR CREAM PIES

Pie shells for Chiffon or Cream Pies should be thoroughly baked to a golden brown. For detailed instructions on how to prepare and bake one-crust pie shells, see page 62. Pie shells can be baked several days in advance and stored in the refrigerator, or baked and frozen indefinitely.

FILLING

The filling should be perfectly blended before pouring into pre-baked and cooled pie shells. Unflavored gelatin is generally used unless otherwise specified in the recipe and must be *entirely* dissolved before using to insure that the filling will stiffen evenly throughout.

In recipes calling for beaten egg whites, they should be beaten to a medium peak. (For detailed instructions on how to beat egg whites properly, see page 14.) Beaten egg whites should be *folded gently* and evenly distributed throughout the mixture; mixing should be kept to an absolute minimum to avoid breaking down the air cells.

Whipped cream used in the mixing process should be beaten until it holds its shape but is not too stiff.

TOPPING AND FINISHING

Whipped cream used for garnishing should be beaten to a stiffer consistency and sweetened in the proportion of 2 tablespoons superfine granulated sugar to each cup of heavy cream. (For detailed instructions on how to whip cream properly, see page 11.)

Place Chiffon or Cream Pies in the refrigerator until the filling is firm before attempting to top with whipped cream or meringue.

A pastry bag fitted with a star tube is the best tool for spreading topping. If one is not available, use a flat, flexible spatula. Spread topping evenly. Finish as directed in the individual recipe.

Note: To avoid rushing, I suggest you prepare the baked pie shell and filling a day in advance. Allow the filled pie shell to remain in the refrigerator overnight. The following day, beat the heavy cream or prepare the meringue topping and finish pie as directed.

PUMPKIN PIE

1½ cups thick canned pumpkin meat
⅔ cup granulated sugar
1 teaspoon all-purpose flour
½ teaspoon salt
¾ teaspoon ground cinnamon
¼ teaspoon ground nutmeg
¼ teaspoon ground cloves
3 eggs, beaten with a fork
1 cup milk
⅔ cup light cream or evaporated milk

Set oven at 425 degrees F.
One 9-inch partially baked pie shell (page 62)

Combine pumpkin meat, sugar, flour, salt and spices. Gradually stir in beaten eggs. Add milk, light cream or evaporated milk. Let the pumpkin mixture stand for 30 minutes at room temperature. Then stir and pour it into the partially baked shell. Bake at 425 degrees F. for approximately 15 minutes. Reduce heat to 400 degrees F. and finish baking for approximately 30 minutes or until a knife, when inserted through the center, comes out clean. Cool before serving. Can be served with or without whipped cream.
YIELD: 6 SERVINGS

SOUR CREAM APPLE PIE

DOUGH

½ cup soft butter
½ cup cream cheese
1½ cups cake flour, sifted
1 pinch salt
1 teaspoon sugar

Set oven at 425 degrees F.
One 10-inch pie plate, greased

Blend butter and cream cheese. Stir in flour, salt and sugar; work all ingredients to form a smooth dough of rolling consistency. Place in refrigerator to chill for approximately 30 minutes. Roll out on a floured board to about ⅛-inch thick. Arrange in the prepared pie plate. Trim the edges and make a rim all around the border of the pie plate as explained on page 62.

FILLING

4 *cooking apples*	½ *teaspoon cinnamon*
⅓ *cup sour cream*	1 *pinch nutmeg*
½ *cup confectioners sugar*	1 *teaspoon lemon juice*

Peel, core and slice the apples approximately ¼-inch thick. Arrange apples in a circle on the bottom of the pie shell with each slice overlapping. Mix together sour cream, confectioners sugar, cinnamon, nutmeg and lemon juice. Blend all ingredients well and spread evenly over the apples. Bake at 425 degrees F. for about 10 minutes. Reduce the heat to 350 degrees F. and finish baking for about 35 minutes or until the apples are tender when pricked with a fork. Serve warm.

YIELD: 8 SERVINGS

APRICOT WONDER PIE

FILLING

4 *cups fresh apricot halves*	½ *cup light brown sugar*
1 *teaspoon lemon juice*	1 *tablespoon cornstarch*
2 *eggs plus* 1 *egg yolk*	½ *cup thick sour cream*

One partially baked 9-inch pie shell (page 62)
Set oven at 450 degrees F.

Prepare the pie shell (page 62). When the shell has cooled, fill it to the top with apricots. Blend well the lemon juice, eggs and extra yolk, brown sugar, cornstarch and sour cream. Pour over the apricots and let soak while preparing the topping.

TOPPING

2 *tablespoons soft butter*	⅛ *teaspoon ground cinnamon*
2 *tablespoons granulated sugar*	⅓ *cup cake flour*

Blend butter, granulated sugar, cinnamon and unsifted flour by rubbing between your fingers until a crumbly consistency is obtained. Dust this mixture over the top of the apricots to cover evenly and entirely. Bake at 450 degrees F. for about 10 minutes; reduce heat to 375 degrees F. and bake for about 35 minutes longer or until golden brown.

YIELD: 6 TO 8 SERVINGS

BANANA CREAM PIE

2 large ripe bananas, sliced thin
3 egg yolks
2/3 cup granulated sugar
1/4 cup corn starch
1 pinch salt
2 cups milk
1 cup light cream
2 tablespoons butter
1 teaspoon vanilla
1 1/2 cups whipped cream
1/3 cup grated sweet chocolate

One 9-inch graham cracker pie shell, baked (page 51)

Line the bottom of the baked pie shell with the sliced bananas. Beat the egg yolks until light. Mix the cornstarch, salt and sugar together in a saucepan and gradually stir in the milk and cream, cooking over medium heat until the mixture comes to a boil. Remove from heat and gradually stir the hot mixture into the egg yolks. Blend well, and then add the butter and vanilla. Pour the hot filling into the prepared pie shell and cool for at least 2 hours. Then garnish with whipped cream, sprinkle with grated chocolate and refrigerate until ready to serve.

YIELD: 6 SERVINGS

RUM CREAM PIE

CUSTARD FILLING

1/2 cup heavy cream
1 tablespoon or 1 envelope unflavored gelatin
1/4 cup hot water
1 cup milk
3 eggs, separated
1/2 cup plus 1 tablespoon granulated sugar
4 tablespoons dark rum

One baked and cooled 9-inch fluted pie shell (page 62)

Whip the cream and place it in the refrigerator to chill. Soak the gelatin in the hot water and let it stand while preparing the following: Scald the milk. Combine the egg yolks and ½ cup sugar in a deep bowl. Gradually, and in a slow stream, pour the scalded milk over the yolks mixture. Place over hot water and cook, stirring, until the mixture becomes thick enough to coat a spoon. DO NOT BOIL. Add soaked gelatin and rum. Remove from heat and cool in refrigerator or over cold water until the mixture starts to set.

Beat the egg whites stiff but not dry, adding 1 tablespoon sugar gradually while beating. Gently fold the egg whites alternately with the whipped cream into the custard mixture. *Do not overmix.* Pour the mixture into the baked and cooled pie shell and let set in the refrigerator for approximately 4 hours or until firm to the touch.

TOPPING:

one 9-inch round sheet cake ⅓-inch thick (use any cake batter of your choice, such as Sponge (page 23) or Chocolate Cake (page 24))
¼ *cup dark rum*
1 *cup heavy cream*
1 *tablespoon granulated sugar*
2 *tablespoons grated sweet chocolate*

One hour or so before serving, cover the pie with a round sheet cake the same size as the pie and approximately ⅓-inch thick. Brush with rum. Beat heavy cream and sugar together until stiff. Spread beaten cream evenly over the soaked sheet cake; cover the pie entirely. Dust with grated sweet chocolate. Serve chilled. Cut pie with a sharp knife dipped in hot water.
YIELD: 6 TO 8 SERVINGS

SOUTHERN PECAN PIE

A perfectly delicious, traditional Southern dessert.

PECAN PASTRY DOUGH

½ *recipe for Pastry Dough (page 54) blended with ⅓ cup finely ground pecans and*
1 *tablespoon cold water*

Set oven at 350 degrees F.
One 9-inch pie plate, greased

Line the prepared pie plate with Pecan Pastry Dough; flute the edges and partially bake as explained in the preparation of partially baked pie shells, page 62. Cool shell.

Meanwhile, prepare the following:

FILLING

2/3 cup superfine granulated sugar
3 eggs
1 cup dark corn syrup
1 teaspoon vanilla extract
1/4 cup melted butter
1 cup halved pecans

Stir the sugar into the eggs. Add the corn syrup, vanilla extract and melted butter. Blend all ingredients thoroughly. Pour into the prepared pie shell. Sprinkle pecan halves on top. Bake at 350 degrees F. for approximately 1 hour or until the point of a knife, when inserted through the center, comes out clean.
YIELD: 6 TO 8 SERVINGS

AMERICANA COCONUT CUSTARD PIE

An extravagant dessert that has been a favorite of guests of the Americana Hotel in Miami Beach, Florida, for years.

one 9-inch partially baked fluted pie shell (page 62)
1 cup shredded coconut
4 eggs
1/3 cup granulated sugar
1 pinch salt
2 cups milk } *scalded*
1 cup light cream } *scalded*
3 drops vanilla extract

Set oven at 450 degrees F.

Spread shredded coconut evenly in a baking pan and toast for approximately 10 minutes at 375 degrees F. until golden brown. Remove from oven and cool.

Beat the eggs until thoroughly blended; stir in the sugar, salt, scalded milk and light cream. Add the vanilla extract. Sprinkle the

toasted coconut on the bottom of the pie shell. Fill completely with the liquid custard mixture. Bake for approximately 12 minutes at 450 degrees F. Reduce heat to 325 degrees F. and bake for another 40 to 45 minutes or until the point of a knife, when inserted through the center of the pie, comes out clean. Cool and chill before serving.
YIELD: 6 SERVINGS

HINTS FOR BETTER MERINGUE PIE TOPPING

In order to stop meringue from sweating, I recommend a very small addition of cornstarch. One-half teaspoon should be enough for one cup of egg whites.

Meringue topping for pie should always be spread over a rather firm, cool filling. If it is to be baked or browned, dust lightly with confectioners sugar before placing in the oven; this helps the formation of a thin crust and will improve the appearance of your pie, act as a protective film against dampness and strengthen the topping considerably.

Oven temperature should not exceed 425 degrees F. when browning the meringue. You must allow time for the meringue to bake inside. Meringue browned in a very hot oven will sweat and shrink rapidly, giving a poor appearance to the finished pie.

When cutting pies or cakes topped with or frosted with meringue, always use a sharp knife dipped in water and wiped with a towel after each slice is cut.

LEMON MERINGUE PIE

one 9-inch baked fluted pie shell (page 62)

FILLING

3 *egg yolks*	1½ *cups milk*
1 *cup sugar*	*grated rind of 1 lemon*
⅓ *cup cornstarch*	2 *tablespoons butter*
1 *pinch salt*	¼ *cup lemon juice*

Set oven at 400 degrees F.

Beat the egg yolks with 2 tablespoons of sugar until thick. In a deep saucepan, blend together remaining sugar, cornstarch and salt; gradually stir in the milk. Bring to a boil. Remove from heat and gradually pour in the beaten egg yolks, stirring rapidly after each addition. Return to heat for at least 1 more minute. Remove from heat; add grated lemon rind, butter and lemon juice. Blend thoroughly. Pour immediately into the baked pie shell and cool.

MERINGUE:

3 egg whites
½ teaspoon lemon juice
6 tablespoons sugar
½ teaspoon cornstarch

Beat the egg whites until foamy and add the lemon juice. Gradually add the sugar and cornstarch and continue beating until stiff. Spread the cooled pie with the meringue and bake at 400 degrees F. for approximately 15 minutes or until golden brown.
YIELD: 6 TO 8 SERVINGS

ORIGINAL KEY LIME PIE
(As told by "The Fisherman" of Key Largo)

one 9-inch baked pie shell (page 62)
6 egg yolks, beaten slightly with a fork
1 can sweetened condensed milk (15 oz.)
½ cup lime juice
grated rind of 1 lime
5 egg whites
5 tablespoons sugar
confectioners sugar

Set oven at 350 degrees F.

Combine egg yolks and condensed milk; blend thoroughly. Add lime juice, grated rind and stir well. Pour into the cooled pie shell. Allow mixture to set for about 20 minutes in a cool place. Meanwhile, beat the egg whites until they form soft peaks; then gradually add the sugar, one tablespoon at a time, and continue beating until the egg whites are stiff. Spread the meringue evenly over the prepared and cooled filling. Dust with confectioners sugar and bake at 350 degrees F. for approximately 15 minutes or until the meringue is golden brown. Cool and serve.
YIELD: 6 TO 8 SERVINGS

AMERICANA KEY LIME PIE

It's spectacular, gorgeous and especially delicious!

one 9-inch baked pie shell (page 62)
1 *tablespoon or 1 envelope unflavored gelatin*
1 *cup sugar*
¼ *teaspoon salt*
4 *eggs, separated*
½ *cup lime juice*
¼ *cup water*
1 *teaspoon grated lime peel*
3 *drops green food coloring*
2 *cups heavy cream, whipped*
1 *tablespoon grated pistachio nuts*
lime wedges to garnish

Thoroughly combine gelatin, ½ cup sugar and salt in a saucepan. Beat together egg yolks, lime juice and water; stir into gelatin mixture. Cook over medium heat, stirring constantly, until mixture comes to a boil. Remove from heat and stir in grated lime peel. Add food coloring sparingly to give a pale green color. Chill in refrigerator or over cold water until the mixture mounds slightly when dropped from a spoon. Stir occasionally to accelerate cooling.

Beat egg whites until soft peaks form; then gradually add remaining ½ cup sugar, beating to stiff peaks. Fold egg whites into cooled gelatin mixture. Fold in 1 cup of whipped cream. Pile into cooled pastry shell and chill until set. Garnish with remaining cup of whipped cream. Dust center with grated pistachio nuts. Garnish each serving with a wedge of lime.

YIELD: 6 TO 8 SERVINGS

CRANBERRY CHIFFON PIE

one 9-inch baked pie shell (page 62)
1 *16-oz. jar or can of unstrained cranberry sauce (approximately 1½ cups)*
2 *tablespoons lemon juice*
½ *cup boiling water*
1 *3-oz. package lemon-flavored gelatin*
1 *cup heavy cream*
2 *egg whites*
¼ *cup sugar*
red candied cherries, to garnish

Combine cranberry sauce and lemon juice in a saucepan and heat to boiling point. Remove from heat. Pour hot water over the lemon gelatin and stir well to dissolve. Combine with the cranberry sauce and cool in refrigerator or over cold water until the mixture starts to set. Stir from time to time to accelerate cooling. Whip ½ cup of the heavy cream. Beat the egg whites stiff but not dry, adding the sugar gradually while beating. Gently fold the beaten egg whites alternately with the whipped cream into the cooled cranberry mixture. Pour into the cooled pie shell, and chill in the refrigerator until firm or for approximately 2 hours. Whip the remaining ½ cup of cream to garnish and decorate with red candied cherries.

YIELD: 6 TO 8 SERVINGS

ORANGE CHIFFON PIE

one 9-inch baked fluted pie shell (page 62)
1 *tablespoon or 1 envelope unflavored gelatin*
¾ *cup sugar*
1 *pinch salt*
2 *eggs, separated*
1 *cup orange juice*
grated rind of 2 oranges
2 *tablespoons lemon juice*
1 *pinch cream of tartar*
1½ *cups heavy cream, whipped*
orange sections to garnish (optional)

Stir the gelatin, ½ cup of sugar and salt together in the top of a double boiler. Mix the egg yolks with the orange juice and add to the gelatin mixture. Place over hot water and stir constantly until the gelatin is completely dissolved. Remove from heat and add grated orange rind and lemon juice. Chill in refrigerator or over cold water until the mixture begins to set, stirring from time to time to accelerate cooling. Beat the egg whites rapidly with the cream of tartar; continue beating and gradually add the remaining sugar. Beat until stiff but not too dry. Whip one cup of the heavy cream. Fold first the beaten egg whites and then the whipped cream into the cooled gelatin mixture. Pour into the pie shell and chill in the refrigerator for approximately 2 hours or until firm. Whip the remaining ½ cup of cream to garnish, and decorate with orange sections if desired.

YIELD: 6 TO 8 SERVINGS

RUM CHIFFON PIE

one 9-inch baked, fluted pie shell (page 62)
1½ tablespoons or 1½ envelopes unflavored gelatin
⅓ cup hot water
6 egg yolks
⅔ cup sugar
⅓ cup Jamaica rum
2½ cups heavy cream, whipped
2 egg whites, beaten stiff with
2 tablespoons sugar
½ cup grated sweet chocolate

Dissolve gelatin by sprinkling it over the hot water. Beat egg yolks and ⅔ cup of sugar together until fluffy and pale in color. Stir and strain the gelatin mixture into the egg yolk mixture and mix rapidly to combine all ingredients thoroughly. Add the rum. Cool in refrigerator or over cold water, stirring from time to time to accelerate cooling. When the mixture begins to set, whip 2 cups of the heavy cream. Beat the egg whites together with 2 tablespoons of sugar. Fold into cooled gelatin mixture and follow immediately with the whipped cream, mixing well to blend all ingredients thoroughly. Pour the creamy mixture into the cooled pie shell. Chill in the refrigerator for approximately 2 hours or until firm. Whip the remaining ½ cup of cream to garnish and sprinkle with grated chocolate. YIELD: 6 TO 8 SERVINGS

PUMPKIN CHIFFON PIE

one 9-inch baked pie shell (page 62)
1 envelope or 1 tablespoon unflavored gelatin
¾ cup light brown sugar
½ teaspoon ground cinnamon
⅓ teaspoon ground nutmeg
⅓ teaspoon ginger
½ teaspoon salt
1½ cups mashed canned pumpkin
4 egg yolks
½ cup light cream
3 egg whites
⅓ cup granulated sugar
½ cup whipped cream

Place gelatin, brown sugar, spices, salt, pumpkin, egg yolks and light cream in a deep saucepan. Cook all ingredients over low heat, stirring constantly, until the mixture begins to boil. Remove from heat and place in refrigerator or over cold water to cool, stirring from time to time to accelerate cooling. When the mixture begins to set, beat the egg whites stiff, adding the sugar gradually while beating. Fold into the cooled pumpkin mixture. Pour into the cooled pie shell and chill in the refrigerator for at least 2 hours or until firm. Garnish with whipped cream.

YIELD: 6 TO 8 SERVINGS

NESSELRODE CHIFFON PIE

one 9-inch baked and fluted pie shell (page 62)
1 tablespoon or 1 envelope unflavored gelatin
2/3 cup granulated sugar
2 tablespoons cornstarch
1 cup scalded milk
6 egg yolks
2 tablespoons brandy
1 3-oz. jar Nesselrode mixture (mixed, chopped, glazed fruits)
2 cups heavy cream, whipped
6 glazed cherries

Place gelatin, sugar and cornstarch in a deep saucepan; gradually add the hot milk while stirring rapidly. Place over low heat and bring all ingredients to a boil. Boil for approximately 1 minute. Remove from heat. Beat egg yolks until fluffy and pale in color; add the brandy and Nesselrode mixture. Stir rapidly into the hot mixture. Blend all ingredients well. Cool in refrigerator or over cold water, stirring from time to time to accelerate cooling. When the mixture begins to set, fold in 1 cup of the whipped cream. Pour into the cooled pie shell and place in the refrigerator for at least 2 hours or until firm. Garnish with the remaining whipped cream and decorate with red glazed cherries.

YIELD: 6 TO 8 SERVINGS

COFFEE CHIFFON PIE

one 9-inch baked fluted pie shell (page 62)
1½ cups strong coffee
1 tablespoon or 1 envelope unflavored gelatin
½ cup granulated sugar
3 eggs, separated
1½ cups heavy cream, whipped
½ cup grated sweet chocolate

Place coffee, gelatin, ¼ cup of sugar and the egg yolks in a saucepan and stir well to blend all ingredients. Place over hot water and beat constantly until gelatin is well dissolved. Chill in refrigerator or over cold water until the mixture begins to set, stirring from time to time to accelerate cooling. Beat the egg whites stiff but not dry, adding the remaining sugar gradually while beating. Fold into gelatin mixture, followed by ⅔ cup of the whipped cream. Fold into a baked pie shell. Chill in the refrigerator for at least 2 hours or until firm. Garnish with the remaining whipped cream and sprinkle with finely grated sweet chocolate.

YIELD: 6 TO 8 SERVINGS

CHOCOLATE CHIFFON PIE

Extra light, fluffy and so luscious to look at!

one 9-inch fluted baked pie shell (page 62)
1 *tablespoon or 1 envelope of unflavored gelatin*
⅔ *cup sugar*
1 *cup milk*
2 *eggs, separated*
7 *oz. or approximately 1 cup grated semi-sweet chocolate*
1 *teaspoon instant coffee*
1½ *cups heavy cream, whipped stiff*
3 *tablespoons grated sweet chocolate*
1½ *cups whipped cream to garnish*

Blend gelatin and ⅓ cup sugar in the top half of a double-boiler. Place over hot water. Add milk, egg yolks and grated chocolate and stir rapidly to dissolve all ingredients. Stir in instant coffee and remove from heat. Place over cold water or in refrigerator to chill, stirring from time to time to accelerate cooling. When the mixture starts to set, beat the egg whites stiff but not dry, adding remaining sugar gradually while beating. Gently fold egg whites alternately with 1½ cups of the whipped cream into the chocolate mixture. Pour into the cooled pie shell and chill in the refrigerator for approximately 1 hour or until set. Garnish with 1½ cups of whipped cream and sprinkle with grated sweet chocolate.

YIELD: 6 TO 8 SERVINGS

STRAWBERRY CHIFFON PIE
(with frozen strawberries)

one 9-inch baked, fluted pie shell (page 62)
2/3 cup plus 2 tablespoons granulated sugar
1 tablespoon or 1 envelope unflavored gelatin
juice of 1 lemon
1 10-oz. package frozen strawberries with juice
2 egg whites
1 1/4 cups heavy cream, whipped
6 whole strawberries, to garnish

Blend 2/3 cup sugar, gelatin, lemon juice and strawberries in a deep bowl. Place over hot water and cook until all ingredients are well dissolved. Stir constantly to avoid burning. Cool the mixture by placing the bowl in the refrigerator or over cold water. Stir from time to time to accelerate cooling. When the mixture begins to set, beat the egg whites until stiff but not dry, adding the remaining 2 tablespoons of sugar gradually while beating. Immediately fold into the strawberry mixture alternately with 3/4 cup of the whipped cream. Pour into the cooled pie shell and chill in the refrigerator at least 2 hours or until set. Garnish with the remaining whipped cream and decorate with whole strawberries.

YIELD: 6 SERVINGS

STRAWBERRY CHIFFON PIE
(with fresh strawberries)

one 9-inch baked, fluted pie shell (page 62)
2 1/2 cups fresh ripe strawberries
1/2 cup granulated sugar
1 tablespoon or 1 envelope unflavored gelatin
1/4 cup hot water
2 egg whites
1/3 cup granulated sugar
1 3/4 cups heavy cream, whipped

Wash and hull the strawberries under cold water until clean. Put aside 8 large ones to decorate the finished pie. Slice the remaining strawberries and combine with the sugar. Let them soak for about 30 minutes or so and then strain the juice into a deep saucepan.

Sprinkle the gelatin over the hot water to soften; then blend with strawberry juice and heat over hot water until dissolved. Add the sliced strawberries to the gelatin and chill until the mixture starts to set; stir from time to time to accelerate cooling. Beat the egg whites and sugar together until stiff. Fold the beaten egg whites into the cooled gelatin mixture and follow immediately with ¾ cup of the whipped cream. Pour into the pie shell and refrigerate until firm. Garnish with the remaining whipped cream and decorate with the whole strawberries.

YIELD: 6 TO 8 SERVINGS

TARTS

Without a doubt, tarts are to Europeans what pies are to Americans; the everyday dessert!

Tarts are more elegant, however. And what could be simpler than an open pie where the crust is at the bottom and the filling on top?

Time is the most important factor for housewives when it comes to the preparation of an elaborate or even simple meal. With the making of tarts, this problem is easily overcome because most of the ingredients can be prepared well in advance and, luckily, baked several hours prior to the arrival of guests.

In this chapter, you will acquaint yourself with some of the most renowned traditional European tarts and tartlets. You are about to discover a new and easy way to present your favorite fruits in an elegant way.

Throughout this book, you will frequently hear me stress *plan in advance, relax* and *have patience.* I firmly believe that by following this advice, you will not only attain success but you will also come to realize that a hostess can look forward to *enjoying* her company. The hectic confusion that often occurs when the housewife has to do the cooking, baking and entertaining, can be kept at an absolute minimum if you follow my suggestions. Adhere to the simple rules and, with a little experience, you will be amazed at how quickly tarts or tartlets can be prepared.

Tart dough has to be chilled before it is rolled and folded over the greased mold. So why not prepare the dough one day ahead of time;

wrap it up in aluminum foil and store it in the refrigerator until needed. If a prebaked tart shell is called for in the recipe, you can bake it the previous day; if this is the case, allow your dough to chill in the refrigerator for 1 hour or so and then proceed as explained in the *Making and Baking of Tart Shells* (page 79). Cool and store it in a place where there is little risk of breakage because the shells are fragile.

Cream, such as Pastry Cream or Frangipane Cream used for tarts or tartlets, can also be cooked or mixed in advance. Store creams in the refrigerator or freezer in a tightly covered stainless steel or chinaware bowl. Remove cream from refrigerator approximately 1 hour before using. Stir well with a wooden spoon to smooth and soften before placing cream into the prepared tart shell. Several hours before your scheduled meal, preheat the oven; assemble everything as explained in the individual recipe and bake according to directions. The final preparations, not including baking, will take no longer than 25 to 30 minutes.

Note: Molds for tarts or tartlets are available in any hardware or department store. Unless otherwise specified tarts are generally baked in round tins or aluminum molds, 9 or 10 inches in diameter and 1½-inches deep.

TART DOUGH

- 2 *cups* (7 *oz.*) *sifted all-purpose flour*
- 3 *tablespoons superfine granulated sugar*
- 1 *pinch or* ⅛ *teaspoon double-acting baking powder*
- 1 *egg beaten with a fork*
- *grated rind of* 1 *lemon*
- 7 *tablespoons soft butter*
- 1 *to* 2 *tablespoons milk, as needed*

Sift flour, sugar and baking powder in a round-bottomed bowl or on a pastry board and make a hole or well in the center. Drop the beaten egg, lemon rind and soft butter into the well and knead all ingredients together, to form a dough of rolling consistency. If dough appears to be too stiff, add 1 tablespoon of cold milk; if too soft, add 1 tablespoon of flour. Form the dough into a ball, wrap in waxed paper or foil, and place in the refrigerator to cool for at least 2 hours or until firm. This dough is also widely used in the making of individual tartlets.

YIELD: ONE 9- OR 10-INCH TART SHELL OR 12 INDIVIDUAL TARTLETS.

TO LINE A TART MOLD:

Roll out the chilled tart dough in a circle approximately 1/8-inch thick and about 14 inches in diameter on a floured board. Roll the dough over a floured rolling pin, place the pin over the greased mold and unroll the dough. Gently press around the sides of the mold with your fingers; avoid breaking the dough. Trim the dough evenly about 3/4-inch beyond the edge of the pan; flute the border with your thumb and forefinger to make a rim. Pinch the rim with a pastry pincher or with your fingers. Chill for at least 30 minutes before placing any filling into the shell.

TO BAKE A TART SHELL:

Some recipes call for a prebaked shell. If this is the case, prick the bottom and sides of the dough well with a fork, and cover entirely with wax paper. Fill the empty shell with dry beans or uncooked rice to prevent the dough from rising during the baking. Bake at 400 degrees F. When the crust begins to brown (approximately 15 minutes) remove the paper and the beans or rice and bake another 15 minutes or until the shell shrinks slightly from the mold and begins to brown evenly. Cool before unmolding.
Total baking time: 25 to 35 minutes

LEFTOVER TART DOUGH:

It can be wrapped in waxed paper or foil and stored in the refrigerator for several days. It can also be used for making cookies. Roll out the dough on a floured board to approximately 1/4-inch thick. Cut out with a fancy cutter and brush with a beaten egg. Dust with granulated sugar and, if desired, decorate each cookie with a glazed cherry or nuts in the center. (Wet the nuts to be sure they stick.) Bake at 375 degrees F. for approximately 10 minutes or until golden brown.

TO UNMOLD BAKED TART SAFELY:

Cool thoroughly at room temperature for at least 1 hour or more. To unmold, proceed as follows:

1. Loosen sides by running the point of a knife all around the edges between the dough and mold.
2. Place a flat strong cardboard or flat tray over the baked and cooled tart.
3. Hold it tightly against the mold and quickly turn it upside down.
4. Remove cake pan.
5. Place a flat serving tray or plate over the bottom dough.
6. Put your finger underneath the cardboard and return the tart to an upright position.

GLAZE FOR FRUIT TARTS

To glaze and give a really professional finish to all your Tarts and Tartlets, use the following recipes. The glaze can be prepared in advance and stored in the refrigerator. When needed, simply heat to lukewarm over a slow flame or over hot water.

APRICOT GLAZE

1 *cup clear apricot preserves* ¼ *cup water*

In a deep saucepan, heat the apricot preserves and water until the ingredients come just to the boil. Strain and cool to lukewarm. Keep warm over hot water. Gently coat the surface of the fruit, using a flat pastry brush.

CURRANT JELLY GLAZE

1 *cup currant jelly* 3 *drops red food coloring*
1 *tablespoon water*

Boil the jelly and water until the ingredients are melted. Add food coloring and cool to lukewarm. Keep warm over hot water. Gently coat the surface of the fruit using a flat pastry brush.

PEAR TART ANDALOUSE

1 Tart Dough recipe (page 78)
3 tablespoons apricot jam
5 to 6 fresh pears
2 cups dry red wine
1 cup water
2½ cups granulated sugar
1 stick cinnamon
1 cup Vanilla Pastry Cream (page 289)
Rum Icing

Set oven at 400 degrees F.
One 9-inch round tart mold, greased

Line the tart mold with tart dough as explained on page 79. Spread the bottom with apricot jam. Peel, halve and core the fresh pears. Prepare the following syrup: Boil the wine, water, sugar and stick of cinnamon together for 1 minute. Pour the prepared pears into the hot syrup and simmer gently for 10 to 15 minutes or until the pears become tender but remain firm. Cool the pears in the syrup. In the meantime, prepare half the recipe for Vanilla Pastry Cream (about 1 cup). Drain the pears thoroughly and lay them in the tart shell, bottom side down and as close to each other as possible. When the pastry cream is thoroughly cooled, spread it over the pears to cover them entirely. Bake in a preheated 400 degrees F. oven for about 40 minutes or until golden brown. Cool, unmold and brush with warm Rum Icing (following recipe).
YIELD: 6 SERVINGS

Note: Tart dough and Pastry Cream can be prepared a day in advance and stored in the refrigerator.

RUM ICING FOR TART ANDALOUSE

½ cup superfine granulated sugar
¼ cup water
1 pinch cream of tartar
1 cup confectioners sugar
1 teaspoon red food coloring
1 teaspoon Jamaica rum

Boil the sugar with water and cream of tartar. When the syrup thickens after 1 minute or so of continuous boiling, remove from heat and add enough sifted confectioners sugar to form a mixture the consistency of a very soft frosting. Add the red food coloring and rum. Brush quickly over the tart while the icing is still warm.

DUTCH APPLE TART

1 *Tart Dough recipe (page 78)*
5 *or* 6 *large baking apples*
¼ *cup butter*
4 *tablespoons granulated sugar*
1 *tablespoon cornstarch*
1 *pinch ground cinnamon*
1 *cup Vanilla Pastry Cream made with brown sugar (page 289)*
Apricot Glaze (page 80)
1½ *cups whipped cream (optional)*

Set oven at 400 degrees F.
One 9-inch round tart mold, 1½-inches deep

Line the tart mold with the dough as previously explained (page 79). Place in the refrigerator while preparing the following: Peel, core and slice the apples ¼-inch thick. Combine the apples and butter in a saucepan. Cover and cook over medium heat for approximately 5 minutes or until the apples begin to soften. Stir from time to time to avoid burning. Then sprinkle sugar blended with cornstarch and cinnamon over the apples. Stir well to mix all ingredients and continue cooking for 2 more minutes. Remove from heat and cool. Pour the cooled mixture into the prepared tart shell, filling it to within ¼-inch from the top. Bake at 400 degrees F. for about 40 minutes or until golden brown. Cool thoroughly.

Cook half of the Vanilla Pastry Cream recipe (page 289) using brown sugar instead of granulated sugar. Pour the hot pastry cream over the baked and cooled tart. Let cool for 20 minutes or until the cream has formed a solid crust. Brush entirely with hot Apricot Glaze (page 80) and, if desired, garnish with whipped cream just before serving.

YIELD: 6 TO 8 SERVINGS

Note: Another very attractive way to finish Dutch Apple Tart is to dust the top of the cooled pastry cream evenly with granulated sugar and burn it in a lattice pattern with a hot iron rod. Iron has to be heated red hot and must be applied directly against the cream and sugar to caramelize the sugar. Then brush entirely with hot Apricot Glaze (page 80).

MERINGUE APPLE TART

Follow the recipe for Dutch Apple Tart (page 82). Spread the baked and cooled tart evenly with the following topping instead of pastry cream.

MERINGUE TOPPING FOR TART

½ cup egg whites at room temperature (approximately 4 whites)
1 *pinch cream of tartar*
1 *cup superfine sugar*
1 *teaspoon cornstarch*

Beat the egg whites and cream of tartar together until fluffy. Add sugar and cornstarch, approximately 2 tablespoons at a time, while beating. When the meringue is stiff and the sugar completely dissolved, spread carefully and evenly on top of the cooled apple tart and brown quickly at 450 degrees F. for about 3 minutes.

LATTICE APPLE TART

1 *Tart Dough recipe (page 78)*
5 *baking apples*
¼ cup butter
⅓ cup brown sugar
juice of 1 lemon
1 *egg yolk*
1 *tablespoon milk*
Currant Jelly Glaze (page 80)
whipped cream to garnish (optional)

Set oven at 425 degrees F.
One 9-inch round tart mold, 1½ inches deep

Line the tart mold with the dough as previously explained (page 79). Place in the refrigerator while preparing the following: Peel, core and slice the apples ½-inch thick. Combine apples and butter in a saucepan. Cover and cook over medium heat for approximately 5 minutes, stirring from time to time to prevent burning. When apples begin to soften, dust with brown sugar and squeeze the lemon juice over them. Continue cooking for 2 minutes longer. Remove from heat. Cool the apple mixture thoroughly. Pour into the prepared shell and fill to ¼-inch from top. Roll out the remaining tart dough to approximately ⅛-inch thick and cut out strips about 10 inches long and not more than ¼-inch wide. Set the strips over the apples, about ½-inch apart. Press well at both ends and trim any overhanging strips. Place a second layer of strips crosswise to form a lattice pattern. Brush the dough with the egg yolk blended with milk. Bake at 425 degrees F. for about 30 minutes or until done. Cool thoroughly. Unmold, then brush the top entirely with ½ cup red Currant Jelly Glaze (page 80). If desired, serve garnished with whipped cream. YIELD: 6 TO 8 SERVINGS

FRENCH APPLE TART

1 *Tart Dough recipe (page 78)*
½ *cup thick apple sauce*
⅓ *cup bread or cake crumbs*
5 *baking apples*
2 *tablespoons brown sugar*
rum
Apricot Glaze (page 80)
1 *cup whipped cream, to decorate*

Set oven at 425 degrees F.
One 9-inch round tart mold, 1½-inches deep
Brown paper, heavily greased

Line the tart mold with the dough as previously explained (page 79). Chill for approximately 30 minutes. Then spread the bottom evenly with apple sauce and dust with bread or cake crumbs. Peel, core and slice the apples approximately ¼-inch thick. Pile them on top of the crumbs in a circular pattern overlapping each other, to at least 1 inch beyond the border of the mold. (Apples will shrink during baking.) Dust evenly with brown sugar. Bake at 425 degrees F. for approximately 20 minutes. Then cover the apples with heavily greased brown paper (this will create steam and help the apples to

cook well). Reduce the heat to 400 degrees F. and finish baking for 25 minutes more or until golden brown. Remove from the oven and cool. Unmold. Sprinkle with a few dashes of rum and brush with Apricot Glaze. Decorate with whipped cream and serve.
YIELD: 6 TO 8 SERVINGS

STRAWBERRY TART

1 *prebaked 9-inch tart shell (page 79)*
1½ *cups Vanilla Pastry Cream (page 289)*
½ *cup lady finger crumbs or thin layer of Sponge Cake (page 23)*
1 *tablespoon kirsch*
2 *pints fresh strawberries*
Currant Jelly Glaze (page 80)

Prepare the prebaked tart shell as previously explained (page 79) and cool thoroughly. Gently pour the prepared pastry cream into the tart shell. Cool for 5 minutes or until a thin crust forms over the top of the cream. Dust with lady finger crumbs or place a thin layer of Sponge Cake over the cream. Sprinkle with kirsch. Hull and wash the strawberries and arrange in the tart shell in an orderly fashion, close to each other and in an upright position. Brush the fruit entirely with warm Currant Jelly Glaze. Cool and serve.
YIELD: 6 TO 8 SERVINGS

Note: Fresh blueberries are also used in the same manner for this very fine tart.

PARISIAN STRAWBERRY TART

Surprisingly delicious to look at and succulent to eat!

one prebaked 9-inch tart shell (page 79)
2 *pints fresh strawberries*
12 *small lady fingers*
few dashes of kirsch
¾ *cup Vanilla Pastry Cream (page 289)*
1 *cup Currant Jelly Glaze (page 80)*

Prepare the prebaked shell as previously explained (page 79) and cool thoroughly. Wash and hull the strawberries and set aside. Line the bottom of the cooled shell with small lady fingers and sprinkle with kirsch. Cover with cooled pastry cream and arrange the strawberries on top in an upright position. Brush with Currant Jelly Glaze.
YIELD: 6 TO 8 SERVINGS

Note: Fresh blueberries can also be used in the making of this outstanding dessert.

APRICOT TART

1 *recipe for Tart Dough (page 78)*
⅓ *cup Frangipane Cream (page 288)*
½ *cup crumbled lady fingers*
1 *1-quart (32-oz.) can apricot halves*
rum
Apricot Glaze (page 80)
⅓ *cup sliced roasted almonds*

Set oven at 425 degrees F.
One 9-inch round tart mold 1½-inches deep

Line the tart mold with the dough as previously explained (page 79). Spread the bottom evenly with Frangipane Cream. Sprinkle ½ cup crumbled lady fingers over the cream. Drain the apricot halves and arrange on top of the crumbs close together and in an orderly fashion. Sprinkle with a few dashes of rum and bake at 425 degrees F. for 10 minutes; reduce the heat to 400 degrees F. and continue baking for another 30 minutes or until golden brown. Cool, unmold and brush the fruit with Apricot Glaze. Sprinkle with sliced roasted almonds.
YIELD: 6 TO 8 SERVINGS

BLUEBERRY TART

1 *recipe for Tart Dough (page 78)*
⅓ *cup bread crumbs*
1½ *pints fresh blueberries*
¼ *cup granulated sugar*
1 *pinch ground cinnamon*
1 *egg*
2 *tablespoons heavy cream*
2 *tablespoons confectioners sugar*

Set oven at 375 degrees F.
One 9-inch tart mold, 1½-inches deep

Line the mold with the dough as previously explained (page 79). Sprinkle the bottom of the mold with bread crumbs. Clean and wash the blueberries and drain thoroughly. Arrange the fruit over the bread crumbs. Sprinkle with granulated sugar mixed with cinnamon. Bake at 375 degrees F. for 10 minutes. Remove tart from the oven and cool for 10 minutes. Blend well the egg with heavy cream. Pour the egg mixture over the berries. Return to the oven and continue baking for 25 minutes or until golden brown. Cool. Unmold. Dust with confectioners sugar.
YIELD: 6 TO 8 SERVINGS

COCONUT MANGO TART

This delicious tropical fruit combined with coconut and Jamaica rum is an unforgettable dessert.

1 *prebaked 9-inch tart shell (page 79)*
1 *dozen lady fingers*
2 *tablespoons Jamaica rum*
4 *large ripe mangos*
Apricot Glaze (page 80)
¼ *cup toasted, shredded coconut*
whipped cream to garnish (optional)

Prepare the prebaked shell as previously explained (page 79) and cool thoroughly. Cover the bottom of the tart shell with lady fingers. Sprinkle with Jamaica rum. Peel and slice the mangos and arrange the slices in an orderly fashion, overlapping each other. Brush entirely with Apricot Glaze and sprinkle heavily with chopped, shredded, toasted coconut. If you wish, garnish with whipped cream and serve.

YIELD: 6 TO 8 SERVINGS

BANANA TART

1 *prebaked 9-inch tart shell (page 79)*
6 *bananas*
1⅓ *cups Vanilla Pastry Cream (page 289)*
1 *dash of nutmeg*
1 *tablespoon rum*
¼ *cup lady finger crumbs*
Apricot Glaze (page 80)

Prepare the prebaked shell as previously explained (page 79) and cool thoroughly. Pass 1 ripe banana through a fine strainer and blend the banana purée with cooled pastry cream, ground nutmeg and rum. Spread the mixture evenly in the bottom of the prepared tart shell. Sprinkle with lady finger crumbs. Slice the remaining ripe but firm bananas approximately ⅛-inch thick and arrange in overlapping circles on top of the pastry cream. Immediately brush the fruit heavily with Apricot Glaze and chill in the refrigerator for 30 minutes.

YIELD: 6 TO 8 SERVINGS

TARTLETS

An endless variety of small, attractive, individual pastries are made with tartlet shells. The proper way to line tartlet molds with dough is to first brush the molds lightly with soft butter or shortening. Roll the desired amount of chilled Tart Dough (page 78) or Pie Dough (page 54) on a floured board to approximately ⅛-inch thick. (I prefer tart dough as it is crisper and actually does not take any longer to prepare than pie dough.) Cut out with a round fluted cutter approximately 3-inches in diameter. Place a circle of dough over the tartlet mold and line the mold all the way to the edge using your fingers to even the dough as much as possible; cut away any excess dough sharply with the palm of your hand.

TO BAKE TARTLET SHELLS

If prebaked tartlet shells are called for, prick the bottom of the tartlet with a fork. Place a paper cup inside the empty shell and fill it ¾ full with dry beans or uncooked rice to prevent the dough from rising. Bake at 400 degrees F. for about 15 minutes. Remove the tartlets from the oven and lift out the paper cups; return the shells to the oven and continue baking for another 10 to 15 minutes or until golden brown. Unless otherwise specified, tartlet shells should always be baked until crisp. Cool thoroughly before handling. Total baking time: 25 to 30 minutes.

TO PARTIALLY BAKE TARTLET SHELLS

If partially-baked tartlet shells are called for, line the tartlet molds as directed above. Prick the bottom of the tartlet with a fork. Place a paper cup inside the shell and fill it ¾ full with dry beans or uncooked rice to prevent the dough from rising. Bake at 400 degrees F. for approximately 15 minutes. Remove from the oven; lift out paper cups. Cool before adding desired filling.

Note: The housewares section of any large department store or bakery supply house will have a great variety of tartlet molds available. I would suggest the use of tartlet molds with fluted edges, approximately 2½-inches top diameter and 1¼-inches deep for individual tartlets.

MACAROON TARTLETS

10 *partially baked and cooled tartlet shells (page 79)*
2 *eggs, separated*
½ *cup sugar*
1 *cup finely chopped macaroons*
1 *tablespoon melted butter*
2 *tablespoons milk*
grated rind of 1 lemon
10 *teaspoons currant jelly*

Set oven at 325 degrees F.

Partially bake and cool the tartlet shells as previously explained (page 79). Beat the egg yolks and sugar together until fluffy. Stir in the chopped macaroons, melted butter, milk and lemon rind. Beat the egg whites stiff but not dry. Fold gently into the yolk mixture. Drop one teaspoon of currant jelly into the bottom of each partially baked tartlet shell. Fill to the top with the macaroon mixture. Bake at 325 degrees F. for approximately 25 minutes or until golden brown.

YIELD: 10 SERVINGS

FRESH BLUEBERRY TARTLET

4 *baked tartlet shells*
1 *cup fresh blueberries*
4 *tablespoons hot currant jelly*
1 *cup heavy cream, whipped*

Prepare, bake and cool the tartlet shells as previously explained (page 79). Wash and drain the blueberries. Heat the jelly over low heat and combine with the washed blueberries. Divide the mixture evenly among the shells. Garnish each one heavily with whipped cream.

YIELD: 4 SERVINGS

FRENCH APPLE TARTLET

½ *recipe for Tart Dough (page 78)*
2 *cups Vanilla Pastry Cream (page 289)*
3 *small apples*
Apricot Glaze (page 80)

Set oven at 425 degrees F.
Six 2½-inch round tartlet molds, 1½-inches deep, greased

Line the greased molds with the dough as previously explained (page 79). Fill each shell ½ full with Vanilla Pastry Cream. Peel, core and cut the apples in two. Slice each half with a sharp knife, but do not separate the slices. Place half an apple into each mold (if too large, trim carefully with a knife). Bake at 425 degrees F. for approximately 35 minutes or until golden brown. Cool, unmold and brush with Apricot Glaze.

YIELD: 6 SERVINGS

TARTLETS DUCHESSES

½ recipe for Tart Dough (page 78)
2 cups Frangipane Cream (page 288)
3 small apples
3 cups Italian Meringue (page 281)
1 cup Fondant Icing colored with a few drops of red food coloring (page 279)
Apricot Glaze (page 80)

Set oven at 425 degrees F.
Six 2½-inch round tartlet molds, 1½-inches deep, greased

Line the greased molds with the dough as previously explained (page 79). Fill each shell ½ full with Frangipane Cream. Peel, core, and cut the apples in two. Slice each half with a sharp knife, but do not separate the slices. Place half an apple into each mold (if too large, trim carefully with a knife). Bake at 425 degrees F. for approximately 35 minutes or until golden brown. Cool and unmold. Reset the oven to 300 degrees F. Using a pastry bag fitted with a round tube approximately ½-inch in diameter, pipe the meringue onto the cooled tarts in a long pear shape or mounded to approximately 3 inches high. Return the tarts to the oven for approximately 10 minutes. Meanwhile, heat the Fondant Icing. Remove tarts from the oven and spoon the icing evenly over the meringue to coat entirely. Or, if you prefer, simply brush the meringue with Apricot Glaze.

YIELD: 6 SERVINGS

FRUIT TARTLETS

The following recipes for fruit tartlets are quick to assemble and handy for any occasion. Tartlet shells are baked in advance and filled with cooled Vanilla Pastry Cream (page 289); drained fruits are placed on top and brushed with glaze.

All the following five recipes require prebaked and cooled tartlet shells. Quantity can be multiplied by as many servings as you desire. (To bake tartlet shells, see page 79.)

STRAWBERRY TARTLETS

Always a favorite!

Fill shells with 5 or 6 fresh strawberries and approximately 2 tablespoons Vanilla Pastry Cream (page 289) for each tartlet. Brush with Currant Jelly Glaze (page 80).

CHERRY TARTLETS

Same initial preparation as for above. Combine drained canned black cherries with warm currant jelly to bind. Place cherries in a pyramid over the pastry cream in cooled shells, and brush with Currant Jelly Glaze (page 80). Sprinkle with sliced pistachio nuts. Use 8 to 10 cherries and 2 tablespoons of Vanilla Pastry Cream (page 289) for each tartlet.

PINEAPPLE TARTLETS

Same initial preparation as above. Place 1 drained pineapple ring over the pastry cream in the cooled shell; drop a red maraschino cherry in the center. Glaze with hot Apricot Glaze (page 80). Use 1 pineapple slice, 1 maraschino cherry and 2 tablespoons of Vanilla Pastry Cream (page 289) for each tartlet.

PEAR TARTLETS

Same initial preparation as above. Place 1 drained canned pear on the pastry cream in the cooled shell. With a small brush dipped in light green food coloring, brush one side of the pear to color it slightly. Repeat the same operation using red food coloring on the other side of the pear. Brush with hot Apricot Glaze (page 80). Use one pear and 2 tablespoons Vanilla Pastry Cream (page 289) for each tartlet.

PEACH TARTLETS

Same recipe as for pear tartlets, but omit the food coloring. Use half a peach and 2 tablespoons of Vanilla Pastry Cream (page 289) for each tartlet.

BAKED ALASKA TARTLETS

6 *baked tartlet shells (page 79)*
1/4 *cup currant jelly*
1 *pint good commercial ice cream, flavor of your choice*
3 *egg whites*
1/8 *teaspoon salt*
2/3 *cup fine granulated sugar*
2 *drops vanilla extract*
6 *red glazed cherries*

Set oven at 450 degrees F.

Warm the jelly just enough to liquefy and spoon it into the cooled tartlet shells. Fill each shell with ice cream. Place in freezer to harden for approximately 15 minutes.

Beat the egg whites and salt together until soft peaks form. Gradually add the sugar and then the vanilla extract and continue beating until the egg-white mixture is stiff but not dry. Spread the meringue over the ice cream in the prepared shells using a spatula or a pastry bag fitted with a star tube. Decorate each one with a red glazed cherry.* Place in the refrigerator until needed. When ready to serve, bake the tartlets at 450 degrees F. for no more than 3 minutes. As soon as the meringue starts to brown, remove from the oven and serve.

YIELD: 6 SERVINGS

* *Note:* Tartlets can be prepared to this point and stored in the freezer compartment for a day or two before browning the meringue.

FRANGIPANE TARTLETS
(almond tartlets)

1 recipe for Tart Dough (page 78)
*½ cup almond paste**
⅓ cup granulated sugar
1½ tablespoons soft butter
½ teaspoon vanilla extract
½ teaspoon green food coloring
2 whole eggs, beaten with a fork
slice blanched almonds } *to garnish*
confectioners sugar } *to garnish*

Set oven at 350 degrees F.
8 2½-inch round tartlet molds, 1½-inches deep, greased

Line the greased shells with tart dough as previously explained (page 79). Knead the almond paste together with the sugar. Add the butter, vanilla extract and green food coloring. Gradually add the beaten eggs and blend well after each addition to obtain a smooth, lump-free paste. Fill each unbaked tartlet shell and sprinkle with sliced blanched almonds. Bake at 350 degrees F. for approximately 25 minutes or until golden brown. Cool and dust with confectioners sugar.
YIELD: 6 SERVINGS

* *Note:* Almond paste can be bought at any bakery or specialty food store. This unsweetened paste is sold in sealed cans or in bulk at retail stores.

Cookies

MAKING COOKIES

Cookies and children go together but most grown-ups are children at heart when it comes to cookies.

The following recipes offer some very delectable European-born and native-American "goodies"; many of which have been passed along to me by famous professionals and personal friends.

Regardless of the type of cookies you intend to make, the following information should be of value to you.

1. Read the recipe *twice*.
2. Assemble all required utensils and necessary ingredients.
3. All ingredients should be at room temperature.
4. Preheat the oven at least 15 minutes in advance.
5. In recipes calling for sifted flour, flour must be measured *after* it is sifted. However, there are the rare cases where the recipe calls for flour (omitting the word sifted); in these instances, measure the required amount of flour *before* sifting.
6. A dough of the proper consistency is essential for crisp cookies. Depending upon the quality of the flour and the size of the eggs used, a little more or less flour may be necessary. Make notations next to

the recipe as necessary to eliminate repeated mistakes and to make your future preparations less tedious and more successful.

7. To avoid coarse, hard to handle dough, mix only enough to blend all ingredients thoroughly after the addition of flour. Any additional flour is generally added alternately with liquid (if any). This helps to make a crisp and tender batch of cookies.

8. All cookies—refrigerator, dropped or squeezed—should be of uniform size and thickness in order for them to bake evenly.

TYPE OF COOKIES

REFRIGERATOR OR ICE BOX COOKIES The dough is of a rolling consistency and is placed in the refrigerator or freezer to harden. Refrigerator cookies will keep for weeks in a cool place.

ROLLED COOKIES While rolling cookie dough in sheets or strips, flour for dusting must be used sparingly and thoroughly brushed off before placing cookies on the baking sheet. The dough is chilled in the refrigerator for better handling and should be rolled a small quantity at a time.

PRESSED OR SQUEEZED COOKIES By pressing or squeezing dough from a cookie press or pastry bag fitted with a plain or star tube, many intriguing designs can be made. Remember, practice and patience are requisites of success. Cookie dough for pressed or squeezed cookies should be rather soft and at room temperature.

MACAROON COOKIES See page 134.

SHEET COOKIES Sheet cookies, like brownies, are easy and quick to prepare. The dough must be thoroughly cooled before it is cut.

BAKING OF COOKIES

Bake cookies according to directions, giving close attention to the approximate baking time. This time may vary somewhat, depending upon the quality of the ingredients, the thickness of the dough and the type and size of oven being used.

TO KEEP COOKIES CRISP

Use a container with a loose cover. In case of humid or rainy weather, dry the cookies in a cool oven (200 degrees F.) for about 10 minutes just before serving.

TO KEEP COOKIES SOFT

Use an airtight container. Place a few slices of fresh apple in container with the cookies and change the fruit from time to time to ensure freshness.

Note: The majority of cookie recipes have been tested with butter. As we all know, butter enhances the flavor and texture of any cookie; however, other shortening may be substituted for butter if you wish.

PETITS FOURS

These little ice cakes presented in miniature paper cups are often decorated with Royal Icing (page 280). A great variety of color blends can be achieved, and glazed fruits, whole nuts or silver dragees can be used to decorate these petite delicacies.

PREPARATION AND FINISHING OF PETITS FOURS

Bake any plain or chocolate cake in an 8 x 8 x 2 greased baking pan lined with paper. The batter should be no more than ⅓-inch thick. Bake according to directions given in the recipe; remove from the pan and cool thoroughly. With a sharp knife, cut the cake into 1-inch squares, small rectangles, diamonds, crescents or oblongs. Place each little cake on a flat screen.

Warm some plain Fondant Icing (page 279) over hot water. Color and flavor to taste. Use plain white fondant icing first; then color some yellow or green; perhaps even a little grated sweet chocolate can be used because the colors blend so nicely. Dip a tablespoon into the warm icing and pour some over each of the petits fours, coating them entirely. Allow to dry for 20 minutes or so. Then decorate with glazed fruits or, if you wish, with Royal Icing (page 280) or whole walnuts. Place the cakes in individual paper cups and arrange them on a serving tray or plate.

YIELD: ABOUT 5 DOZEN PETITS FOURS

FILLED PETITS FOURS

Bake any plain or chocolate cake in an 8 x 8 x 2 greased baking pan lined with paper. The batter should be no more than ⅓-inch thick. Bake according to directions given in the recipe. Remove from the pan and cool. Cut the cake into various shapes: 1-inch square, rectangles, crescents, diamonds, etc. Split each piece with a sharp knife and sandwich them together with Buttercream (page 284) flavored to your taste. Proceed to ice and decorate the cakes as explained in preparation and finishing of Petits Fours (page 97).

REFRIGERATOR ICE BOX COOKIES

REFRIGERATOR COOKIES

1 *cup shortening, half butter and half Crisco*
½ *cup granulated sugar*
½ *cup light brown sugar*
1 *egg*
3 *tablespoons milk*
1 *teaspoon vanilla extract*
2¼ *cups sifted all-purpose flour*
½ *teaspoon baking soda*
½ *teaspoon salt*
¼ *teaspoon ground nutmeg*
¼ *teaspoon ground cinnamon*
½ *cup finely ground almonds*

Set oven at 375 degrees F.
One 10 x 10-inch baking sheet, greased and floured

Cream the shortening together with both kinds of sugar, then mix in the egg, milk and vanilla extract. Sift all the remaining ingredients together and add them to the butter mixture. Blend well but do not overmix. Form the dough into sausage shaped rolls approximately 2 inches in diameter. Wrap the rolls in waxed paper and chill until firm (in the freezer for approximately 1 hour or in the refrigerator for approximately 2 hours). Slice the chilled dough into cookies approximately ¼ inch thick and bake on the prepared pan at 375 degrees F. for approximately 6 minutes, or until golden brown.
YIELD: APPROXIMATELY 6 DOZEN COOKIES

ALMOND BREAD COOKIES

½ cup butter at room temperature
1 cup well-packed dark brown sugar
1 tablespoon honey
1 egg, beaten with a fork
2½ cups sifted cake flour
¼ teaspoon baking soda
½ cup whole blanched almonds

Set oven at 350 degrees F.
One large baking sheet, lightly greased

Cream the butter, brown sugar and honey together thoroughly. Add the beaten egg. Blend all ingredients well. Sift the flour and soda together twice. Stir it into the butter mixture and mix thoroughly. Stir in the almonds. Chill dough in the refrigerator until firm, then shape it into long rolls approximately 1½ inches in diameter. Wrap the rolls in wax paper and chill in the freezer or refrigerator until hard. Cut into slices ⅛-inch thick. Arrange the cookies approximately 1 inch apart on the prepared baking sheet. Bake at 350 degrees F. for about 12 minutes or until golden brown.
YIELD: APPROXIMATELY 6 DOZEN COOKIES

AMERICANA COOKIES

½ cup butter at room temperature
½ cup brown sugar
½ cup granulated sugar
1 egg, beaten with a fork
1½ cups sifted all-purpose flour
½ teaspoon baking soda
½ teaspoon ground cinnamon
⅓ teaspoon salt
1 teaspoon grated lemon rind
½ cup finely chopped walnuts

Set oven at 375 degrees F.
One large baking sheet, greased

Cream the butter and sugars together well. Add the beaten egg and continue beating until light and fluffy. Sift the flour, baking soda, cinnamon and salt together, and stir it into the egg batter alternately with the lemon rind and nuts. Work the mixture into a smooth dough. Place the dough in the refrigerator for approximately 15 minutes or until firm. Form it into long rolls, about 1½ inches in diameter. Wrap the rolls in wax paper and chill in the freezer for approximately 1 hour. Cut into slices about ¼-inch thick. Arrange the slices on the prepared baking sheet 2 inches apart, and bake at 375 degrees F. for about 8 minutes or until golden brown.

YIELD: APPROXIMATELY 5 DOZEN COOKIES

DATE ICE BOX COOKIES

To the above recipe add ½ cup finely chopped dates.

COCONUT ICE BOX COOKIES

Use ½ cup slightly toasted, shredded coconut instead of the walnuts in the above recipe.

CHOCOLATE COOKIES

To the above recipe add 1 oz. or 1 square unsweetened chocolate (melted over hot water) simultaneously with the sifted ingredients.

OLD-FASHIONED COOKIES

½ cup Crisco and ½ cup butter, combined
1½ cups light brown sugar
⅓ cup granulated sugar
2 eggs
3½ cups sifted all-purpose flour
1 pinch salt
¾ teaspoon baking soda
¾ teaspoon cream of tartar
1½ cups finely chopped candied fruits

Set oven at 375 degrees F.
One large baking sheet, greased

Cream the Crisco, butter, brown sugar and granulated sugar together. Add the eggs. Stir in the remaining ingredients and knead to a smooth dough of rolling consistency. Shape the dough into long rolls; wrap the rolls in waxed paper and place them in the refrigerator to harden for approximately 2 hours. Cut into slices ¼-inch thick. Place the cookies on the prepared baking sheet and bake at 375 degrees F. for 8 minutes or until golden brown.

YIELD: APPROXIMATELY 9 DOZEN COOKIES

CHOCOLATE PINWHEELS OR HALF AND HALVES

½ cup butter
¾ cup granulated sugar
1 teaspoon vanilla extract
½ teaspoon grated lemon rind
1 large whole egg
1¾ cups sifted all-purpose flour
½ teaspoon baking powder
¼ cup finely ground walnuts or pecans
½ teaspoon salt
1 oz. unsweetened chocolate, melted
milk, to brush dough

Set oven at 375 degrees F.
One 10 x 10-inch baking sheet, ungreased

Cream the butter, sugar, vanilla extract and lemon rind together. Stir in the egg. Sift together the flour, baking powder, ground nuts and salt and add this to the butter mixture. Blend all ingredients well, but do not overmix. Divide the dough into two equal parts and mix the chocolate into one part.

To form pinwheels: Wrap both halves of the dough in waxed paper and chill in the refrigerator for at least 1 hour, or until firm enough to roll. Roll out each half of the chilled dough on waxed paper to form a rectangle approximately 12 x 10 inches. Brush one half of the dough with milk and place the other half on top of it. Press gently with your hands to secure both pieces together, and cut away any uneven parts. Roll the dough as you would a jelly roll and place in the freezer or refrigerator until firm. Slice cookies approximately ⅙ inch thick and bake at 375 degrees F. for 8 to 10 minutes.

To form half and halves: Form each half of the dough into a sausage-shaped roll approximately 2 inches in diameter (do not roll out). Wrap each half in waxed paper and chill in the freezer or refrigerator until firm. Then cut each roll in half lengthwise with a sharp knife. Brush each cut surface with milk and press the plain and chocolate halves together. Chill again until firm. Slice cookies approximately 1/6 inch thick and bake at 375 degrees F. for 8 to 10 minutes.

YIELD: APPROXIMATELY 5 DOZEN PINWHEELS OR HALF AND HALVES

COCONUT DELIGHT

½ cup soft butter
½ cup superfine granulated sugar
1 egg, separated
grated rind of 1 lemon
1 pinch salt
1 cup sifted all-purpose flour
⅓ cup finely chopped candied cherries
1 cup chopped shredded coconut
confectioners sugar to dust cookies

Set oven at 350 degrees F.
One large baking sheet, greased

Cream the butter and granulated sugar together until light; add the egg yolk, lemon rind, salt and sifted flour. Mix all ingredients gently into a smooth dough. Then blend in the finely chopped cherries and chill the dough in the refrigerator for approximately 1 hour. Shape the chilled dough into small balls the size of a quarter and place them side by side on waxed paper until all dough has been used.

Beat the egg white until foamy; dip each ball into the egg white and immediately roll it in the chopped coconut. Place the cookies on the prepared baking sheet and bake at 350 degrees F. for about 20 to 25 minutes or until golden brown. Remove from the oven, dust with confectioners sugar and cool.

YIELD: APPROXIMATELY 3½ DOZEN COOKIES

DROP COOKIES

CHOCOLATE CHIP COOKIES

½ cup soft butter
½ cup brown sugar
½ cup granulated sugar
1 egg, beaten with a fork
2 tablespoons cold milk
1⅓ cups sifted cake flour
½ teaspoon baking soda
1 4-oz. package small semi-sweet chocolate chips
⅔ cup finely chopped pecans

Set oven at 400 degrees F.
One large baking sheet, greased and floured

Cream the butter and sugars together until light; add the beaten egg and cold milk and blend well. Sift the flour and baking soda together and stir into the egg mixture. Fold in the chocolate chips and nuts. Drop the cookies 1½ inches apart onto the prepared baking sheet using a teaspoon or a pastry bag fitted with a plain round tube. Bake at 400 degrees F. for approximately 15 minutes or until golden brown.

YIELD: APPROXIMATELY 4 DOZEN COOKIES

CHOCOLATE CHIP COOKIES

½ cup soft butter
½ cup granulated sugar
½ cup brown sugar
1 egg, beaten with a fork
3 drops red food coloring
2 oz. or 2 squares unsweetened chocolate, melted over hot water
1¼ cups sifted all-purpose flour
⅓ teaspoon baking powder
1 teaspoon almond extract
½ cup finely chopped nuts
½ cup semi-sweet chocolate bits

Set oven at 375 degrees F.
One large baking sheet, greased

Cream the butter and sugars together until light. Add the beaten egg and continue creaming. Stir in the red food coloring and melted chocolate. Sift the flour and baking powder together and fold into the egg batter alternately with the almond extract, nuts and chocolate bits. With a teaspoon or pastry bag fitted with a round tube, drop the dough onto the prepared baking sheet. Bake at 375 degrees F. for approximately 10 minutes or until firm.

YIELD: APPROXIMATELY 4 DOZEN COOKIES

TEA DROPS

½ cup butter
½ cup granulated sugar
3 eggs
2 teaspoons grated orange rind
2 cups sifted all-purpose flour
⅓ cup currant raisins

Set oven at 360 degrees F.
One large baking sheet, greased and lined with paper

Cream butter, then gradually add the sugar and eggs. Beat until light and fluffy. Add the orange rind. Fold in the flour alternately with the raisins. Blend all ingredients thoroughly. Using a teaspoon or a pastry bag fitted with a round tube, drop the dough in portions the size of a quarter onto the prepared baking sheet. Bake at 360 degrees F. for approximately 10 to 12 minutes.

YIELD: APPROXIMATELY 4 DOZEN COOKIES

AMERICANA PECAN NUT DROPS

2 eggs, beaten
½ cup brown sugar
½ cup granulated sugar
⅔ cup cake flour
¼ teaspoon salt
¼ teaspoon baking powder
¾ cup finely chopped pecans
3 tablespoons apricot jam
confectioners sugar, to dust cookies

Set oven at 400 degrees F.
One large baking sheet, greased

Beat the eggs and sugars together until light and fluffy. Sift the flour, salt and baking powder together and fold into the egg batter alternately with the nuts. With a teaspoon or a pastry bag fitted with a round plain tube, drop the cookies onto the prepared baking sheet, spacing them approximately 2 inches apart. Bake at 400 degrees F. for about 6 minutes or until the edges start to brown. Remove from the sheet while still warm and sandwich together in pairs with apricot jam in the center. Dust with confectioners sugar.

YIELD: APPROXIMATELY 36 COOKIES

FRUIT KISSES

½ cup glazed finely diced mixed fruits
⅓ cup good brandy
4 egg whites
1 cup fine granulated sugar

Set oven at 250 degrees F.
One large baking sheet, greased and floured

Soak the fruits in brandy overnight. Then drain thoroughly and dry with a towel. Beat the egg whites until stiff, adding the sugar gradually while beating. Fold in the drained diced fruits. With a tablespoon, drop the cookies, approximately 2 inches apart, onto the prepared baking sheet. Bake at 250 degrees F. for about 40 to 50 minutes or until dry. Remove immediately from the sheet and store in a dry place.

YIELD: APPROXIMATELY 6 DOZEN COOKIES

ALMOND KISSES

3 egg whites
1 pinch salt
1⅓ cups sugar
½ teaspoon vanilla extract
1⅔ cups sliced almonds

Set oven at 325 degrees F.
One large baking sheet, greased and floured

Beat the egg whites, salt, sugar and vanilla extract over hot water until lukewarm or until the sugar is dissolved. Remove from heat and whip until thick and fluffy. Stir in the sliced almonds and, with a tablespoon, drop the batter onto the prepared baking sheet. Bake at 325 degrees F. for approximately 25 minutes. Remove the cookies immediately from the sheet and store in a warm place.

YIELD: APPROXIMATELY 2 DOZEN COOKIES

Note: The almond cookies can be dipped into melted sweet chocolate for an equally festive appearance. The sliced almonds can also be replaced by chopped pecans or shredded coconut.

PECAN CHERRY KISSES

¾ cup chopped red glazed cherries
½ cup chopped pecans
1 tablespoon cake flour
3 egg whites
1¼ cups granulated sugar

Set oven at 250 degrees F.
One large baking sheet, lined with waxed paper

Blend the cherries, pecans and cake flour together well. Beat egg whites until stiff, adding the sugar gradually while beating. Gently fold the egg whites into the batter. With a tablespoon, drop the batter onto the prepared baking sheet. Bake at 250 degrees F. for approximately 40 minutes. Cool. Store in a dry place.
YIELD: APPROXIMATELY 4½ DOZEN COOKIES

LACE COOKIES

So crispy, and light as a feather!

½ cup light corn syrup
½ cup butter
¾ cup brown sugar
1 cup sifted all-purpose flour
1⅓ cups finely chopped blanched almonds

Set oven at 325 degrees F.
One large baking sheet, well greased

Place the corn syrup, butter and brown sugar in a deep saucepan over medium heat and bring to a slow boil. Remove from heat. Blend the flour and nuts together and gradually add to the warm ingredients. Stir well. Drop the batter in portions about the size of a quarter onto the prepared baking sheet, leaving enough space between each cookie for expansion. Bake at 325 degrees F. for 8 minutes or until golden brown.

Remove from heat and cool before lifting the cookies from the sheet with a thin flexible spatula. Place on waxed paper to complete cooling. If you wish you can ice the bottoms of the cookies with melted sweet chocolate or roll them, while still warm, into a cigarette shape around a thick pencil. If the cookies become too hard to roll, return them briefly to the oven to soften.

YIELD: APPROXIMATELY 4 DOZEN COOKIES

SOUTHERN LACE COOKIES

¼ cup butter
1 cup brown sugar
1 cup granulated sugar
2 eggs
½ cup all-purpose flour
¾ teaspoon baking powder
1 cup finely chopped pecans
½ cup finely chopped almonds

Set oven at 375 degrees F.
One large baking sheet, greased and floured

Cream the butter and sugars together. Add the eggs and continue beating for approximately 3 or 4 minutes. Sift the flour and baking powder together and add it to the egg mixture alternately with the nuts. Blend all ingredients thoroughly. Chill in the refrigerator for about 1 hour. Drop the cookies 2 inches apart onto the prepared baking sheet. Bake at 375 degrees F. for approximately 6 to 8 minutes or until golden brown. Remove from the sheet while still warm and place on waxed paper or aluminum foil to cool.

YIELD: APPROXIMATELY 5 DOZEN COOKIES

FLORENTINE COOKIES

A specialty of Vienna, these delectable cookies have always been a favorite in America.

1 cup heavy cream
1 cup granulated sugar
1 cup finely chopped blanched almonds
6 ozs. candied fruits, chopped fine
⅓ cup flour
⅓ cup melted sweet chocolate

Set oven at 300 degrees F.
One large baking sheet, greased

In the order they are listed above, blend the first five ingredients together into a smooth batter. *Do not overmix.* With a tablespoon, drop the cookie mixture onto the prepared baking sheet, spacing them at least 2 inches apart. Flatten the cookies with a fork dipped in cold water and bake at 300 degrees F. for approximately 10 minutes or until the edges begin to color. Remove from the pan and place on waxed paper or aluminum foil to cool.

Melt the sweet chocolate over hot water, stirring rapidly. Cool to lukewarm and spread the bottom of each cooled cookie with the chocolate mixture. Let stand in a cool place until the chocolate hardens. Store in a tightly covered jar.

YIELD: APPROXIMATELY 4 DOZEN COOKIES

RAISIN DROPS

¼ cup Crisco and ¼ cup butter, combined
½ cup brown sugar
½ cup granulated sugar
2 eggs
½ cup molasses
2½ cups sifted cake flour
2 teaspoons double-acting baking powder
¼ teaspoon salt
½ teaspoon cinnamon
½ teaspoon nutmeg
1 cup seedless raisins

Set oven at 375 degrees F.
One large baking sheet, greased and floured

Cream the Crisco, butter and sugars together. Add the eggs and blend thoroughly. Stir in the molasses. Add remaining ingredients leaving the raisins for last, and mix well. Drop the cookies onto the prepared baking sheet, approximately 1½ inches apart, using a pastry bag fitted with a large plain tube or a teaspoon. Bake at 375 degrees F. for about 12 minutes or until done.

YIELD: APPROXIMATELY 5 DOZEN COOKIES

CURLED WAFERS

¾ cup granulated sugar
½ cup cake flour
3 egg whites
1½ tablespoons finely chopped nuts
1 teaspoon grated lemon rind

Set oven at 350 degrees F.
One large baking sheet, greased

Mix all ingredients together into a smooth dough. Drop onto the prepared baking sheet using a pastry bag fitted with a plain tube. Leave enough space for the cookies to expand. Bake at 350 degrees F. for 10 to 12 minutes or until the edges begin to brown. Remove from heat and while still warm curl the wafers around a pencil into a cigarette shape. If they harden too quickly, return them briefly to the oven to soften. Cool.

YIELD: APPROXIMATELY 4 DOZEN COOKIES

MADELEINES

A favorite of the French tea houses, these delectable petits fours were created by Avice, pastry chef to Prince Talleyrand (1754–1838). They are baked in special fluted molds, available in many gourmet kitchen equipment shops.

2 eggs plus 4 egg yolks
½ cup granulated sugar
1 cup sifted cake flour
grated rind of 1 lemon
4 tablespoons melted, clarified butter

Set oven at 350 degrees F.
2 dozen Madeleine molds, greased and floured

Place the eggs and extra yolks and the sugar in a bowl and beat at moderate speed for about 12 minutes or until the batter is thick and pale in color. Remove from mixer and stir in the sifted flour and grated lemon rind. Gently fold in the melted butter; avoid pouring in the sediment and residue. With a tablespoon, or a pastry bag fitted with a plain tube, drop the batter into the prepared molds and bake at 350 degrees F. for approximately 15 minutes or until golden brown. Unmold immediately and cool.

YIELD: APPROXIMATELY 2 DOZEN COOKIES

LADY FINGERS

3 eggs, separated
½ cup plus 3 tablespoons granulated sugar
1 teaspoon vanilla extract
⅔ cup sifted cake flour
2 tablespoons confectioners sugar

Set oven at 350 degrees F.
One large baking sheet, greased and floured

Combine the egg yolks, ¼ cup of sugar and vanilla extract and beat until light and fluffy. Add the flour. Beat the egg whites until stiff, adding ¼ cup sugar gradually while beating. Combine with egg yolk mixture by folding in the egg whites gently. Press the batter through a pastry bag fitted with a plain round tube onto the prepared baking sheet in portions approximately 3 inches long. Blend the remaining 3 tablespoons of sugar and the confectioners sugar together and sprinkle over lady fingers. Let stand for about 5 minutes. Bake at 350 degrees F. for about 8 minutes or until golden brown. Store in tightly sealed jar.

YIELD: APPROXIMATELY 2 DOZEN LADY FINGERS

Note: In pastry shops lady fingers are baked on a piece of heavy cardboard used only for this purpose. They are removed with a flexible spatula while hot. The reason for this is simply that the lady-finger mixture, being rather light, is very sensitive to bottom heat. I recommend this method if a clean piece of cardboard at least ¼-inch thick is available.

WHIPPED CREAM GINGER SNAPS

1 cup all-purpose flour
⅔ cup granulated sugar
1 tablespoon ground ginger
½ cup dark molasses
½ cup melted butter
½ cup heavy cream, whipped

Set oven at 275 degrees F.
One large baking sheet, greased

Sift the flour, sugar and ginger together twice. Boil the molasses in a deep saucepan. Remove from heat and stir in the melted butter. While stirring constantly, add the sifted ingredients and mix to a smooth batter. With a tablespoon or pastry bag fitted with a round tube, drop the cookies at least 3 inches apart onto the prepared baking sheet. Bake at 275 degrees F. for approximately 15 minutes or until the edges start to brown. Immediately remove from the sheet and roll each cookie around a broomstick, small rolling pin or the handle of a wooden spoon until it is the shape of a cigarette. Cool and fill with whipped cream. Store in a tight container in refrigerator.

YIELD: APPROXIMATELY 5 DOZEN COOKIES

Note: If cookies start to harden while rolling, return them to the oven for a few minutes to soften.

BRANDY SNAPS

2 cups sifted all-purpose flour
1 cup granulated sugar
2 teaspoons ground ginger
⅔ cup molasses
1 cup melted butter
½ cup heavy cream, whipped
1 teaspoon brandy
⅓ cup grated sweet chocolate

Set oven at 275 degrees F.
One large baking sheet, greased

Sift the flour, sugar and ginger together twice. Boil the molasses in a deep saucepan. Remove from heat and stir in the melted butter. While stirring constantly, add the sifted ingredients and mix to a smooth batter. With a tablespoon or pastry bag fitted with a round tube, drop the cookies, at least 3 inches apart, onto the prepared baking sheet. Bake at 275 degrees F. for approximately 15 minutes, or until the edges start to brown. Immediately remove from the pan and roll each cookie around a broomstick, small rolling pin or the handle of a wooden spoon until it is shape of a cigarette. Cool.

Combine the whipped cream, brandy and grated sweet chocolate and fill the cooled cookies. Store in a tightly closed container in the refrigerator or freezer until needed. Remove from the freezer approximately 10 minutes before serving.

YIELD: APPROXIMATELY 10 DOZEN COOKIES

HERMITS

2½ cups sifted flour
1½ teaspoons double-acting baking powder
½ teaspoon ground cinnamon
⅓ teaspoon ground mace
¾ cup soft butter
1⅓ cups dark brown sugar
2 eggs plus 1 egg yolk
½ cup chopped walnuts or pecans
1½ cups seedless raisins
½ cup small diced red glazed cherries
confectioners sugar to dust cookies

Set oven at 375 degrees F.
One large baking sheet, greased and floured

Sift the flour, baking powder and spices together. Cream the butter and sugar together thoroughly. One by one, add the eggs and extra egg yolk, beating well after each addition and scraping the sides and bottom of the bowl frequently to insure a smooth batter. Stir in the flour, nuts, raisins and diced cherries and blend all ingredients thoroughly. With a tablespoon drop the cookies 2 inches apart onto the prepared baking sheet. Bake at 375 degrees F. for approximately 15 minutes or until golden brown. When cool, dust heavily with confectioners sugar.

YIELD: APPROXIMATELY 5 DOZEN COOKIES

PALAIS DE DAMES

½ cup butter
½ cup granulated sugar
3 eggs plus 1 egg yolk
½ teaspoon grated lemon rind
1 cup sifted all-purpose flour
⅓ cup currant raisins

Set oven at 400 degrees F.
One large baking sheet, greased and floured

Cream the butter and sugar together until light. Add the eggs and extra egg yolk one at a time, beating well after each addition. Stir in the lemon rind. Fold in the sifted flour and currant raisins. With a tablespoon or a pastry bag fitted with a plain round tube, drop the cookies onto the prepared baking sheet. Each cookie should be about the size of a quarter. Bake at 400 degrees F. for approximately 12 minutes or until the edges start to brown.

YIELD: APPROXIMATELY 4 DOZEN COOKIES

SPRITZ COOKIES

¼ lb. or 1 stick butter
⅓ cup superfine granulated sugar
2 egg yolks
1 cup sifted cake flour (approximately)
1 pinch salt
½ teaspoon grated lemon rind
halved pecans or glazed cherries

Set oven at 375 degrees F.
One large baking sheet, greased and floured

Cream the butter and sugar together until very light and fluffy. Add the egg yolks one at a time, scraping the sides and bottom of the bowl after each addition. Add the sifted flour, salt and lemon rind. *Do not overmix,* but blend all ingredients well. This batter should be forced through a cookie press onto the prepared baking sheet, but if one is not available, squeeze the mixture through a pastry bag fitted with a No. 3 star tube. Garnish the center of each cookie with a pecan half or a glazed candied cherry. Bake at 375 degrees F. for about 8 to 10 minutes or until the edges start to brown.

YIELD: APPROXIMATELY 3 DOZEN COOKIES

Note: Depending on the size of the egg yolks available, a little more or less flour may be necessary for the above formula. If the batter is too soft, add a little more sifted flour; if too stiff to be pressed through a pastry bag or cookie press, add a tablespoon of milk.

PEANUT BUTTER SPRITZ COOKIES

6 tablespoons Crisco
6 tablespoons butter
3 tablespoons peanut butter
½ cup confectioners sugar
1 egg yolk
grated rind of 1 lemon
2 cups sifted cake flour
1 pinch salt

Set oven at 375 degrees F.
One large baking sheet, greased and floured

Cream the Crisco, butter, peanut butter and sugar together until light and smooth. Add the egg yolk and lemon rind and blend well. Sift the cake flour and salt together; add to the egg mixture and work to a smooth batter. Force through a cookie press or pastry bag, fitted with a star tube, onto the prepared baking sheet. Bake at 375 degrees F. for approximately 10 minutes or until golden brown.

YIELD: APPROXIMATELY 7 DOZEN COOKIES

CATS' TONGUES
(Langues de Chats)

¼ lb. butter
½ cup fine granulated sugar
4 egg whites
1 cup sifted cake flour

Set oven at 425 degrees F.
One large baking sheet, lightly greased and floured

Cream the butter and sugar together until light. Add the egg whites, one at a time, beating well after each addition. Scrape the sides and bottom of the bowl from time to time to avoid lumps. Stir in the sifted flour and blend all ingredients well to obtain a smooth batter. Place the dough in a pastry bag fitted with a ⅙-inch round pastry tube and squeeze in portions about 3 inches long onto the prepared baking sheet. Bake at 425 degrees F. for 8 minutes or until the edges start to brown.

YIELD: APPROXIMATELY 4 DOZEN COOKIES

Note: The mixture should be of a rather soft consistency; depending on the size of the eggs used, a little more or less flour may be necessary. In order to test the consistency of the mixture, drop a little dot (using a tablespoon) onto a greased pie plate and place it in the oven. If the mixture expands and becomes too thin during baking, add a little more flour to the batter. If the mixture does not expand enough, add a little more egg white or heavy cream to soften the batter to the proper consistency.

ANISE COOKIES

4 eggs
1⅓ cups sugar
3 cups unsifted all-purpose flour
½ teaspoon double-acting baking powder
4 teaspoons anise seeds

Set the oven at 350 degrees F.
One large baking sheet, greased and floured

Cream the eggs and sugar together until the mixture becomes thick and the approximate consistency of whipped cream. Sift the flour with the baking powder. Gently fold the sifted ingredients and the anise seeds into the egg mixture. Drop cookies the size of a quarter approximately 1 inch apart onto the prepared baking sheet using a teaspoon or a pastry bag fitted with a plain round tube. Let stand at room temperature overnight. Then bake at 350 degrees F. for approximately 10 to 12 minutes.

YIELD: APPROXIMATELY 5 DOZEN COOKIES

ANISE SPONGE COOKIES

3 eggs
3 tablespoons granulated sugar
1 cup plus 1 tablespoon sifted all-purpose flour
1 tablespoon anise seeds

Set oven at 325 degrees F.
One large baking sheet, greased and floured

Beat the eggs and sugar vigorously over hot water until warm (approximately 110 degrees F.). Remove from heat and continue beating until cold and thick (consistency should be that of whipped cream). Combine the sifted flour with the anise seeds and fold into the egg mixture. Place the batter in a pastry bag fitted with a plain round tube about ½-inch in diameter and squeeze cookies the size of a quarter onto the prepared baking sheet, spacing them about 2 inches apart. Allow the cookies to dry for 6 hours at room temperature. Then bake at 325 degrees F. for 10 to 12 minutes or until golden brown.

YIELD: APPROXIMATELY 4 DOZEN COOKIES

SPONGE DROP COOKIES

4 eggs
1⅓ cups granulated sugar
grated rind of 1 lemon
1⅓ cups sifted all-purpose flour
1 teaspoon baking powder
1 cup sliced or chopped almonds

Set oven at 350 degrees F.
One large baking sheet, greased and floured

Warm the eggs and sugar together over hot water to an approximate temperature of 110 degrees F. Beat with a wire whisk or electric beater for about 10 minutes or until thick. Add the lemon rind. Sift the flour and baking powder and fold carefully into the egg mixture using a flat skimmer or wooden spoon. With a tablespoon drop cookies the size of a fifty-cent piece onto the prepared baking sheet. Cover each cookie entirely with sliced or chopped nuts. Bake at 350 degrees F. for approximately 10 minutes.

YIELD: APPROXIMATELY 2 DOZEN COOKIES

BUTTERSCOTCH DROP WAFERS

1 cup firmly packed dark brown sugar
⅓ cup butter, at room temperature
1 egg
⅓ cup thick buttermilk
½ teaspoon vanilla extract
½ cup finely chopped pecans or walnuts
1½ cups sifted all-purpose flour
½ teaspoon double-acting baking powder
1 pinch baking soda
⅓ teaspoon salt
⅓ teaspoon ground cinnamon (optional)

Set oven at 350 degrees F.
One large baking sheet, lightly greased

Cream the sugar and butter together until light. Combine the egg, buttermilk and vanilla extract and stir into the butter mixture. Add the nuts. Sift the flour, baking powder, soda, salt and cinnamon together and blend into the nut mixture. Let the batter stand at room temperature for approximately 15 minutes. With a teaspoon drop cookies the size of a quarter, about 1 inch apart, onto the prepared baking sheet. Bake at 350 degrees F. for approximately 10 minutes or until golden brown.

YIELD: APPROXIMATELY 4 DOZEN COOKIES

CHINESE ALMOND COOKIES

1 cup rice flour
½ cup superfine granulated sugar
1⅔ cups finely ground almonds
⅓ cup soft butter
1 tablespoon water
1 teaspoon almond extract
30 whole almonds (approximately), to garnish

Set oven at 350 degrees F.
One large baking sheet, greased

Blend all ingredients together to form a dough of rolling consistency. Form the dough with your hands into little balls, each the size of a quarter. Place a whole almond in the center of each ball. Place the cookies on the prepared baking sheet and bake at 350 degrees F. for 15 to 18 minutes.

YIELD: APPROXIMATELY 2½ DOZEN COOKIES

ROLLED COOKIES

LEBKUCHEN

1⅔ cups granulated sugar
½ cup butter
⅓ cup molasses
⅔ cup honey
½ cup sliced, blanched almonds
½ cup chopped candied fruit (citron or orange peel)
5 cups sifted cake flour (approximately)
1 teaspoon salt
1 teaspoon baking soda
1 teaspoon allspice
1 teaspoon ground cinnamon
1 teaspoon grated lemon rind
2 large eggs
½ cup confectioners sugar
½ cup water

Set oven at 400 degrees F.
One large baking sheet, greased

Place the granulated sugar, butter, molasses and honey in a saucepan and warm over low heat until all ingredients are completely dissolved. Remove from heat and allow to stand until lukewarm. Stir the almonds and candied fruit into the lukewarm syrup. Sift the flour, salt, baking soda, allspice and cinnamon together. Sprinkle the lemon rind over the sifted ingredients. Beat the eggs with a fork and add them alternately with the sifted ingredients to the syrup. The mixture should be of a soft rolling consistency. You may need a little more or less flour depending upon the size of the eggs used. Chill in the refrigerator for 2 hours or until firm. Then roll to approximately ⅓-inch thick on a floured board. Cut the dough into 2-inch squares and bake at 400 degrees F. for approximately 10 minutes.

Boil the confectioners sugar and water together until the syrup reaches a temperature of 235 degrees F. on a candy thermometer. Brush immediately over the hot cookies.

YIELD: APPROXIMATELY 5 DOZEN COOKIES

LECKERLI

½ *cup sugar*
½ *cup honey*
1 *cup candied orange and lemon peel, diced*
¾ *cup blanched sliced almonds*
2⅓ *cups sifted cake flour*
½ *teaspoon ground nutmeg*
1 *teaspoon ground cinnamon*
1 *teaspoon baking soda*
½ *teaspoon salt*
1 *teaspoon grated lemon rind*
½ *cup confectioners sugar*
½ *cup water*

Set oven at 350 degrees F.
One large baking sheet, greased

Bring the sugar and honey just to a boil. Remove from heat and add the candied peels and almonds. Cool the syrup to lukewarm. Sift the flour, nutmeg, cinnamon, baking soda and salt together. Sprinkle grated lemon rind over the flour and gradually stir the sifted ingredients into the syrup. Knead the mixture to form a dough of rolling consistency. Place the dough in a bowl; cover with aluminum foil and let stand at room temperature for at least 1 day.

Roll the dough out to approximately ⅓-inch thick on a floured board and cut into round or square shapes. Bake at 350 degrees F. for

10 to 12 minutes or until golden brown. Meanwhile, boil the confectioners sugar and water together until the syrup reaches a temperature of 235 degrees F. on a candy thermometer. Brush immediately over the hot cookies.

YIELD: APPROXIMATELY 2½ DOZEN COOKIES

SPRINGERLI

⅓ cup anise seeds
4 eggs
2 cups sifted superfine granulated sugar
2 drops anise oil
4 cups sifted cake flour
½ teaspoon baking soda
½ teaspoon ground cinnamon

Set oven at 375 degrees F.
One large baking sheet, greased and sprinkled with the anise seeds
One *springerli* mold

Beat the eggs until light and fluffy, adding the sugar gradually while beating. Continue beating until the mixture reaches the consistency of whipped cream. Add the anise oil. Sift the flour, soda and cinnamon together and fold gently into the egg batter. Let the dough rest for 30 minutes then roll out to approximately ⅓-inch thick on a floured board.

Flour a *springerli* mold* and press it firmly on the cookie dough to make a clear print of the design. Remove the mold carefully and cut the cookies around the design. Place the cookies on the prepared baking sheet and let them stand overnight in a cool place. Bake at 375 degrees F. for approximately 5 minutes. Reduce the heat to 300 degrees F. and continue baking for approximately 20 minutes longer or until golden brown. Store in a tightly sealed container.

YIELD: APPROXIMATELY 4 DOZEN COOKIES

* *Note: Springerli* molds come mainly from Switzerland, Germany and Holland. They are made of wood and embossed with a design that will leave an imprint when pressed into the dough.

CHOCOLATE WALNUT CRESCENTS

¼ lb. or 1 stick butter
½ cup confectioners sugar
1 teaspoon almond extract
1¼ cups sifted all-purpose flour
¾ cup finely chopped walnuts
½ cup melted sweet chocolate

Set oven at 350 degrees F.
One large baking sheet, lined with greased waxed paper

Cream the butter, sugar and almond extract together until light. Add the sifted flour alternately with the nuts. Shape the dough with your fingers into small crescents. Bake at 350 degrees F. for approximately 20 minutes or until golden brown. Cool. Dip both ends of each crescent into the melted sweet chocolate and place on aluminum foil until the chocolate is set. Store in a cool place.

YIELD: APPROXIMATELY 2½ DOZEN COOKIES

ALMOND BATONS

¾ cup soft butter
⅓ cup plus 1 tablespoon granulated sugar
1 teaspoon grated lemon rind
2 cups sifted cake flour
1 egg white, beaten with a fork
⅓ cup finely chopped almonds
1 pinch ground cinnamon

Set oven at 350 degrees F.
One large baking sheet, greased

Cream the butter and ⅓ cup of sugar together until light. Add the lemon rind and sifted cake flour. Work all ingredients to a smooth dough of rolling consistency. Place in refrigerator to chill for approximately 2 hours. Roll out in long strips the width of a finger and cut into 2-inch-long bars. Brush with beaten egg white. Mix the remaining tablespoon sugar, almonds and cinnamon together and sprinkle over the cookies. Bake at 350 degrees F. for about 12 minutes or until golden brown.

YIELD: APPROXIMATELY 4 DOZEN COOKIES

CINNAMON COOKIES

⅔ cup butter
1 cup granulated sugar
grated rind of 1 lemon
1 egg separated, plus 1 egg yolk
4 teaspoons light cream
2 cups sifted cake flour
1 teaspoon baking powder
1 pinch salt
½ teaspoon ground cinnamon

Set oven at 375 degrees F.
One large baking sheet, greased

Cream the butter, ¾ cup of sugar and the lemon rind until light and fluffy. Add the egg yolks and cream well. Stir in the light cream. Sift the flour, baking powder and salt together twice. Mix all ingredients to form a smooth dough of rolling consistency. Chill the dough in the refrigerator for at least 1 hour. Roll out to about ⅛-inch thick on a floured board. Brush with egg white slightly beaten with a fork. Mix the remaining ¼ cup of sugar with the cinnamon and dust the dough evenly. Cut out in squares or rectangular shapes. Bake on the prepared baking sheet at 375 degrees F. for about 8 minutes or until golden brown.

YIELD: APPROXIMATELY 3 DOZEN COOKIES

HONEY COOKIES

1 egg
½ cup granulated sugar
¼ cup milk
1 cup honey
4 cups cake flour
½ teaspoon ground cinnamon
1 pinch ground nutmeg

Set oven at 350 degrees F.
One large baking sheet, greased

Blend the egg, sugar and milk together well. Heat the honey to lukewarm and mix it into the liquid ingredients. Sift the flour and stir into the honey mixture along with the spices, and gradually knead the mixture to a smooth, firm dough of rolling consistency. Chill in refrigerator for at least 2 hours or until firm. Roll out to about ⅓-inch thick on a floured board and cut out with a fancy cookie cutter. Bake at 350 degrees F. for about 15 minutes or until golden brown.

YIELD: APPROXIMATELY 6 DOZEN COOKIES

GINGERBREAD MEN

½ cup butter
½ cup Crisco
¾ cup light brown sugar firmly packed
1 cup molasses
4½ cups sifted flour
1 teaspoon baking soda
½ teaspoon ground nutmeg
½ tablespoon ground ginger
1 teaspoon salt
½ cup raisins

Set oven at 375 degrees F.
One large baking sheet, greased

To make these cookies successfully, the butter and Crisco should be melted slowly in a deep, large saucepan. As soon as the ingredients are melted (do not boil), remove them from heat and add the sugar and molasses; stir well until the sugar is melted. Sift the flour, baking soda and all the spices together. Stir approximately 3 cups of flour into the molasses mixture and work until smooth; gradually incorporate the rest of the flour until a dough of rolling consistency is obtained. Allow the dough to stand in a cool place for about 30 minutes. Roll out on a floured board to about ⅛-inch thick. Cut into the desired shape and decorate with raisins. Bake at 375 degrees F. for approximately 8 minutes.
YIELD: APPROXIMATELY 6 DOZEN MEDIUM-SIZED COOKIES

CINNAMON SUGAR COOKIES

1 cup butter
1⅓ cups granulated sugar
2 eggs
4½ cups sifted cake flour
2 teaspoons baking powder
1 pinch salt
1 pinch cinnamon
1 cup sour cream
1 teaspoon grated lemon rind
granulated sugar

Set oven at 400 degrees F.
One large baking sheet, greased

Cream the butter with sugar until light and fluffy. Add the eggs one at a time, mixing well after each addition. Sift the flour with the baking powder, salt and cinnamon and add, alternately with the sour cream, to the egg mixture. Stir in the grated lemon rind and mix all ingredients to a smooth dough of rolling consistency. Chill in refrigerator for about 1 hour or until firm. Roll out to approximately ¼-inch thick on a floured board. Cut out with a fancy cookie cutter. Sprinkle each cookie with granulated sugar and bake at 400 degrees F. for about 12 minutes or until golden brown.

YIELD: APPROXIMATELY 6 DOZEN COOKIES

AMERICANA SABLES COOKIES

Melt in your mouth and so quick to prepare—children will adore them!

1⅓ cups butter
⅔ cup granulated sugar
3 egg whites
4 cups all-purpose flour
1 tablespoon grated almonds

Set the oven at 350 degrees F.
One large baking sheet, ungreased

Cream the butter and sugar together until light. Add the egg whites gradually, scraping the sides and bottom of the bowl frequently to ensure proper mixing. Add the flour and grated nuts and blend to obtain a dough of rolling consistency. A little more or less flour may be necessary depending upon the quality of the flour used and the size of the eggs. Chill in refrigerator for at least 3 hours or until firm. Roll out to approximately ⅛-inch thick and cut into any desired shape using a plain or fancy cookie cutter. Bake at 350 degrees F. for about 12 minutes or until the cookies begin to brown. Do not overbake.

YIELD: APPROXIMATELY 8 DOZEN COOKIES

Note: Before baking, cookies can be decorated with candied fruits or nuts or dusted with granulated sugar.

CHOCOLATE WAFERS
(Sables au Chocolat)

2¼ cups sifted all-purpose flour
1 cup superfine granulated sugar
½ cup butter at room temperature
2 eggs
3 hard-cooked egg yolks
2 oz. or 2 squares sweet chocolate, melted
1 tablespoon cocoa
apricot jam or Chocolate Buttercream (page 284)
½ cup confectioners sugar

Set oven at 350 degrees F.
One large baking sheet, ungreased

Sift the flour and sugar together onto a pastry board. Make a well in the center. Place butter, whole eggs and cooked yolks into the well and work all ingredients together with the tips of your fingers. Add the melted sweet chocolate and cocoa. Blend all ingredients well to a smooth dough of rolling consistency. Knead the dough slightly. Chill in refrigerator for 1 hour or until firm. Roll to approximately ¼-inch thick on a floured board. Cut with a round cookie cutter approximately 2 inches in diameter. Bake the cookies for 10 to 12 minutes at 350 degrees F. Cool thoroughly; sandwich 2 cookies together with apricot jam or Chocolate Buttercream. Dust with confectioners sugar.
YIELD: APPROXIMATELY 4 DOZEN COOKIES

PARISIAN SABLES

Very delicate and so tasty . . .

1½ cups all-purpose flour
1½ teaspoons double-acting baking powder
¼ lb. butter
¾ cup superfine granulated sugar
3 egg yolks
1 teaspoon grated rind of lemon

Set the oven at 350 degrees F.
One large baking sheet, ungreased

Sift the flour together with the baking powder. Blend the butter and sugar together. Add the egg yolks, one at a time, to the butter and sugar. Stir in the lemon rind. Add the flour all at once and blend all ingredients to a smooth dough of rolling consistency. Chill in refrigerator for at least 3 hours. Roll out on a floured board to approximately ¼-inch thick. Cut with a fancy cookie cutter and bake at 350 degrees F. for approximately 10 minutes or until golden brown.

YIELD: APPROXIMATELY 3 DOZEN COOKIES

MILANAISES
(French Nut Wafers)

1 *cup unsifted cake flour*
⅛ *teaspoon double-acting baking powder*
2¾ *cups finely ground almonds*
¼ *cup granulated sugar*
1 *pinch salt*
4 *tablespoons soft butter*
1 *tablespoon grated lemon rind*
1 *egg beaten with a fork*
2 *tablespoons light cream*

Set oven at 400 degrees F.
One large baking sheet, greased

Sift the flour with the baking powder and combine with the ground almonds, sugar, salt, butter and lemon rind. Gradually add the beaten egg. Knead all ingredients gently to form a dough of rolling consistency. Chill in refrigerator for approximately 1 hour. Roll out to about ⅛-inch thick on a floured board. Cut out in fancy shapes with a cookie cutter. Place the cookies on the baking sheet and brush with light cream. Make a criss-cross design on each cookie, using a fork. Bake at 400 degrees F. for approximately 10 minutes or until golden brown.

YIELD: APPROXIMATELY 3 DOZEN COOKIES

SAND COOKIES

1 *cup butter at room temperature*
½ *teaspoon vanilla extract*
½ *teaspoon grated orange rind*
1⅓ *cups dark brown sugar*
3 *egg yolks*
2 *cups unsifted all-purpose flour*

Set oven at 350 degrees F.
One large baking sheet, greased

Cream the butter. Add the vanilla, orange rind and sugar and blend well. Add the egg yolks, one at a time, beating well after each addition. Gradually stir in the flour. Chill the dough in refrigerator for about 1 hour. Roll out to approximately ⅛-inch thick on a floured board. Cut into desired shapes. Bake at 350 degrees F. for approximately 10 minutes or until done.

YIELD: APPROXIMATELY 3 DOZEN COOKIES

Note: You may, if you wish, decorate the baked cookies with glazed fruits or with the icing of your choice.

CHRISTMAS COOKIES

½ cup butter
⅓ cup light brown sugar, well packed
⅔ cup honey
2 egg yolks, beaten with a fork
⅓ teaspoon salt
1 teaspoon grated lemon rind
3½ cups sifted cake flour
3 teaspoons baking powder
sprinkles of all colors
diced fruits, raisins and nuts
Royal Icing (page 280)
(sprinkles, fruits, raisins, nuts and icing: to decorate)

Set oven at 350 degrees F.
One large baking sheet, greased

Cream the butter and sugar together until light. Stir in the honey and beaten egg yolks. Add the salt and lemon rind. Sift the flour and baking powder together twice and add to the creamy mixture. Blend well to obtain a dough of rolling consistency. Chill for approximately 1 hour or until firm. Roll out on a floured board to about ⅛-inch thick. Cut out with fancy cutters or your own cardboard patterns. Cover the unbaked cookies with sprinkles; decorate as you wish with Royal Icing, candied fruits, raisins or nuts. Bake at 350 degrees F. for 6 to 8 minutes or until golden brown.

YIELD: APPROXIMATELY 6 DOZEN COOKIES

CHRISTMAS BUTTER COOKIES

½ cup butter
1 cup granulated sugar
1 whole egg or 2 egg yolks
1 teaspoon vanilla or almond extract
1½ cups sifted cake flour
1¾ teaspoons baking powder
¼ teaspoon salt

Set oven at 375 degrees F.
One large baking sheet, ungreased

Cream the butter and sugar together well. Add the egg or yolks and beat until light. Add the vanilla or almond extract. Sift the flour, baking powder and salt together and stir into the egg batter. Work all ingredients together to form a smooth dough of rolling consistency. Chill in refrigerator for at least 1 hour. Roll out to approximately ⅛ inch thick on a floured board. Cut into various shapes with fancy cookie cutters and bake at 375 degrees F. for approximately 8 minutes or until golden brown.

YIELD: APPROXIMATELY 2½ DOZEN COOKIES

TO DECORATE CHRISTMAS BUTTER COOKIES

Frost cookies with the following mixture:

½ cup confectioners sugar
2 tablespoons milk
1 drop vanilla extract
3 drops red or green food coloring
multicolored sprinkles

Blend and beat all ingredients except the sprinkles together and spread on the cooled cookies. Cover with multicolored sprinkles and let stand at room temperature for approximately 30 minutes or until dry.

Note: These cookies may be hung on the Christmas tree as decorations. Before baking, make a hole in the cookie so that a piece of string or a hook can be passed through.

CRISP CHEESE COOKIES

2⅓ cups sifted cake flour
½ lb. soft butter
1 teaspoon grated lemon rind
1 pinch salt
½ lb. cream cheese
1 egg, separated
⅓ cup granulated sugar

Set oven at 375 degrees F.
One large baking sheet, ungreased

Combine the sifted flour, soft butter, lemon rind, salt and cream cheese in a deep bowl. Blend all ingredients well. Add the egg yolk and knead gently to form a smooth dough of rolling consistency. Chill in refrigerator for approximately 1 hour or until firm. Roll out, a small amount at a time, to approximately ⅛-inch thick on a floured board. Cut out with a fancy cookie cutter and arrange on baking sheet. Beat the egg white slightly with a fork and brush over the cookies. Dust with granulated sugar and bake at 375 degrees F. for approximately 8 minutes or until just starting to brown.
YIELD: APPROXIMATELY 5 DOZEN COOKIES

SHEET COOKIES

PECAN FUDGE BROWNIES

½ cup butter
¾ cup plus 2 tablespoons light brown sugar
2 eggs beaten with a fork
2 oz. or 2 squares unsweetened chocolate
½ cup sifted cake flour
3 drops vanilla extract
3 tablespoons seedless raisins
½ cup chopped pecans

Set oven at 350 degrees F.
One 8 x 8 x 2-inch pan lined with greased paper

Cream the butter and sugar together well; gradually add the beaten eggs. Blend all ingredients to a smooth mixture. Melt the chocolate over hot water and add to the creamed mixture. Stir in the sifted flour, vanilla, raisins and pecans. Scrape the sides and bottom of the bowl to insure a perfect blending. Spread the mixture into the prepared pan and bake at 350 degrees F. for approximately 35 to 40 minutes. Cool. Ice with the following icing:

CHOCOLATE ICING FOR PECAN FUDGE BROWNIES

1 cup granulated sugar
½ cup light brown sugar
1½ tablespoons corn syrup
½ cup milk
2 oz. or 2 squares unsweetened chocolate
2 tablespoons butter
1 teaspoon vanilla extract
3 drops red food coloring

Boil the sugars, corn syrup and milk in a deep saucepan over moderate heat until all ingredients are melted. Add the chocolate and continue cooking until the temperature reaches 235 degrees F. and the mixture forms a soft ball; stir from time to time. Remove from heat and cool to lukewarm. Place in a mixing bowl and add the butter, vanilla extract and food color. Beat until smooth and spread icing over the cooled brownies. Cut into squares with a sharp knife dipped in hot water.

YIELD: ENOUGH FOR 16 2-INCH SQUARES

Note: For an alternate brownie icing see Quick Brownie Icing, page 130.

BROWNIES

(Not quite as soft or moist as Pecan Fudge Brownies.)

2 oz. or 2 squares unsweetened chocolate
½ cup soft butter
3 drops red food coloring
¾ cup sifted cake flour
⅓ teaspoon baking powder
½ teaspoon salt
2 eggs
1 cup granulated sugar
¾ cup broken walnuts
3 drops vanilla extract

Set oven at 350 degrees F.
One 8 x 8 x 2-inch greased and floured pan

Melt the chocolate over hot water and cool to lukewarm. Add the butter and food coloring and mix well. Sift the flour, baking powder and the salt together twice. Beat the eggs and sugar with a fork; add the vanilla and blend into the chocolate mixture. Stir in the sifted ingredients and broken walnuts and work to a smooth batter. Pour into the prepared pan and bake at 350 degrees F. for approximately 35 to 40 minutes. Remove from the oven and cool. Ice with the following Quick Icing:

QUICK BROWNIE ICING

½ stick butter (approximately ¼ cup)
1½ oz. or 1½ squares unsweetened grated chocolate
2½ cups sifted confectioners sugar

Melt the butter with the grated chocolate in a deep saucepan. Stir constantly and remove from heat as soon as bubbles appear. Add the sugar and work until smooth, beating vigorously until spreading consistency is reached. Spread the icing over the cooled brownies. Cut into squares with a sharp knife dipped in hot water.

YIELD: ENOUGH FOR APPROXIMATELY 16 BROWNIES

Note: If the icing is too stiff, stir in 1 tablespoon or so of warm milk while beating rapidly. If too soft, stir in additional sifted confectioners sugar.

AMERICANA BROWNIES

Light and moist—the favorite of millions!

½ cup shortening, half butter and half Crisco
1½ cups granulated sugar
3 eggs
3 squares or 3 oz. unsweetened chocolate
1 cup sifted all-purpose flour
½ teaspoon double-acting baking powder
1 pinch salt
1 small pinch ground cinnamon (optional)
½ cup chopped pecans
½ cup chopped walnuts

Set oven at 350 degrees F.
One 9-inch square pan, greased

Cream the shortening, sugar and eggs together until light. Melt the chocolate over hot water and add to the egg mixture. Blend well. Sift the flour, baking powder, salt and cinnamon together and stir into the chocolate mixture. Add the nuts. Pour into the prepared pan and bake at 350 degrees F. for approximately 40 minutes. Cut into squares.

YIELD: APPROXIMATELY 2 DOZEN BROWNIES

Suggested frosting: Quick Brownie Icing, page 130.

RAISIN AND DATE BROWNIES

A cake-type of brownie made with cocoa.

½ *cup butter*
¼ *cup light brown sugar*
¼ *cup granulated sugar*
¼ *cup cocoa powder*
¼ *cup hot milk*
2 *eggs*
1 *cup sifted cake flour*
¼ *cup milk*
⅓ *cup seedless raisins*
⅓ *cup chopped dates*

Set oven at 350 degrees F.
One 8 x 8 x 2-inch pan, greased and floured

Combine the butter and sugars together until light and fluffy. Mix the cocoa powder with the hot milk until smooth and add to the butter. Add the eggs, one at a time, beating well after each addition; scrape the sides and bottom of the bowl to insure a smooth batter. Add the sifted flour alternately with the milk. Stir in the raisins and dates. Pour into the prepared pan and bake at 350 degrees F. for approximately 35 to 40 minutes or until golden brown.

YIELD: APPROXIMATELY 16 BROWNIES

BLACK-AND-WHITE SQUARES

⅓ cup shortening, half butter and half Crisco
1 cup granulated sugar
1 egg plus 2 yolks
½ cup sifted cake flour
½ teaspoon double-acting baking powder
1 pinch salt
¾ cup chopped pecans or walnuts
1½ oz. or 1½ squares unsweetened chocolate, melted

Set oven at 350 degrees F.
One 8 x 8 x 2-inch pan, greased

Cream the shortening and sugar together until light. Add the egg and extra yolks. Blend well to obtain a smooth batter. Stir in the flour, baking powder, salt and chopped nuts and mix thoroughly. Divide the dough into two equal parts. Add the melted chocolate to one part. Spread immediately on the bottom of the pan. Refrigerate to harden approximately 30 minutes. Then spread the remaining white mixture over the chocolate. Bake at 350 degrees F. for about 25 minutes. Cool.
YIELD: ABOUT 3 DOZEN 1-INCH SQUARES

Note: Black-and-white squares may be spread with Chocolate Frosting (page 24) or simply dusted with confectioners sugar.

ALMOND SLICE COOKIES

½ pound butter
¾ cup granulated sugar
1 egg, separated
2 cups all-purpose flour
1 pinch of ground nutmeg
1 pinch of salt
½ cup sliced blanched almonds

Set oven at 375 degrees F.
One 14 x 14 x 2-inch greased pan

Cream the butter and sugar together well. Add the egg yolk, flour, nutmeg and salt. Work all ingredients to a dough of soft but rolling consistency. Roll out to approximately ¼-inch thick on a floured board and place in the prepared pan. Beat the egg white with a fork and brush over the dough. Sprinkle entirely and evenly with almonds.

Bake at 375 degrees F. for about 25 minutes or until golden brown. Cool and cut into desired shapes.

YIELD: APPROXIMATELY 24 PIECES

CIGARETTES

¼ cup soft butter
½ cup superfine granulated sugar
¼ cup light cream
1 cup sifted all-purpose flour
⅓ cup finely grated almonds
1 cup clear apricot jam

Set the oven at 350 degrees F.
One 10 x 12-inch baking sheet, greased

Cream the butter and sugar together until light and fluffy; gradually stir in the cream. Add the flour and blend all ingredients to a smooth dough. Spread evenly, and not less than ⅒-inch thick, on the baking sheet. Sprinkle with almonds and bake at 350 degrees F. for approximately 5 minutes. Cut into squares immediately and roll each square around a stick or wooden broom handle into the form of a cigarette. If the dough becomes too hard to roll return it to the oven to soften. When cool, fill the cigarettes with apricot jam.

YIELD: APPROXIMATELY 40 WAFERS

DATE AND NUT BARS

¼ cup melted butter
1 cup granulated sugar
2 eggs
¾ cup sifted cake flour
⅓ teaspoon double-acting baking powder
1 pinch salt
1 teaspoon grated orange rind
¾ cup chopped dates
1 cup chopped pecans or walnuts
¼ cup confectioners sugar

Set oven at 375 degrees F.
One 8 x 8 x 2-inch pan, greased and lined with paper

Blend the melted butter and sugar together. Beat the eggs with a fork until fluffy. Sift the flour, baking powder and salt together and sprinkle the orange rind over it. Add the sifted ingredients alternately with the beaten eggs to the butter mixture. Blend until smooth.

Do not overmix. Stir in the dates and nuts. Pour into the prepared pan and bake at 375 degrees F. for approximately 20 minutes or until golden brown. Cool to lukewarm and cut into the shape of long fingers. Roll each piece in confectioners sugar.

YIELD: APPROXIMATELY 3 DOZEN PIECES

MACAROONS

HINTS FOR THE MAKING AND BAKING OF MACAROONS

The availability of ready-made almond paste and coconut flakes* has made the preparation of all kinds of macaroons a great deal easier than it once was.

* *Note:* Almond paste and coconut flakes are available in any local retail bakery or specialty store. One pound of almond paste yields about 1¾ cups. Bakery supply houses sell coconut flakes which means simply a very fine mixture of unsweetened coconut powder.

PREPARING ALMOND PASTE MACAROONS:

Break the almond paste into small pieces or slice it with a sharp knife. Knead the paste with the sugar on a wooden board until the ingredients are well blended. Place the mixture in a deep bowl and add the unbeaten egg whites gradually until a very smooth, lump-free paste is obtained. For Almond Crescents (page 138) the completed mixture should be rather stiff and of a rolling consistency. For Plain Almond Macaroons (page 136), the completed mixture should be of a stiff consistency but not as stiff as the mixture for Fancy Macaroons (page 137). Depending on the size of the eggs being used, a little more or less almond paste may be necessary. Almond paste or coconut macaroons are dropped from a tablespoon or squeezed through a pastry bag onto a baking sheet lined with brown paper. They should be approximately the size of a quarter and spaced about 2 inches apart.

BAKING ALMOND PASTE AND COCONUT MACAROONS:

Read the recipe carefully. Almond paste macaroons are generally baked immediately after being dropped onto the baking sheet. The reason for this is that a draft or long standing will cause a crust to form and the macaroons will crack during the baking process. However, coconut macroons, in order to hold their shape during baking, should stand to dry for a few minutes before being placed in the oven.

Follow the instructions given in each recipe. *All* macaroons should be baked in double pans, which means two pans of the same size fitted one inside the other. This is done to avoid overbaking the underside of the macaroons. If two pans the same size are not available, I recommend you line the baking sheet with two pieces of heavy brown paper instead of one.

TO REMOVE THE MACAROONS FROM THE PAPER:

Immediately after removal from the oven, place the paper and the macaroons on a wet board. Macaroons will lift easily after 2 minutes or so. Cool thoroughly and store in a tight container.

PLAIN COCONUT MACAROONS

4 *oz. flaked coconut*
¾ *cup granulated sugar*
2½ *tablespoons cake flour*
3 *egg whites*
1 *teaspoon almond extract*

Set oven at 325 degrees F.
One large baking sheet, greased and lined with heavy brown paper, and placed on top of a second baking sheet of the same size.

Combine all ingredients in a deep bowl. Cook over hot water, stirring constantly until your finger, when dipped into the mixture, cannot tolerate the heat. Remove from heat and cool for 10 minutes. Using a tablespoon, or pastry bag fitted with a round tube, drop in portions about the size of a quarter spaced 2 inches apart onto the baking sheet. Let stand at room temperature for 5 minutes. Bake at 325 degrees F. for 12 to 15 minutes.

YIELD: APPROXIMATELY 2 DOZEN MACAROONS

ALMOND MACAROONS
(made with almond paste)

½ lb. almond paste
½ cup superfine granulated sugar
½ cup confectioners sugar
3 egg whites (approximately ⅓ cup)
½ teaspoon grated orange rind
granulated sugar, to dust macaroons

Set oven at 325 degrees F.
One large baking sheet, lined with heavy brown paper, and placed on top of a second baking sheet of the same size

Rub the almond paste and sugars together until smooth; gradually add the unbeaten egg whites. Blend all ingredients well and scrape the sides and bottom of the bowl from time to time to obtain a lump-free mixture. Add the grated orange rind. Place mixture in a pastry bag fitted with a round tube about ½-inch in diameter. Squeeze in portions the size of a quarter onto the baking sheet. Flatten the surface of the macaroons with a wet towel and dust with granulated sugar. Bake at 325 degrees F. for approximately 18 minutes or until brown. Place the brown paper and macaroons on a wet board; macaroons will lift easily from the paper after 2 minutes or so. Store in a tight container.

YIELD: APPROXIMATELY 2 DOZEN MACAROONS

ALMOND MACAROONS
(made with ground almonds)

2⅓ cups ground blanched almonds (approximately 1⅓ cups whole almonds)
1⅓ cups granulated sugar
5 egg whites

Set oven at 300 degrees F.

One large baking sheet, lined with heavy brown paper, and set on top of a second baking sheet of the same size

Grind or grate the almonds as thin as possible. Mix all the ingredients together in a deep saucepan and cook over a very low flame or in a double boiler, stirring constantly, for 10 to 15 minutes or until your finger, when dipped into the mixture, cannot tolerate the heat. Remove from heat and with a teaspoon or a pastry bag fitted with a plain round tube drop the macaroons 2 inches apart onto the baking sheet. Let stand at room temperature for about 10 to 15 minutes until a thin crust has formed over the macaroons. Bake at 300 degrees F. for about 20 minutes or until golden brown.

YIELD: APPROXIMATELY 3½ DOZEN MACAROONS

FANCY MACAROONS

One recipe for Almond Macaroons made with almond paste (page 136)

candied fruits, to decorate

Set oven at 400 degrees F.

One large baking sheet, lined with heavy brown paper, and set on top of a second baking sheet of the same size

Follow the recipe for Almond Macaroons using 2 egg whites instead of 3. Squeeze the mixture through a pastry bag fitted with a star tube onto the baking sheet. Decorate with candied fruits. Let stand at room temperature to dry for at least 5 to 6 hours. Bake at 400 degrees F. for approximately 12 minutes or until golden brown.

YIELD: APPROXIMATELY 2 DOZEN MACAROONS

CHOCOLATE COCONUT MACAROONS
(made with shredded coconut)

2 egg whites
1 pinch cream of tartar
½ cup granulated sugar
1 teaspoon sifted cocoa
5 oz. or 5 squares semi-sweet chocolate, melted over hot water
1⅔ cups chopped shredded coconut

Set oven at 350 degrees F.
One large baking sheet, lined with heavy brown paper, and set on top of a second baking sheet of the same size

Beat the egg whites and cream of tartar together until medium peaks form. Add the sugar gradually and continue beating until stiff but not dry. Stir in the cocoa and chocolate. Fold in the coconut. Using a teaspoon or a pastry bag fitted with a round tube, drop in portions approximately the size of a quarter, spaced 2 inches apart, onto the prepared baking sheet. Bake at 350 degrees F. for approximately 15 to 20 minutes or until golden brown.
YIELD: APPROXIMATELY 2 DOZEN MACAROONS

ALMOND CRESCENTS

½ lb. almond paste
½ cup confectioners sugar
½ cup granulated sugar
¼ cup egg whites (approximately 2 to 3 eggs)
1 egg white beaten with a fork
1 cup sliced almonds
Apricot Glaze (page 80)

Set oven at 400 degrees F.
One large baking sheet, lined with heavy brown paper, and set on top of a second baking sheet of the same size

Rub the almond paste together with the sugars until smooth. Add the ¼ cup egg whites gradually until a dough of rolling consistency is obtained. Roll the dough into a long cylinder the size of a broom handle. Cut into 24 equal parts and shape each piece with your finger into a crescent. Dip each crescent into the beaten egg white and roll entirely in sliced almonds. Place the crescents 2 inches apart on the baking sheet and let stand at room temperature to dry for approximately 3 hours or until a crust has formed over them. Bake at 400 degrees F. for approximately 5 minutes or until the almonds start to brown. Brush quickly with clear Apricot Glaze.

YIELD: APPROXIMATELY 2 DOZEN CRESCENTS

Note: Like other macaroons, depending on the size of the eggs used, a little more or less egg white may be necessary to obtain a dough of proper consistency, of approximately the same texture as a pie dough.

CHOCOLATE COCONUT MACAROONS
(made with flaked coconut and almond paste)

1/3 cup almond paste
1 1/2 cups granulated sugar
1 tablespoon cocoa powder
6 oz. finely flaked coconut
1/2 cup egg whites

Set oven at 375 degrees F.
One large baking sheet, lined with heavy brown paper, and set on top of a second baking sheet of the same size

Rub the almond paste with 1/2 cup of the granulated sugar until smooth. Gradually add the remaining sugar and the cocoa; blend all ingredients well. Add the coconut and the egg whites one tablespoon at a time. Mix well after each addition to obtain a smooth dough. Cook the mixture over hot water stirring constantly until hot enough so that your finger, when dipped into the mixture, cannot tolerate the heat. Remove from heat and, using a tablespoon or a pastry bag fitted with a plain tube, drop in portions the size of a quarter onto the baking sheet. Bake at 375 degrees F. for 10 to 12 minutes or until golden brown.

YIELD: APPROXIMATELY 3 DOZEN MACAROONS

ALMOND DELIGHT

½ lb. almond paste
½ cup confectioners sugar
2 egg whites
1 cup sliced almonds
¼ cup clear apricot jam
1 teaspoon Jamaica rum

Set the oven at 375 degrees F.
One large baking sheet, lined with heavy brown paper, and set on top of a second baking sheet of the same size

Rub the almond paste, sugar and one egg white together until a firm paste is obtained. Roll this into a long cylinder the size of a broomstick and cut into 24 equal pieces; shape each piece into a ball. Dip each ball quickly into the remaining egg white and roll it entirely in the sliced almonds. Place the macaroons 2 inches apart on the prepared baking sheet. Make a depression in the center of each cookie with your thumb and fill with apricot jam blended with rum. Let stand at room temperature for 3 hours. Bake at 375 degrees F. for about 15 minutes or until golden brown.
YIELD: 2 DOZEN MACAROONS

Note: For a better-looking cookie, press the center as explained above. Bake the cookies and fill them with jam just before serving. Currant jelly or any other jam of your choice may be used successfully if this method is chosen.

ITALIAN MACAROONS

2 cups whole blanched almonds
1 cup granulated sugar
1 teaspoon grated orange rind
2 egg whites slightly beaten with a fork
1 drop almond extract
confectioners sugar to dust cookies

Set oven at 375 degrees F.
One large baking sheet, lined with heavy brown paper, and set on top of a second baking sheet of the same size

Grind the almonds very fine. Blend all ingredients together and with a tablespoon or pastry bag fitted with a plain tube, drop the macaroons, 2 inches apart, onto the baking sheet. Dust heavily with confectioners sugar and let stand at room temperature for 1½ hours. Bake at 375 degrees F. for about 25 minutes or until golden brown. To remove, place the paper and macaroons on a wet board. After 2 minutes or so the macaroons will lift off easily.

YIELD: APPROXIMATELY 2 DOZEN MACAROONS

Breads & Breakfast Pastries

CROISSANTS

Light and tasty croissants are the unforgettable "pièce de résistance" of a Continental breakfast.

Unfortunately the preparation is lengthy and rather complicated for the inexperienced cook; but the final results are well worth the effort.

To facilitate the rolling and make-up of the croissants the dough should always be handled away from heat and, if possible, in a cool place. Milk must be added to the dough gradually as the amount will vary according to the quality of the flour used. For successful and easy handling, the mixed dough should be the *same* consistency and pliability as the butter.

Knead the butter on a wooden board to take out as much water as possible. Remember that butter should always be kept firm; if it is too hard it will break through the dough, and if it is too soft, it will separate from the dough.

2 cakes or 2 pkgs. yeast
¼ cup lukewarm water
4 cups sifted all-purpose flour
1 pinch salt
1½ tablespoons granulated sugar
1 egg yolk
1½ cups milk (approximately)
1½ cups butter
¼ cup melted butter

Set oven at 400 degrees F.
One 10 x 10-inch baking sheet, greased

Soften the yeast in the lukewarm water and gradually add one cup of flour; work to a smooth paste and form into a ball. Cover entirely with the remaining flour and let rise in a warm place (approximately 80 degrees F.) for about 1 hour, or until doubled in bulk. Add the salt, sugar and egg yolk; gradually stir in the milk and the remaining flour.

Knead all ingredients well for approximately 5 minutes into a pliable and smooth dough of a rolling consistency. (Remember you may need a little more or less milk depending upon the quality of flour used.) Cover the dough with a cloth and let rise for about 1 hour at room temperature. Punch down the dough and place in the refrigerator to chill.

Remove the water from the butter by kneading it to a pliable and elastic consistency on a wooden board.

After the dough has cooled and rested in the refrigerator for approximately 1 hour, roll it out on a floured board in an oblong 3 times longer than it is wide, and approximately ½-inch thick. Dot the rolled dough entirely with pieces of butter of uniform size. Fold ⅓ of the rolled dough back to the center; fold the other end over and seal both ends by pressing slightly with your fingers; roll up gently to its original size and let rest in the refrigerator for 20 minutes. Repeat the same rolling and folding. Cover the dough with a wet cloth and let rest in the refrigerator for approximately 30 minutes. Roll out once more; fold it back to its original size and let chill in the refrigerator overnight.

The next day, roll the dough out to approximately ⅛-inch thick on a floured board. Cut in strips about 5 inches wide; cut each strip into a 5-inch square, and cut each square into triangles. Roll the triangles beginning at the wide end opposite the point. Shape into crescents and arrange on the baking sheet. Be sure to secure the tips of the triangles under the crescents or they will pop loose during the baking process. Brush gently with the melted butter and let rise in a warm place (85 degrees F.) until doubled in bulk. Bake at 400 degrees F. for about 20 to 25 minutes. Serve hot.

YIELD: 24 CROISSANTS

BRIOCHES

For a delicious Continental breakfast, try light-as-a-feather brioches.

2 cakes or packages yeast
1/3 cup lukewarm milk
4 cups all-purpose flour (approximately)
1 pinch salt
3 tablespoons granulated sugar
6 eggs
1½ cups soft butter
2 egg yolks, beaten

Set oven at 425 degrees F.
Twenty-four muffin tins, greased

Place the yeast, warm milk and approximately 1 cup of flour in a mixing bowl and beat well to blend thoroughly. Scrape sides and bottom of the bowl. Cover the dough with the remaining flour, salt and sugar (do not mix) and let all ingredients rise at room temperature for about 1 hour or until doubled in bulk. Add the eggs gradually and mix all ingredients vigorously for at least 10 minutes, to a smooth and elastic dough. Add the butter bit by bit while beating with an electric mixer at moderate speed* and mix to a smooth dough for approximately 3 minutes. *Do not overmix after butter has been added.* Let the dough rise again in the bowl for approximately 2 hours or until doubled in bulk. Stir down and place in the refrigerator overnight or for at least 5 hours.

Punch down the dough, form it into a long roll shape and cut out pieces the size of a Ping-Pong ball. Make a hole halfway down through the center of each ball and insert in this space a smaller ball of dough which has been rolled in the shape of a pear (this makes the head of the brioche).

Arrange the brioches in the muffin tins and allow them to rise in a warm place until doubled in size. Brush the tops with the beaten egg yolks and bake at 425 degrees F. for about 15 minutes or until done.

For large brioches, fill a buttered mold half full and bake brioches at 425 degrees F. for 30 to 35 minutes or until done.

This dough can be kept in the refrigerator for 2 or 3 days and baked when needed, but it must be kept covered with a wet towel or aluminum foil to avoid crust formation.

YIELD: APPROXIMATELY 24 BRIOCHES

**Note:* If no electric mixer is available, knead the dough against a pastry board at least 50 times until it is elastic and detaches itself cleanly from the board and fingers.

BRIOCHE PARISIENNE

1 *recipe for Brioche dough (page 144)*
1 *egg yolk*
1 *teaspoon cold water*
2 *cups stewed prunes*
2 *tablespoons apricot jelly*
1 *teaspoon kirsch liqueur*
2 *tablespoons hot apricot jelly*

Set oven at 375 degrees F.
One 2-quart mold, greased

Prepare the Brioche dough and place inside the mold. Allow to rise in a warm place until double in size. Brush the top with the egg yolk beaten with the cold water. Bake at 375 degrees F. for about 35 to 40 minutes or until done. Cool, and remove from mold. Slice off the top and hollow out the center to leave only a crust approximately 1 inch thick. Fill the cavity with the stewed prunes mixed with 2 tablespoons of apricot jelly and the kirsch liqueur. Replace the cover. Coat entirely with hot apricot jelly. Decorate with candied fruits. Serve with Apricot Sauce (page 291).

YIELD: 8 SERVINGS

WAFFLES AND PANCAKES

RUSSIAN BUCKWHEAT PANCAKES (Blinis)

3/4 *package compressed or dried yeast*
3 *tablespoons lukewarm water*
1 1/2 *cups milk at room temperature*
1 *egg, separated*
3/4 *cup buckwheat flour*
1 1/3 *cups sifted all-purpose flour*

Soften the yeast in the water. Beat the egg yolk and gradually stir it into the yeast along with the milk. Add the flours. Beat all ingredients until smooth. Cover and let rise in a warm place (80–85 degrees F.) for at least 2 hours.

Beat the egg white stiff and fold it quickly into the yeast batter. With a tablespoon, drop the batter in portions the size of a half dollar onto a hot greased pan or griddle. Cook on both sides until brown. Serve with caviar and sour cream.

YIELD: APPROXIMATELY 4 DOZEN BLINIS

GERMAN APPLE PANCAKE

4 *cooking apples, peeled and sliced about 1/8 inch thick*
2 *tablespoons lemon juice*
3 *tablespoons butter*
6 *whole eggs*
a pinch of salt
1 *cup milk*
3/4 *cup all-purpose flour*
1 *tablespoon lemon juice*
confectioners sugar, to garnish

Set oven to 450 degrees F.

Combine the prepared apples with the lemon juice. Melt the butter in a large frying pan. Add the apples and cook until tender. Beat the eggs and add the salt, milk and flour gradually. Blend to a smooth batter. Pour over the apples and place in a 450 degrees F. oven. Bake for approximately 25 minutes. Reduce heat to 375 degrees F. and continue baking about 5 more minutes, until crisp. Serve hot, sprinkled with lemon juice and confectioners sugar.

YIELD: 6 TO 8 SERVINGS

PLAIN WAFFLES

2 *cups sifted cake flour*
3 *teaspoons baking powder*
the point of a knife of salt
2 *tablespoons granulated sugar*
2 *eggs, beaten*
1 1/2 *cups milk*
1/3 *cup melted butter*

Sift the flour, baking powder, salt and sugar together twice into a deep bowl. Stir the eggs and milk together and gradually add them to dry ingredients. Stir in the butter. Let the batter rest for approximately 1 hour. Pour batter into a hot oiled waffle iron. Bring cover down and bake for approximately 4 minutes or until crisp.

YIELD: APPROXIMATELY 6 MEDIUM-SIZED WAFFLES

DELIGHTFUL WAFFLES

This is perhaps the finest waffle mixture ever made.

- 1 *cup or 2 sticks butter*
- 1½ *cups brown sugar*
- 4 *eggs, separated*
- 3 *cups sifted all-purpose flour*
- ½ *tablespoon double-acting baking powder*
- ½ *teaspoon rum or Cognac*
- ½ *teaspoon vanilla extract*

Melt the butter and blend with sugar. Beat the egg yolks and stir into the butter mixture. Sift the flour and baking powder together. Add the sifted ingredients, liqueur and vanilla extract to the yolk mixture. Beat the egg whites stiff and fold gently into the batter. Bake on a hot, oiled waffle iron for approximately 4 minutes or until crisp.

YIELD: APPROXIMATELY 3 DOZEN ULTRA DELICIOUS WAFFLES

AMERICANA WAFFLES

- 1⅓ *cups all-purpose flour*
- 2 *teaspoons baking powder*
- ½ *teaspoon salt*
- 1 *tablespoon sugar*
- 1 *cup milk*
- 2 *eggs, separated*
- 6 *tablespoons melted butter*

Sift the flour, baking powder, salt and sugar together twice into a deep bowl. Beat the egg yolks and gradually stir into the flour along with the milk and butter. Blend well. Beat the egg whites until stiff and fold gently into the batter. Let the batter rest for 1 hour. Cook on a hot, oiled waffle iron until crisp or approximately 4 minutes.

YIELD: ABOUT 4 WAFFLES

CHEESE WAFFLES

Stir ⅓ cup grated cheese into the batter.

CHOCOLATE WAFFLES

Sift ¼ cup cocoa with the dry ingredients. Add 2 additional tablespoons milk to the batter.

NUT WAFFLES

Stir ⅓ cup chopped walnuts or pecans into the batter.

MUFFINS AND CUPCAKES

BASIC MUFFIN RECIPE

2 cups sifted cake flour
2½ teaspoons double-acting baking powder
1 teaspoon salt
2 tablespoons granulated sugar
1 cup milk
1 egg, beaten with a fork
3 tablespoons melted butter

Set oven at 400 degrees F.
One dozen muffin tins, greased

Blend the sifted flour, baking powder, salt and sugar and sift into a deep bowl. Gradually stir in the milk, egg and butter. Blend all ingredients well. *Do not overmix.* Fill muffin tins ⅔ full. Bake at 400 degrees F. for approximately 20 minutes or until golden brown.

YIELD: APPROXIMATELY 12 TENDER MUFFINS

BLUEBERRY MUFFINS

Stir 1 cup fresh blueberries into the basic muffin recipe. Frozen blueberries, thawed and drained, or drained canned blueberries may be substituted for fresh.

CHEESE CORN MUFFINS

Substitute 1 cup yellow corn meal for 1 cup of the cake flour in the basic muffin recipe. Add ⅔ cup shredded sharp cheese to the dry ingredients before adding the liquid.

RAISIN OR DATE MUFFINS

Add ⅔ cup seedless raisins or finely chopped dates to the dry ingredients.

ORANGE OR LEMON MUFFINS
Add grated rind of 1 lemon or 1 orange to the dry ingredients. Use only ¾ cup milk and add ¼ cup orange or lemon juice.

CUPCAKES

½ cup butter or vegetable shortening
1 cup granulated sugar
3 eggs
1¾ cups sifted cake flour
2 teaspoons double-acting baking powder
3 drops vanilla extract
½ cup milk

Set oven at 400 degrees F.
20 muffin tins

Cream the butter or shortening and sugar together until smooth. Add the eggs gradually while beating and continue to beat until the batter becomes fluffy. Sift the flour and baking powder together. Stir into the milk about 3 drops of vanilla extract. Add the flour and milk alternately to the batter and mix just enough to blend all ingredients. Drop the batter into paper cups, set the cups into the muffin tins and bake at 400 degrees F. for approximately 20 minutes. Cool and ice with frosting of your choice.
YIELD: 20 CUPCAKES

HINTS FOR DEEP FRYING

DEEP FRYING

Electric deep fryers with temperature controls are the most reliable for deep frying. If not available, a pan 5 to 6 inches deep and at least 8 inches in diameter can be used. It should be made of heavy-weight metal. A frying basket is very helpful to place your food in as it can be easily removed. The handle of such a basket should be made out of material that does not conduct heat. A frying thermometer with a clamp that fits over the edge of the pan is also an asset for accuracy in determining the proper temperature for all fried foods (365 to 375 degrees F.). If no thermometer is available, check the temperature by dropping a 1-inch square of bread in the hot fat. It should brown in 60 seconds at 365 degrees F.

During the many demonstrations and lectures I have conducted, one of the most often-asked questions referred to the appropriate fat for frying. In this book all recipes have been tested with "Crisco" which is available in any grocery store and which can be reused. To reuse, strain the used fat through cheesecloth into an empty can and keep it in the refrigerator after it has cooled. Add a little fresh shortening each time you deep fry to replace the amount which was used up.

DOUGHNUTS

CAKE DOUGHNUTS

Light, easy and delicious!

4 eggs
⅔ cup granulated sugar
½ cup milk
⅓ cup melted shortening
3¾ cups sifted cake flour
3 teaspoons double-acting baking powder
a pinch of salt
a pinch of ground nutmeg
granulated sugar

A deep fryer with oil heated to 365 degrees F.

Blend the eggs and sugar together thoroughly. Stir in the milk and shortening. Add the flour, baking powder, salt and nutmeg and mix thoroughly to obtain a pliable dough of rolling consistency. Place in refrigerator to chill for about 1 hour.

Roll the dough out on a floured board to a little less than ½-inch thick. Cut with a doughnut cutter. Fry in deep fat until golden brown. While hot sprinkle with granulated sugar.

YIELD: APPROXIMATELY 32 DOUGHNUTS

CINNAMON DOUGHNUTS

Combine one part cinnamon and one part superfine granulated sugar and sprinkle over hot doughnuts.

ORANGE OR LEMON DOUGHNUTS

Spread the hot doughnuts with icing made of ½ cup confectioners sugar mixed with 1½ tablespoons orange or lemon juice.

COCONUT DOUGHNUTS

Dip the cooled doughnuts in Fondant Icing (page 279) and sprinkle with shredded coconut. If fondant is not available, make a glaze by adding 3 tablespoons warm water to 1 cup confectioners sugar.

YEAST DOUGHNUTS

1 *pkg. cake yeast or* 1 *envelope dry yeast*
1 *cup lukewarm milk*
3½ *cups sifted cake flour*
⅓ *cup shortening*
1 *teaspoon salt*
¼ *cup granulated sugar*
1 *egg*
granulated sugar to dust

A deep fryer with oil heated to 365 degrees F.

Dissolve the yeast in the milk. Add 1½ cups of the flour to the dissolved yeast and beat until smooth. Cover the mixture with a wet cloth and let it rise in a warm place until it doubles in bulk. Cream the shortening, salt and sugar together. Add the egg and continue creaming until light. Stir in the yeast mixture. Add the remaining flour and blend all ingredients well. Place the dough in a deep bowl, cover with a wet cloth, and let rise until it doubles in bulk. Roll out the dough to a little less than ½-inch thick on a floured board. Cut it with a doughnut cutter and allow the doughnuts to rise for approximately 40 minutes. Fry in deep hot fat at 365 degrees F. until golden brown. Drain on absorbent paper. Dust with granulated sugar.
YIELD: ABOUT 1½ DOZEN DOUGHNUTS

BISMARCKS

Roll out the dough to approximately ½-inch thick. Cut it out in 3-inch circles. Let rise and fry as explained above.

TWISTS

Roll out the dough to ½-inch thick. Cut in strips ¾-inch by 10 inches. Twist the strips into a corkscrew shape. Let rise and fry as explained above.

CHOCOLATE DOUGHNUTS

¼ cup butter
½ cup granulated sugar
3 egg yolks
1 teaspoon vanilla extract
2 squares or 2 oz. of chocolate, melted
3 cups sifted cake flour
1 teaspoon baking soda
1 pinch salt
1 tablespoon baking powder
1 cup milk
1 cup Chocolate Fondant Icing (page 279)

A deep fryer with oil heated to 365 degrees F.

Cream the butter and sugar together. Add the egg yolks one at a time, mixing well after each addition. Stir in the vanilla and chocolate. Sift the flour, baking soda, salt and baking powder together twice. Add the flour mixture alternately with the milk to the yolk mixture. Blend thoroughly to form a pliable dough of rolling consistency. Chill in refrigerator for approximately 20 minutes. Roll the dough out to a little less than ½-inch thick on a floured board. Cut with a doughnut cutter and fry for about 3 minutes or until golden brown. When cool dip into the Chocolate Fondant Icing.
YIELD: APPROXIMATELY 1½ DOZEN DOUGHNUTS

CROQUIGNOLES

French yeast doughnuts served hot, dusted with confectioners sugar.

⅓ cup granulated sugar
3 tablespoons salad oil
½ cup milk
1 pinch salt
1 package active dry yeast
½ cup lukewarm water
4 cups sifted all-purpose flour
3 eggs
confectioners sugar to dust doughnuts

A deep fryer with oil heated to 375 degrees F.

Blend the sugar, salad oil, milk and salt in a large, deep mixing bowl. Sprinkle the yeast over the water and stir well to dissolve. Add to the milk mixture. Beat the eggs with a fork and stir, alternately with the flour, into the other ingredients. Mix to a smooth paste. Knead the dough for 5 minutes or until it becomes elastic. Place the dough in an oiled pie tin. Brush it with vegetable oil and let rise in a warm place for approximately 1 hour or until the dough has doubled in bulk. Punch it down and roll out on a floured board to about 1/3-inch thick and cut in 3-inch squares. Stretch each square slightly with your fingers and fold it in half. Fry until thoroughly brown. Drain on absorbent paper. Dust with confectioners sugar and serve very hot.

YIELD: ABOUT 3 DOZEN DOUGHNUTS

DANISH PASTRY AND COFFEE CAKES

AMERICANA DANISH PASTRY DOUGH

3/4 cup butter *2 tablespoons all-purpose flour*

Blend the butter and flour together and shape into a ball. Place in the refrigerator to cool while preparing the following dough:

3/4 package dried yeast or 3/4 package compressed yeast
1/4 cup lukewarm water
2 tablespoons granulated sugar
1/4 teaspoon salt
1/2 cup milk
1 egg plus 1 egg yolk
1/4 teaspoon vanilla extract
1/2 teaspoon grated lemon rind
1/2 teaspoon ground mace
2 to 2 1/2 cups sifted all-purpose flour

Dissolve the yeast in the water. Combine the sugar, salt and milk. Beat the egg and extra yolk with a fork and add to the milk mixture. Stir in the vanilla, lemon rind and mace and gradually add enough flour to obtain a pliable dough of rolling consistency. Knead the dough until smooth. (A very important factor in making successful Danish pastry is that the dough be of the same consistency as the butter that is rolled into it.)

Cover the dough with a towel and allow it to rise in a warm place (80–85 degrees F.) until doubled in bulk. Roll out the dough to approximately 1/3-inch thick. Dot it evenly with half the prepared butter, leaving a 2-inch unbuttered edge. Fold the dough in half and seal the edges with the palm of your hand, enclosing the butter tightly inside. Pat the dough lightly with your hands and roll it out gently to about 1/3-inch thick. Fold it in half and let stand in a cool place for approximately 10 minutes. Repeat, rolling and folding 3 more times, letting the dough rest at least 15 minutes after each folding.

The precautions that apply to the handling of puff pastry dough apply also to the handling of Danish pastry dough. Detailed explanations are given on page 169.

YIELD: ABOUT 16 INDIVIDUAL DANISH PASTRIES

AMERICANA DANISH PASTRIES

1 *recipe for Danish Pastry Dough (page 153)*
Danish Pastry Filling of your choice (page 155)
1 *egg, beaten*
½ *cup sliced filberts or almonds*

Set oven at 375 degrees F.
One 10 x 10-inch baking sheet, greased

Roll out Danish Pastry Dough on a floured board to approximately ¼ inch thick. Cut into 3-inch squares and place a heaping tablespoon of Danish Pastry Filling in the center of each square. Fold 2 opposite corners to the center and press gently to seal tightly. Place the pastries on the baking sheet and brush with beaten egg. Sprinkle with sliced nuts. Let stand in a warm place until doubled in bulk. Bake at 375 degrees F. for about 20 minutes or until golden brown.

YIELD: 16 DANISH PASTRIES

CHEESE FILLING FOR DANISH PASTRIES

1 *cup cream cheese or*
1 *cup cottage cheese, drained*
1 *egg yolk*
2 *tablespoons sugar*
1 *tablespoon flour*
1 *teaspoon lemon juice*
1 *tablespoon seedless raisins*

Pass cheese through a fine sieve. Stir in the remaining ingredients and blend until smooth.

YIELD: ENOUGH FILLING FOR APPROXIMATELY 8 PASTRIES

ALMOND FILLING FOR DANISH PASTRIES

¼ cup butter
½ cup almond paste
¼ cup granulated sugar
1 egg yolk
1 teaspoon cornstarch

Cream the butter and almond paste together thoroughly. Add the sugar and beat until smooth. Stir in the egg yolk and cornstarch.
YIELD: ENOUGH FILLING FOR APPROXIMATELY 8 PASTRIES

PRUNE FILLING FOR DANISH PASTRIES

*½ cup thick prune jam**
1 tablespoon granulated sugar
1 teaspoon lemon juice

Combine all ingredients to a smooth mixture.
YIELD: ENOUGH FILLING FOR APPROXIMATELY 8 PASTRIES

* *Note:* Prune jam can be bought in any food store.

SCHNECKEN

1 recipe for Danish Pastry Dough (page 153)
½ cup butter, melted
⅓ cup granulated sugar, mixed with
1 teaspoon cinnamon
⅓ cup finely chopped pecans
3 tablespoons raisins
1 egg, beaten
1 recipe for Streusel Topping (page 158)
confectioners sugar, to dust

Set oven to 375 degrees F.
One 10 x 10-inch baking sheet, greased

On a floured board, roll out the dough in a rectangular shape approximately 10 inches long and 8 inches wide. Brush the dough with butter and sprinkle it evenly with the sugar and cinnamon, chopped pecans and raisins. Roll it up like a jelly roll and cut it into ¾-inch slices. Place flat on baking sheet and brush with beaten egg. Cover the pastries entirely with Streusel Topping and allow them to rise in a warm place (80–85 degrees F.) until doubled in bulk. Bake at 375

degrees F. for approximately 20 minutes or until golden brown. Dust with confectioners sugar.
YIELD: 16 SCHNECKENS

AMERICANA RUSSIAN COFFEE CAKE

1 recipe for Danish Pastry Dough (page 153)
1 recipe for Almond Filling (page 155)
⅓ cup mixed diced fruits
⅓ cup raisins
3 tablespoons finely chopped pecans
1 egg, beaten
1 recipe for Streusel Topping (page 158)
confectioners sugar, to dust

Set oven to 350 degrees F.
One greased pound-cake mold, 9 x 4 x 3 inches

On a floured board, roll out the dough into a 9-inch square. Spread it with Almond Filling and sprinkle evenly with the diced fruits, raisins and pecans. Roll the dough up like a jelly roll and place it in a greased pound-cake mold. Brush with beaten egg and cover entirely with Streusel Topping. Let the dough rise in a warm place (80–85 degrees F.) until doubled in bulk. Bake at 350 degrees F. for approximately 35 minutes or until golden brown. Cool for 25 minutes before unmolding. Dust with confectioners sugar.
YIELD: 8 SERVINGS

STRUDEL DOUGH

2 cups all-purpose flour
½ cup water
5 tablespoons vegetable oil
1 egg
1 pinch salt
3 tablespoons bread crumbs
3 tablespoons melted butter
strudel filling of your choice (page 155)
confectioners sugar, to dust

Set oven at 375 degrees F.
One 10 x 10-inch baking pan, greased

Sift the flour into a deep bowl. Add the water, 4 tablespoons of the oil, egg (lightly beaten with fork) and salt. Blend all ingredients to obtain a dough of smooth consistency. Keep working the dough to an elastic consistency. If no electric mixer is available, it will take a little longer to accomplish this; the best method is to smack the dough against a table time after time until the proper consistency is reached. It should take approximately 5 minutes of continuous kneading. Shape the dough into a ball. Place it on a pie tin brushed with ½ tablespoon oil, brush the surface with the remaining oil and cover with a cloth. Let the dough rest for about 1 hour in a warm place before proceeding to stretch it.

HOW TO STRETCH STRUDEL DOUGH

Cover a table approximately 36″ long x 18″ wide with a tablecloth. Dust the cloth evenly with all-purpose flour. Remove the dough from the pie tin and place it in the center of the tablecloth. Roll it out with a rolling pin as thin as possible. Place your fingers underneath the rolled dough and pull gently in all directions. This should be done gradually and carefully to avoid breaking the dough. (The quality of a good strudel is determined by the thinness of the dough. Some experienced chefs obtain amazing results; the dough is stretched so thin you have to look twice to actually see it.) Once the dough is properly stretched, let it dry for approximately 3 to 5 minutes before sprinkling it with the bread crumbs and 2 tablespoons of the melted butter. With a sharp knife or scissors, cut away any excess dough that may hang over the edges of the table. Place the prepared strudel filling down the entire length of the dough, approximately 3 inches in from the edge of the table. Fold the 3 inches of dough over the filling; lift the tablecloth and the dough will roll itself into the shape of a jelly roll.

Cut the strudel to fit the baking pan. Grease the pan well and place dough gently into it. Brush entirely with the remaining melted butter and bake at 375 degrees F. for about 45 minutes or until golden brown. Cool to lukewarm, dust with confectioners sugar and cut into desired portions.

YIELD: APPROXIMATELY 12 SERVINGS

Note: Any size table can be used to roll the dough, but bear in mind that the dimensions given above would apply to this particular quantity of dough stretched to the proper thinness.

APPLE STRUDEL FILLING

6 large, tart apples (approximately 2½ lbs.)
¾ cup seedless raisins
⅓ cup currant raisins
½ cup bread crumbs
¾ cup granulated sugar
¾ teaspoon ground cinnamon
juice of 1 lemon

Peel, core and slice the apples approximately ½-inch thick and combine with all other ingredients.

YIELD: APPROXIMATELY 12 SERVINGS

CHEESE STRUDEL FILLING

One 1-pound package cottage cheese, drained and pressed through a fine sieve, blended with 2 whole eggs, ½ cup granulated sugar, 2 tablespoons cornstarch, 1 teaspoon lemon rind and ½ cup seedless raisins. (Cream cheese can be substituted for cottage cheese. Cream cheese does not need to be pressed through a sieve.)

YIELD: APPROXIMATELY 12 SERVINGS

CHERRY, PINEAPPLE OR OTHER FRUIT STRUDEL FILLINGS

Approximately 3 cups well-drained, canned fruits combined with ½ cup bread crumbs, ½ cup sugar, 1 tablespoon lemon juice, ½ teaspoon ground cinnamon and, if desired, ½ cup finely chopped walnuts or pecans.

YIELD: APPROXIMATELY 12 SERVINGS

STREUSEL TOPPING

⅓ cup all-purpose flour
⅓ cup granulated sugar
3 tablespoons butter at room temperature

Mix all the ingredients together by rubbing them into the palm of your hand. Chill in the refrigerator for approximately 15 minutes and crumble over the pastry. Store in a cool place until needed.

YIELD: 1¾ CUPS

Note: Streusel topping will keep in the refrigerator for about a month.

BUTTERSCOTCH CURLS

1¾ *cups melted butter*
1 *cup brown sugar*
3 *tablespoons heavy cream*
1 *cup milk, scalded*
1 *tablespoon grated orange rind*
½ *cup granulated sugar*
1½ *teaspoons salt*
2 *cakes fresh yeast or* 2 *packages granulated yeast*
2 *eggs*
4¾ to 5 *cups all-purpose flour*
1 *teaspoon ground cinnamon*

Set oven to 350 degrees F.
Twenty-four muffin cups, greased

Combine 1 cup of melted butter, ½ cup of brown sugar and the heavy cream into a smooth mixture. Pour it evenly into the muffin cups. Blend the scalded milk, orange rind, sugar, salt and ½ cup of the remaining butter. Cool the mixture to lukewarm. Add the yeast and stir well to dissolve. Beat the eggs with a fork and work until light and fluffy. Add the eggs alternately with the flour to the yeast mixture and knead until smooth and elastic. Let the dough stand in a cool place for approximately 20 minutes. Then, on a floured board, roll it out to about ¼-inch thick. Brush with the remaining melted butter and dust with the remaining brown sugar mixed with cinnamon. Roll the dough up like a jelly roll and slice it approximately 1-inch thick. Place the slices in the prepared muffin tins and allow them to rise in a warm place (80–85 degrees F.) until double in bulk. Bake at 350 degrees F. for approximately 30 minutes or until golden brown.

YIELD: APPROXIMATELY 24 CAKES

PLAIN KUGELHOPF
(German yeast cake)

1 cake yeast or 1 package dry yeast
½ cup lukewarm water
½ cup milk
3 cups sifted all-purpose flour
½ cup butter
¼ cup granulated sugar
1 pinch salt
2 eggs plus 2 egg yolks
1 teaspoon grated lemon rind
½ cup seedless raisins
1 tablespoon confectioners sugar

Set oven at 350 degrees F.
One 10-inch fluted tube pan, well greased

In a deep bowl dissolve the yeast in water. Add the milk and 1 cup of flour and beat well. Place the remaining flour on top and let it rise in a warm place for approximately 45 minutes.

In a separate bowl, cream butter, sugar and salt together; add the beaten eggs and extra yolks. Stir in the grated lemon rind, pour into the flour batter and beat or knead well to a smooth and elastic dough. Stir in the raisins, and pour into the prepared pan. Let the dough rise in a warm place until doubled in bulk. Bake at 350 degrees F. for about 50 minutes or until golden brown. Remove from oven, unmold and cool. Dust the bottom with confectioners sugar and serve upside down.

YIELD: APPROXIMATELY 8 SERVINGS

ORIGINAL KUGELHOPF
(German yeast cake)

¾ cup butter
8 egg yolks, beaten with a fork
2 cups sifted all-purpose flour
¼ cup granulated sugar
1 teaspoon grated lemon rind
¼ teaspoon salt
¾ cake yeast or ¾ of a package dry yeast
¼ cup lukewarm water
¼ cup milk
¼ cup raisins
1 tablespoon confectioners sugar

Set oven at 350 degrees F.
One 10-inch fluted tube pan, well greased

Cream the butter and add the beaten egg yolks alternately with the flour (¼ cup flour each time 1 yolk is added). Beat well to blend.

Add the sugar, lemon rind and salt. Dissolve the yeast in lukewarm water and stir it into the milk. Add the yeast solution and raisins to the flour mixture and blend just enough to obtain a smooth dough. Pour the dough into the prepared pan and allow it to rise in a warm place (80–85 degrees F.) for about 3 to 4 hours or until doubled in bulk. Bake at 350 degrees F. for approximately 50 minutes or until golden brown. Turn the cake out on a wire rack and let it cool to lukewarm before attempting to lift off the mold. Dust the bottom with confectioners sugar and serve upside down.

YIELD: APPROXIMATELY 8 SERVINGS

DRESDEN STOLLEN

2 *packages or 2 cakes of yeast*
¼ *cup lukewarm water*
1 *cup soft butter*
2 *eggs plus 1 egg yolk*
¾ *cup plus 3 tablespoons granulated sugar*
1 *teaspoon salt*
2 *cups milk*
6¼ *cups sifted all-purpose flour*
1 *cup raisins*
½ *cup diced glazed cherries*
½ *cup orange peel*
¾ *cup chopped blanched almonds*
1 *tablespoon melted butter*
3 *teaspoons ground cinnamon*
½ *cup confectioners sugar to dust, or Royal Icing (page 280)*

Set oven at 375 degrees F.
One 10 x 10-inch baking sheet, greased

Dissolve the yeast in the water. Cream the butter, eggs and extra yolk, ¾ cup sugar and salt together. Stir in the dissolved yeast, milk and 4 cups flour. Place on a floured board and incorporate 2 cups flour by working the dough with your hands. Work the dough until smooth and elastic. Place the dough in an oiled bowl, cover with a towel and let rise until it doubles in bulk, or for about 1 hour. Punch the dough down and let rise once more for about 30 minutes. Dust the fruits with the remaining flour and add the fruits and nuts to the dough. Divide the dough into 3 parts and roll out each part into an oval shape. Brush the dough with melted butter and fold it in half. Brush again with melted butter. Sprinkle each piece of stollen with 1 tablespoon of the remaining sugar mixed with 1 teaspoon of ground cinnamon. Allow the stollen to rise on the baking sheet for approximately 25 minutes or until doubled in bulk. Bake at 375 degrees F. for approximately 40 minutes or until golden brown. Dust with confectioners sugar or frost with Royal Icing. Cool and wrap in foil. The stollen will keep for weeks if properly wrapped.

YIELD: 3 CAKES OR APPROXIMATELY 18 SERVINGS

European Favorites

CREAM PUFF PASTE

Shells made from Puff Paste are widely used for a variety of dessert preparations.

THE BATTER

½ cup water	*2 pinches sugar*
¼ cup butter	*½ cup all-purpose flour*
1 pinch salt	*2 medium eggs*

Combine the water, butter, salt and sugar in a deep pan and bring to a boil. Boil gently until all ingredients are melted. Remove from heat and add the flour all at once. Mix rapidly with a wooden spoon to a smooth paste. Return to a slow fire and stir rapidly until the mixture comes away from the sides of the pan. Remove from heat and add the eggs, one at a time, mixing thoroughly after each addition. The batter should be of the same consistency as a thick cream yet solid enough to hold its shape.

YIELD: 8 ÉCLAIR SHELLS, 8 LARGE PUFF SHELLS OR 16 TINY PUFFS

PREPARING CREAM PUFF PASTE FOR BAKING

CREAM PUFFS

Drop the batter onto a lightly greased baking pan from a tablespoon or teaspoon, depending on the size desired.

ÉCLAIRS

Using a pastry bag fitted with a ½-inch round tube, squeeze the cream puff paste in 1 x 3-inch portions onto a greased baking sheet.

BAKING CREAM PUFF PASTE

To speed up preparations at meal time, cream puffs or éclair shells can be baked a day ahead. Once baked thoroughly, puffs or éclair shells should be cooled thoroughly and stored refrigerated in a tightly closed container.

Bake in a 400 degrees F. oven for approximately 10 minutes or until the rising is completed. Then lower the oven temperature to 350 degrees F. and continue baking until done—15 to 25 minutes, depending upon the size of the pastry. If underbaked, Cream Puff Paste will collapse while cooling.

FREEZING PUFF SHELLS

Cream puff or éclair shells freeze well. Remove from the freezer and place in a 400 degrees F. oven for a few minutes to thaw before using.

LEFTOVER CREAM PUFF PASTE

Cream Puff Paste should be baked as soon as mixed. If, however, it is not used immediately, brush the surface with vegetable oil or butter, cover with waxed paper to prevent a skin from forming, cool and store in the refrigerator or freezer. When you are ready to use it, warm up Cream Puff Paste over hot water, stir rapidly with a wooden spoon, and proceed to bake as usual.

FILLING AND FROSTING CREAM PUFFS OR ÉCLAIR SHELLS

Cream puffs or éclair shells are usually filled by splitting the shells in two. In some cases, however, they can be filled in the following manner:

Punch a hole in the bottom of the cooled puff or éclair shell with the end of a pencil or the handle of a small wooden spoon. Fit a pastry bag with a small round tube approximately ¼-inch in diameter and squeeze the desired filling into the shell. When filled this way the shells are less likely to fall apart when they are dropped into the frosting or icing.

Cream puffs and éclairs are generally filled with Vanilla Pastry Cream (page 289), whipped cream or ice cream. They are most often frosted with Chocolate Fondant Icing (page 279) or simply dusted with confectioners sugar.

QUICK CHOCOLATE FROSTING FOR ÉCLAIRS

Melt 2½ oz. or 2½ squares unsweetened chocolate over warm water. Stir in ¼ cup granulated sugar and 3½ tablespoons water and bring to a boil. Remove from heat, cool to lukewarm and beat to spreading consistency. If necessary, place over hot water to keep soft while icing the éclairs.

ÉCLAIRS CHANTILLY

Bake the éclair shells as previously directed (page 164). Cool and split. Dip the top half in melted chocolate. Garnish the bottom half with a thick layer of whipped cream and replace the iced cover.

ÉCLAIRS DUCHESSE

Bake the éclair shells as previously directed (page 164). Cool. Fill with Vanilla Pastry Cream (page 289) and frost with Caramel Sugar (page 287).

CREAM PUFFS CARIBBEAN

Bake and cool the regular sized cream puffs as previously explained (page 164). Split the shells and fill the bottom with shredded coconut, blended with Vanilla Pastry Cream (page 289). Garnish heavily with whipped cream. Replace the cover and ice with melted sweet chocolate.

CREAM PUFFS GRILLÉS

Using a tablespoon, drop the Cream Puff Paste (page 163) onto a greased and floured baking sheet. Brush with beaten egg and cover heavily with sliced almonds. Place 1 teaspoon granulated sugar on each puff, and bake according to directions on page 164. When cool, split in two and fill with whipped cream or Vanilla Pastry Cream (page 289). Replace the cover and dust with confectioners sugar.

CROQUE-EN-BOUCHE

Bake small cream puff shells the size of a Ping-Pong ball according to directions on page 164. Cool and fill with Vanilla Pastry Cream (page 289). Cook 1 cup granulated sugar over a low fire until golden brown, stirring constantly to avoid burning. Dip the puffs in the hot syrup and pile them on top of each other to form a pyramid, using an oiled cone-shaped mold for support. When cool, remove the mold.

Note: If you wish, Croque-en-Bouche may be served garnished with whipped cream.

RELIGIEUSES

Bake an equal number of large- and small-sized cream puff shells according to directions on page 164. Fill the shells with Vanilla Pastry Cream (page 289). Ice the large puffs with chocolate and the small ones with Fondant Icing flavored with coffee (page 279). Place the small puffs on top of the large ones and decorate all around the base with Mocha Flavored Buttercream (page 284).

TRIPLE CREAM PUFFS

A very unusual-looking puff! Prepare Cream Puff Paste according to directions on page 163 and in groups of 3 small puffs not larger than a Ping-Pong ball, set close enough together so that they will bake as one shell. Bake as directed. Cool and split in two. Fill with Pastry Cream flavored to your taste (page 289), whipped cream or ice cream, and dust with confectioners sugar.

SWAN CREAM PUFFS

Drop Cream Puff Paste (page 163) in oval shapes onto a greased baking pan using a tablespoon or pastry bag fitted with a round tube and bake according to directions on page 164. Reserve approximately ⅓ cup Cream Puff Paste to form the necks and heads of the swans. With the help of a paper cone or pastry bag fitted with a small round tube, pipe the dough onto a greased baking sheet in the shape of a wide question mark. Press harder at the start of the question mark to form the head of the bird. Bake at 325 degrees F. for about 10 minutes. Meanwhile, split the cooled cream puffs in half. Fill the bottom half with drained crushed pineapple or any other fruit of your choice and garnish heavily with Coffee-Flavored Whipped Cream (page 11). Cut the top part of the cream puff in two, lengthwise, to form the wings. Secure them in an upward position on each side of the whipped cream. Insert the neck at the front of the filled puff. Dust with confectioners sugar.

PAINS DE LA MECQUE

On a greased and floured pan, form the Cream Puff Paste (page 163) into rings approximately 3 inches in diameter, using a pastry bag fitted with a ½-inch star tube. Dust heavily with coarse granulated sugar and bake at 400 degrees F. for approximately 30 minutes or until done. Cool, split in two and garnish with whipped cream.

POLKAS

Roll out Tart Dough (page 78) to approximately ¼-inch thick. Cut circles approximately 3 inches in diameter and prick with a fork. Pipe a border of Cream Puff Paste (page 163) all around the edge of each circle using a pastry bag fitted with a plain tube about ½-inch in diameter. Brush the Cream Puff Paste with 1 egg, beaten with a fork. Bake at 400 degrees F. for about 30 minutes, or until done. When cool, fill the centers with Vanilla Pastry Cream (page 289) and top with 1 teaspoon granulated sugar. Burn the sugar with a *red hot* curling iron.

PARIS BREST

1 *recipe for Cream Puff Paste (page 163)*
1 *egg, beaten*
½ *cup sliced blanched almonds*
1 *cup Vanilla Pastry Cream (page 289)*
3 *tablespoons of Praline Powder (page 288)*
1 *cup whipped cream*
confectioners sugar, to dust

Set oven at 375 degrees F.
One 10 x 10-inch baking sheet, greased and floured

Using a plate or pie tin as a guide, trace a circle on the baking sheet approximately 8 inches in diameter. With a pastry bag fitted with a round tube ¾-inch in diameter, squeeze out Cream Puff Paste dough approximately 1 inch high and 1½ inches wide. Brush the circle with beaten egg; dust with sliced blanched almonds and bake at 375 degrees F. for about 40 minutes or until crisp. Remove from heat and cool. Split the circle in half horizontally and fill the bottom with 1 cup Vanilla Pastry Cream flavored with the Praline Powder. Garnish the pastry cream with the whipped cream and replace the cover. Dust with confectioners sugar and serve chilled.
YIELD: 6 SERVINGS

Note: Cream Puff Paste, as explained on page 164, can be prepared a day or two in advance.

HINTS ON PUFF PASTRY

Most culinary historians have concluded that Claude Gelée, or Le Lorrain, born in France in the year 1600, is the person we have to thank for puff pastry.

But the puff pastry was certainly not created by one man alone. As far back as the Greeks, Romans and Charles Quint, King of France (1500–1558), some indications have been discovered that puff pastry was already known but, of course, not perfected to the extent it is today.

An endless variety of French pastries are made with puff pastry. I have listed some of the most popular ones on the following pages. Because of the large amount of butter it requires, puff pastry certainly is one of the most expensive doughs ever made and also one whose preparation takes a great deal of special care.

It is important that you use a good quality all-purpose flour and that you brush off any excess flour that may have accumulated on the dough after each folding.

Be sure to rest the dough properly between foldings, and be sure to roll it in a cool place, away from heat.

PUFF PASTRY

1 *lb. cold sweet butter*
1 *lb. all-purpose flour*
1 *teaspoon salt*
1½ *cups* ice *water* (*approximately*)

Knead the butter with your hands on a pastry board to remove the water. Squeeze it tightly and work it to a pliable and smooth consistency. Form it into a square approximately ½-inch thick and place it in the refrigerator to chill. Sift the flour and salt together into a deep bowl; make a hole in the center and pour the ice water gradually while beating constantly. If no electric mixer is available, pour with your left hand and work all ingredients to a rather stiff dough using the fingertips of your right hand. Add only enough cold water to obtain a dough of the *same consistency as the butter* but remember that the dough will soften slightly after a few minutes of rest.

Cover the dough with a wet towel and let it rest in the refrigerator for approximately 30 minutes. Then roll the dough out on a floured board into a square about ¾-inch thick and place the butter in the center. Fold the 4 sides of the dough over the butter and press the edges firmly with the palm of your hand to secure the butter inside the dough. Roll out again into a rectangle 3 times longer than it is wide. This first rolling has to be done gently to make sure that the butter does not break through the dough. This is the secret of a well-made puff pastry dough. Fold the rectangle in 3: left over right and right over left. The dough has now returned to its original size. This rolling and folding is called, in the "professional world," a *turn*. Let dough rest in a cool place, but not the refrigerator, for approximately 30 minutes. If you rest the dough in a place that is too cold after the first folding, the butter will become too hard and will not mix properly during the rolling process.

Repeat the same rolling and folding one more time. Chill in the refrigerator for about 20 minutes and make 2 more turns, allowing the dough to rest between each rolling and folding by placing it in the refrigerator for at least 20 minutes. Repeat until you have given the dough 6 complete turns in all. Chill for approximately 1 hour after the final turn before trying to roll and cut the dough into the shapes desired.

This "wonder" pastry can be made several days in advance. If stored, the dough should be kept in the refrigerator lying flat on a floured board and covered with a damp cloth until needed.

YIELD: 12 TO 14 PATTY SHELLS OR 16 NAPOLEONS

BAKING

To be fully appreciated, all puff pastry must be baked thoroughly. Unless otherwise indicated in the individual recipe, first place the pastry in a hot oven (400–450 degrees F.) until the rising is completed. Then open the oven door and allow the temperature to drop to 375–325 degrees F. When the oven has cooled to the desired temperature, cover the pastries with heavy brown paper lightly brushed with vegetable oil or shortening, close the oven door and finish baking 15 minutes longer, or until crisp and golden brown.

Note: Many French pastries are made out of puff pastry. In the following pages I will explain to you how they are made but remember: a well-made puff paste is a *must* for a successful finished product.

QUICK PUFF PASTRY

A good recipe for anyone who can't afford the time necessary for the preparation of "real" Puff Pastry.

4½ cups sifted all-purpose flour
3 cups butter
1 teaspoon salt
1 teaspoon lemon juice
2 tablespoons cold water

Knead all ingredients together. Give only 4 turns to the dough and do not rest it between turns. Chill and use immediately.

(For detailed instructions concerning the preparation and rolling of Puff Pastry, see page 169.)

YIELD: 12 PATTY SHELLS

MIRLITONS

1 recipe for Puff Pastry (page 169)
5 teaspoons apricot jam
2 eggs
½ cup granulated sugar
1 teaspoon rum
6 large dry macaroons
3 tablespoons confectioners sugar
½ cup sliced almonds

Set oven at 400 degrees F.
ten individual deep tartlet molds

Line the molds with Puff Pastry (page 169) rolled to about ⅛-inch thick. Place ½ teaspoon of apricot jam in the bottom of each mold. Beat the eggs with sugar and rum until light and fluffy. Crush the macaroons to powder form and stir into the egg mixture. Blend thoroughly and fill the tartlet molds approximately ⅔ full with egg mixture. Dust with confectioners sugar and sliced almonds. Bake at 400 degrees F. for approximately 20 minutes or until golden brown.

YIELD: 10 SERVINGS

Note: Any other jam of your choice may be substituted for the apricot.

CREAM ROLLS
(Lady Luck)

1 recipe Puff Pastry (page 169)
1 egg, beaten
1 recipe Vanilla Pastry Cream (page 289)
½ cup roasted sliced almonds
3 tablespoons confectioners sugar

Set oven at 425 degrees F.
One 10 x 10-inch baking sheet, ungreased

Roll out Puff Pastry approximately ⅛-inch thick and cut into strips 1 inch wide and 10 inches long. Wind each strip around a well-greased metal tube or cone starting at the wide part of the cone. Brush with beaten egg and place 1 inch apart on the baking sheet. Bake at 425 degrees F. for approximately 10 minutes then remove from heat and slip the pastry off the tubes. Reduce the heat to 350 degrees F.; cover the pastry with heavy brown paper and return to the oven for approximately 10 more minutes or until crisp. Cool and fill with Vanilla Pastry Cream. Dip both ends of the rolls into roasted sliced almonds and dust with confectioners sugar.

YIELD: 24 PIECES

PALMIERS
(Palm Leaves)

1 recipe for Puff Pastry (page 169)
granulated sugar

Set oven at 425 degrees F.
One 10 x 10-inch baking sheet, greased

Roll out Puff Pastry on a floured board to approximately ⅛-inch thick, 16 inches long and 5 inches wide, and sprinkle heavily with granulated sugar. Fold each long side toward the center and then fold again to obtain a strip approximately 1 inch wide, ½ inch thick and 16 inches long. Cut the dough crosswise in slices about ½-inch wide and arrange the slices cut-side down on the prepared baking sheet. Bake at 425 degrees F. for 10 minutes or until the bottom is caramelized. Turn and finish baking until golden brown.

YIELD: 24 PALMIERS

APPLE TURNOVERS

5 *large apples*
4 *tablespoons butter*
2 *tablespoons brown sugar*
1 *teaspoon lemon juice*
1 *tablespoon rum*
1 *recipe Puff Pastry (page 169)*
1 *egg, beaten*
1 *cup confectioners sugar*

Set oven at 400 degrees F.
One 10 x 10-inch baking sheet, wet

Peel, core and slice the apples. Fry the apples until tender in the butter. Add the sugar and continue cooking on a low fire until the mixture thickens; stir well to avoid burning. Add the lemon juice and rum. Cool before using.

Roll out the Puff Pastry to approximately ¼-inch thick and cut into a 9-inch circle, using a pie tin or plate as a guide. Spread the center with the cooked apples or use thick applesauce, leaving about a 2-inch rim all around. Wet half the border slightly with cold water and fold the other half over to obtain a semicircle. Seal the edges tightly together and brush entirely with beaten egg and prick here and there with a fork. Arrange the turnovers on the prepared sheet and bake at 400 degrees F. for about 35 minutes or until golden brown. Immediately after removing from the oven, brush with the confectioners sugar diluted with enough water to obtain an icing of brushing consistency. Serve warm.

YIELD: 6 SERVINGS

ALLUMETTES

1 *recipe for Puff Pastry (page 169)*
1 *egg white*
1 *cup confectioners sugar*

Set oven at 375 degrees F.
One 10 x 10-inch baking sheet, wet

Roll out the dough on a floured board to ⅓-inch thick in a rectangle 4 inches wide. Beat the egg white, adding the sugar, until you get a stiff icing. Spread the icing thinly and evenly over the pastry and let it stand to dry for approximately 5 minutes. Using a knife dipped in water, cut the dough crosswise in pieces about 1¾ inches wide and arrange the pieces on the baking sheet. Bake at 375 degrees F. for approximately 15 to 18 minutes. Check the pastry after 5 minutes; if the sugar seems to be coloring too rapidly, cover the Allumettes with heavy brown paper.

YIELD: 2 DOZEN PIECES

NAPOLEONS

1 *recipe for Puff Pastry (page 169)*
1 *recipe for Vanilla Pastry Cream (page 289) or*
1 *cup heavy cream, whipped*
1 *recipe for Apricot Glaze (page 80) or Fondant Icing (page 279)*

Set oven at 425 degrees F.
One 10 x 10-inch baking sheet, lined with greased paper

Roll out the dough on a floured board ⅛-inch thick, 16 inches long and 12 inches wide and lay it on the baking sheet. Prick well with a fork and bake at 425 degrees F. for approximately 10 minutes. Reduce the temperature to 350 degrees F. and continue baking until golden brown. Remove from oven, slip the paper from under the dough and cool. Cut lengthwise into 3 equal strips and sandwich the layers together with cool Vanilla Pastry Cream or whipped cream. Brush top layer with hot Apricot Glaze or with Fondant Icing.

YIELD: 16 NAPOLEONS, EACH 2 INCHES WIDE

AMERICANA NAPOLEONS

Bake as directed above. Fill with Vanilla Pastry Cream. Dust with confectioners sugar and cut into 2-inch bars.

JALOUSIE CAKE

1 *recipe for Puff Pastry (page 169)*
⅓ *cup raspberry or apricot jam*
1 *egg, beaten*
1 *cup confectioners sugar*
water

Set oven at 400 degrees F.
One 10 x 10-inch baking sheet, wet

Roll out two rectangular pieces of Puff Pastry the length of the baking sheet and approximately 5 inches wide, one piece ⅛-inch thick and the other ⅓ inch thick. Lay the thinner sheet on the baking sheet and spread with the jam, leaving a border of about 1 inch down each of the long sides. Lay the thicker piece of dough on top and seal the two together by pressing on each side firmly with your fingers or the palm of your hand. With a razor blade or sharp knife, make small incisions 1 inch apart across the top of the Jalousie. Brush the cake with the beaten egg and prick it here and there with a fork. Bake in a 400 degree F. oven for approximately 10 minutes, turn down the heat to 350 degrees F. and continue baking for 15 minutes longer or until golden brown. Mix the confectioners sugar with enough water to obtain an icing of brushing consistency. Frost the top of the pastry as soon as it is removed from the oven.

YIELD: 6 SERVINGS

PITHIVIERS
(almond cake)

Follow the recipe for Jalousie Cake above but instead of filling the cake with raspberry jam, use the following cream: 6 oz. almond paste blended thoroughly with 2 egg yolks and mixed to a smooth cream with ⅔ cup cooled Vanilla Pastry Cream (page 289) and 2 tablespoons rum.

YIELD: 6 SERVINGS

CONVERSATIONS

1 *recipe for Puff Pastry (page 169)*
1½ *cups Frangipane Cream (page 288)*
1 *cup Royal Icing (page 280)*

Set oven at 375 degrees F.
One 10 x 10-inch baking sheet, wet

Roll out 2 separate pieces of Puff Pastry, one approximately ⅛-inch thick and the other about ⅓-inch thick. Cut a 10-inch circle out of each piece using a pie tin or plate as a guide and reserve the leftover dough. Set the thinner circle of dough on the baking sheet and spread it evenly with the Frangipane Cream leaving a clear rim about 1½ inches all around. Brush the rim with a little cold water, place the thicker layer of dough on top and secure the two pieces together by pressing gently with your fingers. Chill in the refrigerator while preparing the Royal Icing. Spread thinly and evenly over the top of the chilled dough.

Roll the remaining small piece of pastry into strips ⅛-inch wide and 10 inches long. Arrange the strips on the Royal Icing in a lattice pattern and bake at 375 degrees F. for approximately 20 minutes. Then cover the pastry with heavy brown paper and reduce the heat to 325 degrees F. Continue baking for another 20 minutes or until crisp.

YIELD: 8 SERVINGS

Note: For small Conversations, line shallow and straight-edged tartlet molds with Puff Pastry. Fill the molds with Frangipane Cream and cover with a second sheet of Puff Pastry. Proceed as explained above and bake for about 20 minutes at 350 degrees F.

YIELD: 12 INDIVIDUAL CONVERSATIONS

GÂTEAU SAINT-HONORÉ

On Sunday after Mass, it is considered the French traditional "pièce de résistance." Filled with a fluffy, light cream composed of pastry cream and egg whites blended with gelatin, this luscious-tasting cake is a real treat for anyone who likes the unusual and ultimate in desserts.

SAINT-HONORÉ SHELL

Half recipe for Plain Pastry or Pie Dough (page 54)

1 *recipe Cream Puff Paste (page 163)*

Set oven at 425 degrees F.
One 10 x 10-inch baking sheet, lined with heavy greased paper

Roll out the pie dough to approximately ⅛-inch thick. Cut out in a circle approximately 10 inches in diameter using a plate or pot cover as a guide. Arrange the dough on the greased baking sheet and prick generously with a fork. Using a pastry bag filled with the Cream Puff Paste and fitted with a plain round tube, about ½-inch in diameter, squeeze a rim all around the circle and bake at 425 degrees F. for about 15 minutes. Reduce the heat to 350 degrees F. and continue baking for 20 minutes more or until dry and golden brown.

With the remaining Cream Puff Paste squeeze out about 1 dozen small cream puffs, no bigger than the size of a Ping-Pong ball, onto a large, greased and floured baking sheet, using a pastry bag fitted with a small tube. Bake at 375 degrees F. for about 30 minutes, or until golden brown. Remove from the heat and cool thoroughly. The Saint-Honoré Shell can be prepared in advance and stored in a cool dry place.

YIELD: ONE 10-INCH CAKE

CARAMEL SUGAR FOR GÂTEAU SAINT-HONORÉ

Dissolve 1 cup granulated sugar with ⅓ cup water and 1 pinch cream of tartar. Cook over medium heat without stirring until the syrup turns golden brown. Remove from heat and cool for a minute or so before attempting to dip the cream puffs. If the syrup hardens before all the cream puffs have been dipped, set it into a pan filled with hot water and stir to melt the caramel.

CREAM FOR GÂTEAU SAINT-HONORÉ

2 *cups hot Vanilla Pastry Cream (page 289)*
½ *tablespoon or ½ package unflavored gelatin softened in*
2 *tablespoons hot water*
6 *egg whites*
1 *pinch salt*
2 *tablespoons granulated sugar*

Prepare the Vanilla Pastry Cream. Stir in the softened gelatin and mix thoroughly. Pour the mixture into a deep mixing bowl. Beat the egg whites and salt until soft peaks form; gradually add the sugar and continue beating until stiff. Fold approximately ¼ of the egg whites into the hot cream and blend well. Fold in the remaining egg whites. Pour into the center of the prepared Saint-Honoré Shell and chill in refrigerator for 1 hour or until set.

YIELD: ENOUGH FOR ONE 10-INCH SAINT-HONORÉ CAKE

FINISHING AND ASSEMBLING
THE GÂTEAU SAINT-HONORÉ

Fill each small puff with cooled Vanilla Pastry Cream or whipped cream. Dip each puff in Golden Caramel Sugar and arrange them all around the edges of the cake. Fill the center with cream for Saint-Honoré, or whipped cream, and chill. Decorate with red glazed cherries.

YIELD: 8 SERVINGS

FRITTERS

HINTS ON DEEP FAT FRYING FOR FRITTERS

Fill a deep pot about ⅔ full with melted shortening. Heat to the desired temperature (approximately 360 degrees F. for an uncooked mixture like fritters). Do not overcrowd the fritters while frying or the temperature of the fat will be lowered too quickly, causing the dough to absorb too much fat. As the fritters rise to the top, turn them over gently to assure a perfect and even coloring.

When golden brown, lift the fritters out with a wire basket or skimmer and drain off the hot fat before placing the fritters on a table covered with a cloth.

If you strain the fat after each use, it can be used over and over again. When the fat smokes, it means it has been overheated and cannot be used any longer at such a high temperature. To clean fat properly, cook chunks of raw potatoes in it to absorb cooking flavors; then strain through a fine sieve to remove all foreign particles. (For further instructions on deep frying, see page 149.)

FRUIT FRITTERS

Practically any kind of fruit can be used in making fruit fritters, but it is imperative that fruits be thoroughly dried in order that the flour and batter adhere properly. Fritters should fry to a golden brown in approximately 5 minutes. Fruit fritters, in most cases, are served with sauces or simply dusted with confectioners sugar.

FRITTER BATTER FOR FRUITS
(Basic Recipe)

1 cup sifted all-purpose flour
1 teaspoon double-acting baking powder
½ teaspoon salt
1 tablespoon melted butter
½ cup milk
1 tablespoon brandy
1 teaspoon grated orange rind
1 egg plus 1 yolk
1 egg white, beaten stiff

Sift the flour, baking powder and salt together in a deep bowl. Combine the melted butter, milk, brandy and orange rind and stir gradually into the sifted ingredients. Blend well. Beat egg and extra yolk with a fork and add to the flour mixture. Mix all ingredients thoroughly to obtain a batter free of lumps. Beat the egg white stiff but not dry and fold it gently into the prepared batter. Let stand for about 1 hour in a cool place.
YIELD: 12 TO 15 FRITTERS

Note: Beer may be substituted for milk if you wish.

BANANA FRITTERS

Peel 4 large, ripe but firm bananas. Slice approximately ½-inch thick. Squeeze the juice of 1 lemon over them and dust evenly with all-purpose flour. Dip into the fritter batter, coating each banana chunk entirely. Fry in deep fat at 365 degrees F. until golden brown. Drain on absorbent paper. Serve with Liqueur Sauce flavored with rum (page 292).
YIELD: 6 SERVINGS

APPLE FRITTERS

Peel and core 4 firm apples and slice into rings ½-inch thick. Dust the apple rings entirely with all-purpose flour. Dip into fritter batter, coating each apple ring entirely and fry in deep fat at 360 degrees F. until golden brown. Drain on absorbent paper. Dust with a mixture of cinnamon and sugar and serve hot with Custard Sauce (page 293).
YIELD: 4 SERVINGS

ORANGE FRITTERS

Peel 4 large oranges. Remove the white skin gently with the point of a knife and cut into ½-inch-thick slices. Drain well on a towel and dust each slice entirely with all-purpose flour. Dip into fritter batter, coating each slice entirely, and fry at 360 degrees F. until golden brown. Serve hot with Liqueur Sauce (page 292) flavored with Cointreau.

YIELD: 4 SERVINGS

PINEAPPLE FRITTERS

Drain a can of pineapple chunks (1 lb. 12 ozs.). Dust the pineapple with all-purpose flour and dip into fritter batter, coating each chunk entirely. Fry in deep fat at 360 degrees F. until golden brown. Drain on absorbent paper and serve hot with Strawberry Sauce (page 293).

YIELD: 4 SERVINGS

APRICOT FRITTERS

Cut in half 6 ripe, firm apricots and remove the pits. Soak the fruit in brandy or rum overnight. Drain well and proceed as for Apple Fritters (page 179).

YIELD: 2 SERVINGS

STRAWBERRY FRITTERS

Select 12 very large and firm strawberries; sprinkle heavily with granulated sugar and kirsch and let soak for 1 or 2 hours. Drain the fruit well and proceed as for Apple Fritters (page 179).

YIELD: 2 SERVINGS

Note: Use the same procedure for cherries or any other juice fritters.

FRITTERS SUZON

Prepare one recipe for Rice Condé (page 249) and when the rice is cool, form it into balls the size of Ping-Pong balls; fill the center of each ball with finely chopped diced fruits mixed with hot Apricot Glaze (page 80). Enclose the filling well and dip the rice balls in fritter batter. Fry gently at 360 degrees F. until golden brown. Drain on absorbent paper and serve hot, dusted with a mixture of cinnamon and sugar and accompanied by any sauce of your choice (see sauces, page 290). Use 3 balls per serving.

YIELD: 12 TO 15 BALLS

BEIGNETS SOUFFLÉS

Prepare Cream Puff Paste (page 163) using ⅓ cup butter for each cup of liquid. From a teaspoon drop the paste in small portions into hot fat (360 degrees F.). Increase the heat gradually to 275 degrees F. allowing enough time for the dough to rise fully. Sprinkle with a mixture of cinnamon and sugar and serve hot accompanied by Custard Sauce (page 293).

YIELD: 4 SERVINGS

BEIGNETS SOUFFLÉS SURPRISE

Follow the recipe for Beignets Soufflés above but make bigger puffs using a small ice cream scoop instead of a teaspoon. Cut each puff in two and fill with a fruit jam such as raspberry or apricot before serving. Serve with sauce of your choice (page 290).

YIELD: 4 SERVINGS

FRITTERS BOURGEOISE

Cut a stale Brioche (page 144) into slices approximately ½-inch thick. Dip each slice quickly into Custard Sauce (page 293) mixed with 2 tablespoons rum or kirsch. Drain off the excess sauce and dip into fritter batter; proceed as for Apple Fritters (page 179).

YIELD: ONE POUND OF BRIOCHE MAKES 4 SERVINGS

GOLDEN FRITTERS

½ cup sifted all-purpose flour
1 pinch salt
⅓ cup milk
2 eggs, separated
1 tablespoon granulated sugar
3 tablespoons confectioners sugar
1 teaspoon cinnamon

Deep fat heated to 370 degrees F.

Place sifted flour and salt in a bowl. Gradually stir in the milk and beat well to obtain a batter free of lumps. Beat the egg yolks with a fork for approximately 1 minute and add to the batter. Blend all ingredients well. Beat the egg whites, adding the granulated sugar gradually while beating, until stiff but not dry and mix them into the batter. Drop from a tablespoon into the deep fat and fry until golden brown. Remove from heat and drain on absorbent paper. Combine the confectioners sugar and cinnamon and dust over the fritters. Serve warm with Hot Custard (page 293) or Chocolate Sauce (page 291).
YIELD: 6 SERVINGS

FRIED CREAM FRITTERS

4 egg yolks
1 tablespoon brandy
2 tablespoons granulated sugar
3 tablespoons cornstarch diluted in
¼ cup milk
1¾ cups heavy cream
1 vanilla bean or 1 teaspoon vanilla extract
½ cup bread crumbs
2 eggs, beaten
½ cup almonds, finely ground
⅓ cup warm Cognac

Deep fat heated to 360 degrees F.

Blend the egg yolks, brandy and sugar well together and add the cornstarch and milk mixture. Scald the heavy cream and pour gradually over yolk mixture. Add the vanilla bean or vanilla extract and cook over hot water, stirring constantly until the custard thickens. The custard should be near the boiling point but *should not boil.* Pour it into a shallow pan to a depth of 1 inch and chill in refrigerator until it sets. Using a sharp knife dipped in water, divide and cut the cream into small squares. Dip them in bread crumbs and beaten eggs and roll in the almonds. Fry in deep fat until golden brown. Arrange the hot fritters on a heat-proof platter, cover with Cognac, flame, and serve immediately.

YIELD: 4 SERVINGS

BEIGNETS PARISIENS

A French recipe for cream fritters.

2 cups all-purpose flour	*1 teaspoon grated lemon rind*
¼ cup granulated sugar	*½ teaspoon vanilla extract*
6 eggs plus 5 yolks	*3 tablespoons butter*
1 pinch salt	*1 cup bread crumbs*
2 cups hot milk	*½ cup confectioners sugar*

Deep fat heated to 375 degrees F.
One 12 x 5 x 2-inch baking pan, greased

Combine 1 cup of the flour, sugar, five of the whole eggs, yolks, and salt in a deep saucepan. Gradually pour in the hot milk and stir rapidly to mix all ingredients thoroughly. Add the lemon rind and vanilla extract and cook over a medium flame until thick and smooth. When the mixture starts to boil, remove from heat immediately. Stir in the butter. Pour the hot cream mixture into the prepared pan to a depth of approximately ½-inch. Cool until set and cut into squares, diamonds, ovals or rounds. Beat the remaining egg. Dip the beignets in the remaining *flour* and *beaten egg*; roll in *bread crumbs* and fry in deep fat until golden brown. Drain on absorbent paper. Dust with confectioners sugar and serve immediately.

YIELD: 6 SERVINGS

EUROPEAN BEST-SELLER CAKES AND PASTRIES

In Vienna, a meal without dessert is considered a near catastrophe. The Austrians admire sweets in much the same way that they appreciate Mozart, Beethoven or Johann Strauss. And like their music,

Viennese desserts are recognized the world over as truly "sublime."

Anyone who has had the pleasure of strolling along the streets of Vienna undoubtedly has felt the compulsion to stop, look and admire the window displays of a *Konditorei* (a combination pastry shop and tea house), where an endless selection of cakes, tortes and cookies constantly tempts the viewer.

Vienna's best-known dessert is indubitably the famous *Sacher Torte*. Both the Demel Pastry Shop and the Sacher Restaurant claim to have fabricated the original.

To the best of my knowledge, I offer you the following as the genuine and original Sacher Torte, along with other exquisite and incomparable European desserts.

ORIGINAL SACHER TORTE

6 oz. semi-sweet chocolate
¾ cup butter
½ cup granulated sugar
8 egg yolks
1 cup sifted cake flour
7 egg whites
2 tablespoons hot, clear apricot jam

Set oven at 325 degrees F.
One cake pan, 9 inches round and 3 inches deep, greased and floured

Melt the chocolate over hot water and stir well. Cool. Cream the butter and sugar together until fluffy. Add the egg yolks one at a time, alternately with a spoonful of melted chocolate, beating well after each addition. Fold in the sifted flour. Beat the egg whites until stiff but not dry and fold gently into the yolk mixture. Blend all ingredients well and pour into the prepared cake pan. Bake at 325 degrees F. for approximately 45 minutes or until the point of a knife, when inserted through the center, comes out clean. Unmold the cake and cool. Spread the cooled cake with clear apricot jam and set it on a screen.

CHOCOLATE ICING FOR SACHER TORTE

6 oz. sweet chocolate
⅔ cup granulated sugar
⅓ cup hot water
1 teaspoon melted butter

Melt the chocolate over hot water. Boil the sugar and water together until the syrup thickens and forms a strong thread or until the temperature reaches 232 degrees F. on a candy thermometer. Remove from heat and add the melted chocolate gradually. Stir in the melted butter and beat rapidly. As soon as the icing thickens, pour it quickly over the cake. Let dry for 1 hour in a cool place.
YIELD: 8 TO 10 SERVINGS

WALNUT TORTE

½ cup butter
¾ cup fine granulated sugar
8 *egg yolks*
1 *teaspoon almond extract*
1½ *cups sifted cake flour*
7 *egg whites*
3 *tablespoons granulated sugar*
2 *cups heavy cream, whipped*
¾ cup finely chopped walnuts
1 *tablespoon Grand Marnier*
confectioners sugar to dust

Set the oven at 325 degrees F.
Two 9-inch round cake pans, greased and floured

Cream the butter and fine granulated sugar together until fluffy. Add the egg yolks one at a time, beating well after each addition. Stir in the almond extract and gently fold in the sifted flour. Beat the egg whites until stiff but not dry, adding the granulated sugar gradually while beating, and fold into the yolk mixture. Divide the batter evenly into the 2 cake pans and bake at 325 degrees F. for about 35 minutes or until the cake is done and pulls away from the sides of the pans. Cool thoroughly, and sandwich the two layers together with whipped cream blended with chopped walnuts and Grand Marnier. Chill in refrigerator and just before serving dust with confectioners sugar.
YIELD: 6 SERVINGS

BÛCHE DE NOËL
(Christmas Log)

The traditional pastry that all French people look forward to eating during the Christmas holiday.

4 eggs, separated
¼ cup cocoa powder
¼ cup sifted cake flour
¼ cup granulated sugar
2 cups of Mocha or Chocolate Buttercream (page 284)
½ cup Rich Buttercream colored pale green
2 tablespoons cocoa powder

Set the oven at 400 degrees F.
One baking sheet, 9 x 16 inches, lined with wax paper

Beat the egg yolks in a deep bowl until light and fluffy. Combine and sift together the cocoa powder and cake flour. Beat the egg whites until stiff, adding sugar gradually while beating. Fold approximately ⅓ of the beaten egg whites gently into the yolks. Then stir the yolk mixture quickly into the remaining egg whites. Dust the sifted cocoa powder and flour on top of the yolks mixture and fold all ingredients gently together. Avoid overmixing and breaking up the air cells. Spread the batter evenly onto the baking sheet and bake at 400 degrees F. for about 8 minutes or until golden brown. Reverse on a table sprinkled with 2 tablespoons granulated sugar. Cool and peel off the paper. Spread the cooled cake with Mocha or Chocolate Buttercream approximately ½-inch thick. Roll tight like a jelly roll and cut each end at a slight angle. Cover entirely with the remaining buttercream, using a fork to imitate a woody texture, or squeeze the buttercream from a pastry bag fitted with a star tube. Using the pale green buttercream, squeeze out some small leaves to decorate the log and dust with cocoa powder.
YIELD: 4 TO 5 SERVINGS

DOBOS CAKE

8 egg yolks
½ cup plus 3 tablespoons granulated sugar
1 teaspoon water
1 cup sifted cake flour
grated rind of 1 lemon
7 egg whites

Set oven at 350 degrees F.

Seven 9-inch spring-form molds, greased, lined with waxed paper, and greased again

Beat the egg yolks and ½ cup of sugar together until fluffy and thick; stir in the water and fold in the flour and lemon rind. Beat the egg whites until stiff but not dry, gradually adding the remaining 3 tablespoons sugar while beating. Fold the egg whites into the yolk batter and blend all ingredients well.

Divide evenly into the prepared pans, dropping only 4 tablespoons of batter into each pan and spreading it evenly. Bake each layer at 350 degrees F. for approximately 8 minutes or until starting to brown. Remove from the pans, peel off the paper and cool.

CHOCOLATE BUTTERCREAM FOR DOBOS TORTE

6 oz. unsweetened chocolate
5 egg yolks
1 egg white
1 teaspoon vanilla extract
2 drops red food coloring
⅔ cup confectioners sugar, sifted
1⅓ cups sweet butter

Melt the chocolate over hot water, stirring constantly. Remove from heat and add the egg yolks and egg white, one at a time, beating well after each addition. Stir in the vanilla, food coloring and sugar. Cook over hot water for approximately 3 minutes. Remove from the heat and cool. In the meantime, knead the butter on a wooden board to a pliable and creamy consistency. Divide it into large pieces and add to the chocolate mixture. Beat vigorously to a fluffy and creamy consistency. Sandwich together 6 of the 7 cake layers with the frosting. Frost the sides of the cake and put it into the refrigerator to chill.

TO GLAZE AND ASSEMBLE THE DOBOS CAKE

Place 1 cup of granulated sugar and 1 cup of butter in a small saucepan and cook over medium heat, stirring constantly until golden brown. Immediately spread evenly on the surface of the remaining unfrosted cake layer and into 8 equal portions with a sharp knife dipped in hot water before it hardens. Place the pieces carefully, overlapping each other, on top of the frosted and chilled cake. Store in refrigerator until needed.

YIELD: 8 SERVINGS

BIENENSTICH

Roll out on a floured board a 12-ounce piece of Danish Pastry Dough (page 153) large enough to fit the prepared pan. Set it to rest in refrigerator while preparing the following topping:

¼ cup butter
⅙ cup honey
¼ cup granulated sugar
⅔ cup sliced almonds
1 recipe for Vanilla Pastry Cream (page 289)

Set oven at 375 degrees F.
One 10-inch round cake pan, 1½ inches deep, greased

Combine the butter, honey and sugar in a saucepan. Cook over low flame stirring constantly until all ingredients are melted and a golden color. Stir in the almonds and mix gently. Remove from heat and, using a lightly oiled spatula, spread immediately and evenly over the Danish Pastry Dough. Let the cake rise in a warm place (approx. 85 degrees F.) for about 1 hour or until doubled in bulk. Place in preheated oven and bake for 35 minutes or until golden brown. Remove from the oven and cool. Split into two layers. Fill with Vanilla Pastry Cream.
YIELD: 10 SERVINGS

GÉNOISE
(French Sponge Cake)

The favorite cake of most Continental pastry chefs. Texture is light and this cake is used as a base for many layer cakes, petits fours and French pastry. Follow recipe and instructions closely in order to succeed; you will be amazed and proud of the result.

8 *eggs*
1⅓ *cups granulated sugar*
2 *cups sifted all-purpose flour*
½ *cup sweet butter*

Set the oven at 350 F.
Two 9-inch cake pans, at least 2½ inches deep, greased and floured

Combine the eggs and sugar in a mixing bowl. Place over hot water and beat vigorously and steadily with a wire whip for about 5 minutes or until the mixture is warm (approximately 95 degrees F.). The water should be approximately 110 degrees F. and should not boil at any time.

Remove from heat and whip with an electric mixer (this is essential to the complete success of this cake) at moderate speed for about 12 to 15 minutes or until the mixture is cool, has tripled in bulk and becomes thick (approximately the consistency of whipped cream).

In the meantime, sift the flour onto a large piece of paper. Melt the butter thoroughly over low heat and cool to lukewarm. When the egg batter is ready, remove the bowl from the electric mixer and fold the sifted flour in gently and gradually in several stages, using a flat spatula or large spoon. (Folding must be done gently to avoid breaking the air cells in the egg batter.) Sprinkle the butter over the batter (leaving the sediment in the bottom of the pan) and blend all ingredients very carefully.

Divide evenly into the pans and bake at 350 degrees F. for about 40 minutes or until the point of a knife, when inserted through the center of the cake, comes out clean. Turn out immediately onto a large piece of paper lightly sprinkled with granulated sugar. Cool. Sandwich and frost the layers together with the buttercream filling of your choice.

YIELD: 8 SERVINGS

Note: Génoise cakes can be stored in the refrigerator for several days.

CHOCOLATE GÉNOISE
(French Chocolate Sponge)

Follow directions for Génoise (page 188) using the following ingredients:

5 *eggs*
½ *cup granulated sugar*
1 *cup sifted all-purpose flour*
4 *oz. sweet chocolate melted with 4 tablespoons water and cooled to lukewarm*

Add the sifted flour alternately with the melted, cooled chocolate. Bake as directed.

YIELD: 6 SERVINGS

MOCHA LAYER CAKE

Bake 2 9-inch layers of cake as explained in the Génoise recipe (page 188). Cool. Using a sharp knife, split each layer in two horizontally (you will now have 4 layers). Sandwich layers together with Mocha Rum Buttercream (see following recipe). Frost entirely with the remaining buttercream. Dust with grated sweet chocolate. Chill in the refrigerator before serving.

YIELD: 1 9-INCH LAYER CAKE, 3 INCHES HIGH—APPROXIMATELY 6 GENEROUS SERVINGS

MOCHA RUM BUTTERCREAM

1 *cup butter at room temperature*
1 *tablespoon Jamaica rum*
3 *tablespoons instant coffee dissolved in 2 tablespoons boiling water*
2 *cups sifted superfine granulated sugar*
5 *egg yolks*
1 *tablespoon cocoa powder*

Beat butter and rum together until fluffy. Dissolve instant coffee in boiling water. Stir coffee mixture and sugar into creamed butter. Beat rapidly until smooth. Add egg yolks one at a time, beating well after each addition. Stir in cocoa powder.

YIELD: ENOUGH FILLING AND FROSTING FOR 2 9-INCH LAYERS OF CAKE

LINZER TORTE

½ *lb. or 2 sticks butter*
1 *cup granulated sugar*
3 *egg yolks*
1½ *cups sifted all-purpose flour*
¼ *teaspoon double-acting baking powder*
½ *teaspoon salt*
1 *tablespoon grated lemon rind*
1 *pinch ground cinnamon*
1⅓ *cups finely ground pecans or almonds*
1 *tablespoon milk*
1½ *cups raspberry jam*
confectioners sugar

Set oven at 375 degrees F.
One 9-inch round cake pan, 1½ inches deep, lined with paper

Cream the butter and sugar together until light and fluffy. Add the egg yolks, one at a time, beating well after each addition, scraping the sides and bottom of the bowl to ensure a smooth mixture. Sift the flour, baking powder and salt together. Sprinkle the lemon rind and cinnamon on top and blend with the nuts. Stir into the yolk mixture. Add the milk. *Do not overmix.* The dough should be of a rolling, pliable and smooth consistency. Form into a ball and place in refrigerator to chill for approximately 1 hour.

Roll out ⅔ of the dough on a floured board and fit it into the pan. Spread the jam over it. Roll out the remaining dough and cut it into strips approximately ⅓-inch wide. Arrange the strips over the jam in a lattice pattern. Bake at 375 degrees F. for approximately 40 minutes or until done. Cool, unmold and dust with confectioners sugar.

YIELD: 8 SERVINGS

CLAFOUTI
(Cherry Torte)

A traditional cake from the French countryside—a simple but very savory dessert. Children love it!

- *⅔ cup sifted all-purpose flour*
- *1⅓ cups milk*
- *⅓ cup granulated sugar*
- *3 eggs*
- *1 teaspoon vanilla extract*
- *1 teaspoon kirsch (optional)*
- *1 pinch salt*
- *3 cups pitted fresh black cherries*
- *confectioners sugar*

Set oven at 350 degrees F.
One 9-inch baking dish or pie tin, greased

Place the sifted flour into a deep bowl and gradually stir in the milk. Add the sugar and eggs. Mix well until all lumps are dissolved. Add the vanilla, kirsch and salt and blend all ingredients. Pour half the batter into the prepared baking dish or pie tin. Distribute the cherries evenly over the batter, and cover with remaining batter. Bake at 350 degrees F. for approximately 50 minutes or until a knife, when inserted through the center, comes out clean. Remove from heat and dust with confectioners sugar. Serve warm.

YIELD: 4 TO 5 SERVINGS

Note: If fresh cherries are not available, use drained pitted Bing cherries.

CANNOLI

3 cups sifted all-purpose flour (approximately)
⅓ cup granulated sugar
1 teaspoon ground cinnamon
1 teaspoon cocoa powder
1 pinch salt
3 tablespoons shortening
2 eggs, beaten with a fork
4 tablespoons red wine (approximately)
1 egg yolk, beaten

Deep fat heated to 360 degrees F.

Sift the flour, sugar, cinnamon, cocoa powder and salt into a large deep bowl. Add the shortening and blend with a fork until the mixture is broken into pieces the size of small peas. Add the beaten eggs and stir in the wine gradually. Work to a smooth dough of rolling consistency. (If the dough is too stiff, add a little more wine; if it is too soft, add a little more flour.) Place in the refrigerator for 15 minutes to chill. Roll out gently as thin as possible on a floured board. Cut into 5-inch circles, and wrap each circle around a wooden stick about 6 inches long and 1 inch in diameter.* Seal the dough by moistening both ends with beaten egg yolk. Fry cannoli in deep hot fat until golden brown. (For detailed instructions about deep frying, see page 149). Cool, drain the excess fat, remove the sticks gently and fill with the following filling.
YIELD: APPROXIMATELY 24 CANNOLI OR 8 SERVINGS

* *Note:* Sticks are sold for this purpose in good kitchen supply shops.

CANNOLI FILLING

3½ cups ricotta cheese
1½ cups sifted confectioners sugar
1 pinch ground cinnamon
⅓ cup finely chopped candied lemon peel
¼ cup grated semi-sweet chocolate

Work the cheese until smooth. Add the sugar and continue beating until light. Add the remaining ingredients, blend well and chill. The quantity is sufficient to fill 24 cannoli. Dust each cannoli with confectioners sugar before serving.

Note: Chopped candied cherries or pineapple can be substituted for the lemon peel.

BABA AU RHUM

Baba cakes can be baked days in advance and will freeze well.

1 envelope or 1 cake yeast
¼ cup lukewarm water
2 cups sifted all-purpose flour
½ cup butter at room temperature
3 tablespoons granulated sugar
3 tablespoons milk
3 eggs, beaten with a fork
⅓ teaspoon salt
½ teaspoon grated lemon rind
2 tablespoons seedless raisins
hot Rum Syrup (page 194)
hot Apricot Glaze for Babas (page 194)
glazed cherries
whipped cream (optional)

Set oven at 350 degrees F.
Ten individual Baba molds, greased

Sprinkle the yeast over the water and stir to dissolve. Add ½ cup of the flour and blend well. Cover with the remaining flour and let rise in a warm place (approximately 80–85 degrees F.) for about 1 hour. Punch down. Cream the butter and sugar together and stir in the milk, beaten eggs, salt and lemon rind. Add gradually to the yeast mixture. Knead all ingredients briskly to an elastic dough. Add the raisins and form the dough into a ball; cover with a towel and let stand at room temperature for 20 minutes or until the dough starts to rise. Stir down to break up the air cells. Spoon into the prepared Baba molds, filling them approximately ½ full. Let the dough rise for about 30 minutes to the top of the molds. Bake at 350 degrees F. for about 10 minutes. Reduce the heat to 325 degrees F. and continue baking for 15 minutes or until the Baba are firm and begin to shrink from the sides of the molds. Unmold the cakes on a rack or screen and cool. Baba cakes can be wrapped in aluminum foil and frozen. Several hours before serving, soak the Babas in hot Rum Syrup until they are spongy and moist, but don't allow them to become too soggy through over-absorption of syrup. Remove the cakes from the syrup and let stand to dry. Brush entirely with hot Apricot Glaze for Babas and decorate with candied cherries. Garnish with whipped cream if you wish.

YIELD: 10 INDIVIDUAL BABAS 3 INCHES DEEP AND 2 INCHES IN DIAMETER

SAVARIN CAKE

Follow the recipe for Baba au Rhum but omit the raisins. Spoon the dough into a 9-inch ring mold and bake at 350 degrees F. for 35 minutes or until done. Soak in hot Kirsch Syrup. Cool and glaze entirely with hot Apricot Glaze for Babas. Garnish the center with whipped cream.

YIELD: 6 TO 8 SERVINGS

HOT RUM SYRUP

1 cup water
1¼ cups granulated sugar
1 orange sliced in two
1 vanilla bean
½ cup Jamaica rum

Combine all ingredients except the rum in a saucepan. Bring to a boil and stir gently to dissolve the sugar properly. Strain and add the rum.

YIELD: APPROXIMATELY 1½ CUPS

KIRSCH SYRUP

Follow the above recipe for Rum Syrup but substitute kirsch for the rum.

HOT APRICOT GLAZE FOR BABAS

½ cup clear apricot jam
2 tablespoons hot water
3 drops red food coloring

Combine all ingredients in a deep saucepan and bring to a boil. Use immediately while hot.

APPLE CHARLOTTE
(Charlotte aux Pommes)

12 baking apples
⅔ cup melted butter
1 tablespoon lemon juice
⅓ cup granulated sugar
3 tablespoons clear apricot jam
2 teaspoons rum
1 loaf stale white bread
½ cup Apricot Sauce (page 291)

Set oven at 350 degrees F.

This is the classic Apple Charlotte, made for centuries in European kitchens. The preparation is easy but proper baking in deep Charlotte cake pans is rather difficult. I suggest the use of a 1½-quart square baking pan, no deeper than 4 inches and with straight edges.

Peel and core the apples. Slice them no more than ½ inch thick. Place them in a frying pan with ⅓ cup melted butter and the lemon juice. Cover the pan and cook over low heat for about 5 minutes or until the apples are tender. Remove from heat and stir the apples with a wooden spoon; continue cooking, if necessary, until the apples are rather thick. Stir in the sugar, apricot jam and rum. Remove the crust from a square loaf of white bread; slice about ½ inch thick and cut into small triangles. Dip each slice in the remaining melted butter and place them in the bottom of the mold or pan, overlapping each other to cover the bottom entirely. Fill with the cooked apples. Cover with heavy brown paper brushed with butter, and bake at 350 degrees F. about 35 to 40 minutes. Remove from the heat and cool for a few minutes. Unmold and serve with hot Apricot Sauce.

YIELD: 6 TO 8 SERVINGS

MERINGUE CHANTILLY
(Meringue shells with whipped cream)

4 *egg whites at room temperature*
1 *pinch salt*
1 *cup plus 1 tablespoon fine granulated sugar*
4 *tablespoons confectioners sugar*
1½ *cups heavy cream*
8 *candied cherries*

Set the oven at 200 degrees F.
One 10 x 10-inch baking sheet, greased and floured
Eight fluted paper cups

Beat the egg whites with a small pinch of salt until foamy; add the sugar gradually and continue to beat until stiff but not dry. Squeeze the meringue mixture through a pastry bag fitted with a round tube approximately ¾-inch in diameter onto the baking sheet in egg-sized ovals 1½ inches apart. Dust the ovals with 2 tablespoons of confectioners sugar and bake at 200 degrees F. for about 1 hour and 20 minutes or until crispy. The meringues should be a very pale golden color. Remove from the oven; slide a flexible spatula underneath and remove the meringues from the pan. Press slightly with your finger on the flat side to form an oval-shaped hollow. Cool. Whip the heavy cream with 2 tablespoons of confectioners sugar. Sandwich two meringue shells together with whipped cream. Set in paper cups and decorate with candied cherries.

YIELD: 16 SHELLS OR 8 SERVINGS

THE ART OF MAKING HOT SOUFFLÉS

Contrary to public opinion, I believe that soufflés are easier and quicker to prepare than any other dessert from the "Classic Cuisine." Anyone who can boil milk and beat egg whites properly can, with a little experience, become an expert in the making of this unusual and appealing dessert.

The secret of a well-done soufflé is the proper timing between the oven and the actual serving in the dining room. Guests have to wait for this delectable and fluffy dessert, but the short waiting period is always worth the reward. To cut down the waiting time, I would suggest you first prepare the sauce to accompany the soufflé. Soufflés are generally served with a sauce although no definite ruling has been established concerning the choice of sauces to be served with hot soufflés. I would suggest that in most cases the flavor of the sauce be consistent with the flavor of the liqueurs or fruits used in the soufflé, except in the case of hot chocolate soufflés where a vanilla sauce should always be served.

The egg yolk mixture can be prepared well ahead of time, but the egg whites should always be beaten and folded in just prior to placing the soufflé into the preheated oven.

Following is a list of things to remember whenever making a dessert soufflé.

I. Soufflé dishes should be well-buttered and sugared with confectioners sugar.

II. Egg whites should be beaten stiff but *not dry*. (For detailed instructions on how to beat egg whites, see page 14.) The folding of the egg whites should be done very carefully with a wooden spoon or flat skimmer. A complete blending of the egg whites into the yolk mixture is necessary to obtain a successful soufflé. Place the prepared egg yolk mixture in a bowl deep enough to hold the beaten egg whites. (By using a bowl you will facilitate a proper and perfect blending.) Place the soufflé in a preheated oven immediately following the folding of the egg whites. Place the soufflé dish in the center of the oven, leaving sufficient room on the top for the soufflé to rise.

III. Fill the soufflé dish to approximately 1 inch from the top. After the dish has been filled, dust the soufflé mixture heavily with confectioners sugar. This will form a crust during baking and will enhance the appearance of the soufflé.

IV. Proper baking is a very important factor in achieving a well-done soufflé. While the soufflé is in the oven *do not open the door* until the end of the required baking time. Do not allow your curiosity to ruin the soufflé—to overcome the temptation to take just one little peek, entertain your guests or make a good cup of coffee. You have now mastered the most glamorous dessert of the French classic cuisine.

If you think you'll have a problem making your soufflé, think of *my* problem one evening some years ago when I had to prepare six soufflés of six *different* flavors for a party of 48 people in a very famous, internationally-known restaurant. Many distinguished guests and renowned politicians were present at this gala affair. My biggest problem, of course, was to send all the soufflés out of the kitchen at the same time. I succeeded simply by remaining calm and patient, two necessary qualifications in the art of making soufflés.

BAKING TEMPERATURE AND TIME

Baking time varies according to the size of the soufflé dish being used. The approximate rule of thumb to follow is:

1-quart soufflé dish or 2 to 3 servings—20 to 25 minutes at 375 degrees F.

1½-quart soufflé dish or 4 to 5 servings—25 minutes at 375 degrees F.

2-quart soufflé dish or 6 to 8 servings—30 to 35 minutes at 400 degrees F.

SOUFFLÉS

Some soufflés are known as "classics." They can be identified by their traditional names, and the composition is always the same the world over. Credit for these creations justifiably goes to some well-known French chefs and gourmets such as Brillat-Savarin, Carême, Urbain Dubois, Leblanc, Chiboust, Escoffier and many others.

No doubt the classic cuisine is slowly disappearing from our everyday living but fortunately some gourmets' "hideouts" still feature on their menus these fine and unforgettable creations, a heritage from a great past when cooking was an art and eating a privilege. They are just as easy to prepare as any other soufflé; the base remains the same, only the composition has been improved.

Following are the recipes for some of the best-known soufflés of the French classic cuisine. All are made with a base of Vanilla Soufflé.

VANILLA SOUFFLÉ

1/3 cup butter
1/2 cup plus 2 tablespoons granulated sugar
1/3 cup unsifted cake flour
1 1/2 cups milk
3 drops vanilla extract
1 pinch salt
5 eggs, separated
confectioners sugar

Set oven at 400 degrees F.
One 2-quart soufflé dish, well greased and dusted with confectioners sugar

Blend the butter, 1/2 cup granulated sugar and flour to a smooth paste. Place milk in a deep saucepan and boil gently. Remove from the heat, pour in the prepared paste and beat rapidly until all ingredients are well blended. Add the vanilla and salt and mix well. Return to medium heat and cook for about 1 more minute, stirring well to avoid burning. Remove from the heat and pour in a bowl. Gradually add the egg yolks, one at a time, mixing thoroughly after each addition. Now beat the egg whites, adding 2 tablespoons sugar gradually while beating. Egg whites should be beaten until they hold their shape and are stiff but not dry. Fold immediately into the yolk mixture, blending gently but thoroughly with a flat skimmer or large wooden spoon. *Do not overmix.* Pour at once into the soufflé dish, filling it to within 1 inch of the top. Dust with confectioners sugar and bake in a preheated oven at 400 degrees F. for approximately 30 minutes. Suggested sauces: Egg Nog (page 290) or Hot Chocolate (page 291).

YIELD: ONE 2-QUART SOUFFLÉ DISH—6 TO 8 SERVINGS

SOUFFLÉ AIDA

Vanilla Soufflé (page 198) flavored with 2 tablespoons of Curaçao and mixed with 2 fresh oranges, quartered.

SOUFFLÉ AMBASSADRICE

Vanilla Soufflé (page 198) with 2 tablespoons of crushed almond macaroon, 2 tablespoons of sliced blanched almonds and 1 tablespoon of rum added.

SOUFFLÉ HARLEQUIN

A soufflé dish filled half with Vanilla Soufflé (page 198) and half with Chocolate Soufflé (page 203).

SOUFFLÉ HILDA

Vanilla Soufflé (page 198) flavored with 1 tablespoon lemon extract and garnished before serving with fresh wild strawberries.

SOUFFLÉ LUCULLUS

One 9-inch round Savarin Cake (page 194) soaked in Kirsch Syrup (page 194). Place the cake on an oven-proof tray or earthenware dish and fill the center with ½ the recipe for Vanilla Soufflé (page 198). Bake in a 400 degree F. oven for approximately 20 minutes. Remove from heat, brush the cake quickly with Hot Apricot Glaze for Babas (page 194) and serve immediately.

SOUFFLÉ MONT BRY

Vanilla Soufflé (page 198) blended with ⅓ its volume of purée of marrons (chestnuts) (1 small jar of marrons glacés passed through a fine sieve) and flavored with 1 tablespoon kirsch.

SOUFFLÉ MONTMORENCY

Vanilla Soufflé (page 198) flavored with 2 tablespoons kirsch and mixed with ⅓ cup finely diced candied cherries.

SOUFFLÉ PALMYRE

Vanilla Soufflé (page 198) made in a dish lined with 8 lady fingers sprinkled with 2 tablespoons rum.

SOUFFLÉ ROTHSCHILD

Line bottom of the soufflé dish with 8 lady fingers sprinkled with 2 tablespoons Curaçao and fill the mold with Vanilla Soufflé (page 198) mixed with 2 tablespoons small, diced candied fruits. Decorate with glazed cherries just before serving.

SOUFFLÉ ROYAL

Alternate layers of Vanilla Soufflé (page 198) and approximately 10 lady fingers soaked in 2 tablespoons kirsch.

CHEESE SOUFFLÉ

¼ cup butter
3 tablespoons all-purpose flour
1 pinch each salt and pepper
1 cup milk
⅔ cup grated sharp cheddar cheese
⅓ cup grated Parmesan cheese
4 egg yolks
6 egg whites

Set oven at 375 degrees F.
One 1½-quart soufflé dish, greased

Rub the butter, flour, salt and pepper well together. Pour the milk into a deep saucepan and bring to a boil. Remove from heat, add the prepared paste and stir well with a wooden spoon or wire whip to blend. Return to heat and cook for about 2 more minutes, stirring well to avoid burning. Gradually add the grated cheeses and continue mixing all ingredients over low heat until the cheeses are well melted. Remove from heat and cool for approximately 5 minutes. Stir in the egg yolks, one at a time, mixing well after each addition. Beat the egg whites stiff but not dry and fold gently into the cheese mixture. Pour into the prepared soufflé dish and bake at 375 degrees F. for approximately 25 minutes or until firm. Serve hot.

YIELD: 4 SERVINGS

Note: The cheese mixture can be prepared well in advance, but the egg whites must be folded in immediately before baking. If cheese mixture is allowed to cool, baking time will have to be increased a few minutes.

HAZELNUT SOUFFLÉ

A fascinating soufflé—unique for its exquisite flavor!

HAZELNUT POWDER

1 *cup granulated sugar*
1 *cup roasted hazelnuts, chopped fine*

Melt the sugar in a saucepan until golden brown. Remove from heat and add the hazelnuts. Pour into a buttered or oiled pan to cool. When thoroughly cool, crush to a fine powder with a rolling pin or in electric blender. This powder can be made days in advance and stored in a tightly covered container in a dry place.
YIELD: 2 CUPS

SOUFFLÉ MIXTURE

3 *tablespoons butter*
1 *pinch salt*
3 *tablespoons flour*
¾ *cup hot milk*
4 *egg yolks*
⅓ *cup granulated sugar*
¾ *cup hazelnut powder*
2 *tablespoons Chartreuse liqueur*
5 *egg whites*

Set oven at 375 degrees F.
One 1½-quart soufflé mold, greased and dusted with confectioners sugar

Stir the butter, salt and flour together until a smooth paste is obtained. Place the milk in a deep saucepan and boil gently. Remove from heat and pour in the flour mixture. Return to low heat and cook for 1 or 2 minutes more, stirring constantly to avoid burning. Remove from heat and place in a bowl. Gradually add the egg yolks, one at a time, stirring rapidly after each addition. Blend all ingredients well to obtain a smooth paste. Stir in the sugar, ½ cup hazelnut powder and the Chartreuse. Beat the egg whites stiff but not dry and fold gently into the yolks mixture. *Do not overmix.* Pour into the soufflé mold and bake at 375 degrees F. for approximately 25 to 30 minutes. Remove from the oven and dust with the remaining ¼ cup hazelnut powder. Serve immediately.

YIELD: 4 TO 5 SERVINGS

SOUFFLÉ LIQUEUR

A French classic dessert, the ultimate in taste and elegance.

3 tablespoons flour
3 tablespoons butter
3 tablespoons granulated sugar
¾ cup milk
3 drops vanilla extract
5 egg yolks
6 egg whites
¼ cup liqueur of your choice
confectioners sugar

Set the oven at 375 degrees F.
One 1½-quart soufflé dish, greased and dusted with confectioners sugar

Mix the flour, butter, and 2 tablespoons of the sugar to a smooth paste. Place the milk in a deep saucepan and boil gently. Remove from heat and add the vanilla. Stir in the prepared paste and blend rapidly with a whip or wooden spoon until all ingredients are well mixed and form a smooth cream. Return to low heat and cook for 1 or 2 minutes, stirring constantly to avoid burning. Remove from heat and pour into a deep bowl. Gradually add the egg yolks, one at a time, mixing thoroughly after each addition. Add the liqueur of your choice. (The most popular liqueur soufflé is, without a doubt, the Grand Marnier soufflé, because of its fine flavor and aroma.) Beat the egg whites stiff but not dry, adding the remaining tablespoon of sugar gradually while beating. Fold into the yolk mixture immediately, blending all ingredients thoroughly but gently with a flat skimmer or a large wooden spoon. *Do not overmix.* Pour at once into the soufflé dish filling it to within 1 inch of the top. Dust with confectioners sugar and bake at 375 degrees F. for about 25 or 30 minutes. Suggested sauces: Sauce Liqueur—Number 2 (page 292) flavored with liqueur of the same flavor used in the soufflé.

YIELD: 4 TO 5 SERVINGS

CHOCOLATE SOUFFLÉ

2 tablespoons butter
2½ tablespoons all-purpose flour
1 pinch salt
¾ cup milk
2½ squares or 2½ oz. grated unsweetened chocolate
⅓ cup plus 2 tablespoons granulated sugar
½ teaspoon vanilla extract
4 egg yolks
5 egg whites
confectioners sugar
Custard Sauce (page 293)

Set oven at 375 degrees F.
One 2-quart soufflé dish, greased and dusted with confectioners sugar

Melt the butter gently over low heat. Gradually add the flour and salt and stir rapidly with a whip or wooden spoon to blend all ingredients thoroughly. Remove from heat. Bring the milk to a boil and add the grated chocolate. Stir well to dissolve. Pour the chocolate mixture in a slow stream over the flour mixture. Add ⅓ cup of the sugar and blend all ingredients well. Return to medium heat and cook for 1 more minute, stirring rapidly to avoid burning. Remove from heat and pour the cooked mixture into a deep bowl. Stir in the vanilla. Beat the egg yolks with a fork and add them gradually stirring rapidly with a wooden spoon or wire whip. Beat the egg whites stiff but not dry, adding the remaining 2 tablespoons of sugar gradually. Fold in the egg whites carefully; blend well but do not overmix. Pour into the soufflé dish, dust with confectioners sugar and bake at 375 degrees F. for approximately 25 to 30 minutes. Serve immediately accompanied by Custard Sauce.
YIELD: 6 SERVINGS

JAMAICAN SOUFFLÉ

The flavor of bananas and rum well blended bring to your table the enchanting aroma of the Caribbean.

3 tablespoons flour
3 tablespoons butter
4 tablespoons granulated sugar
¾ cup milk
5 eggs, separated
1 large ripe banana, sliced thin
1½ tablespoons rum
confectioners sugar

Set the oven at 375 degrees F.

One 1½-quart soufflé dish, greased and dusted with confectioners sugar

Mix the flour, butter and 3 tablespoons of sugar to a smooth paste. Place the milk in a deep saucepan and boil gently. Remove from heat, pour in the prepared paste and beat rapidly until all ingredients are well blended. Return to low heat and cook 1 or 2 minutes longer. Remove from heat and pour the hot mixture into a bowl. Gradually stir in the egg yolks, one at a time, mixing thoroughly after each addition. Add the sliced banana and rum and blend all ingredients well. Beat the egg whites until stiff but not dry, adding the remaining tablespoon of sugar gradually. Fold into the banana mixture, mixing gently with a flat skimmer in an up and down motion. *Do not overmix.* Pour at once into the soufflé dish, filling it to within 1 inch of the top. Dust with confectioners sugar and bake at 375 degrees F. for approximately 25 to 30 minutes. Serve immediately.
YIELD: 4 TO 5 SERVINGS

Suggested sauce: Strawberry Sauce (page 293) or Custard Sauce (page 293).

LEMON SOUFFLÉ

6 tablespoons milk
1½ tablespoons granulated sugar
1½ tablespoons all-purpose flour
¼ cup butter
juice of 2 lemons
1 teaspoon grated lemon rind
3 eggs, separated
confectioners sugar

Set oven at 375 degrees F.
One 1-quart soufflé dish, greased and dusted with confectioners sugar

Bring the milk and sugar to a boil; remove from heat and stir in the flour. Mix until smooth. Add the butter, return to the fire and cook for about 2 minutes more, stirring constantly to avoid burning. Remove from heat and pour the hot mixture into a deep bowl. Stir in the lemon juice and rind. Add the egg yolks one at a time, beating well after each addition. Beat the egg whites until stiff but not dry and fold into the yolk mixture. *Do not overmix.* Pour into the soufflé dish, dust with confectioners sugar and bake at 375 degrees F. for

20 to 25 minutes. Suggested sauces: Rum Sauce (page 292) or Strawberry Sauce (page 293).
YIELD: 3 SERVINGS

OMELETTE SOUFFLÉ

This light dessert soufflé can easily be classified among the most classic and well known of the "haute cuisine." The preparation is quick and simple; only a few ingredients are needed. For this reason, many European gourmet restaurants feature it on their menu all year round. It truly is a pleasant conclusion to a heavy meal!

8 *egg yolks*
½ *cup granulated sugar*
3 *drops vanilla extract*
10 *egg whites beaten stiff with*
⅓ *cup sugar*
3 *oz. Cognac, Grand Marnier or any other liqueur of your choice*

Set oven at 400 degrees F.
One large ovenproof tray or dish, generously greased and dusted with confectioners sugar

Beat the egg yolks and sugar until thick and pale in color. Add the vanilla. Beat the egg whites until stiff but not dry, adding the ⅓ cup of sugar gradually. Fold gently into the yolk mixture. Do not overmix. Pour the mixture into the prepared tray or dish and smooth the surface evenly with a spatula or flat spoon, shaping it into a mound. Bake at 400 degrees F. for 20 minutes or until golden brown. Flame at the table with liqueur of your choice.
YIELD: 6 TO 8 SERVINGS

FLAMBÉ DESSERTS AND CRÊPES

FLAMBÉ DESSERTS

The name of desserts of this type originated from the French verb "flamber" which means to burn in flame. The flaming adds an exciting finish to many elegant desserts; sometimes it enhances the taste, but generally it is done simply to add brilliance and glamor as the dessert is being served.

Liqueurs used in the preparation of these flaming desserts should be of a high alcoholic content, i.e. brandy, Cognac, rum, etc. Such liqueurs should always be warmed over hot water or low heat before they are poured over the dessert. The food to be served should be placed on a heat-proof platter or in a chafing dish with a long handle. Set the dishes on a serving cart away from curtains, drapes or draft. Pour the warmed spirits around the sides of the food and ignite the alcohol with a long match or lighted straw. Move the platter or pan back and forth slowly to activate the flame. It will flame for a short period of time depending upon the amount of liqueur used. The moment the fire burns out, serve the dessert while still hot.

Flambé desserts are spectacular and professional in appearance yet they are most often quite simple to make.

Note: Flambé desserts have to be served and kept hot. Keep the platter or chafing dish over a Sterno warmer while serving. The light under the platter should be lowered just before the liqueur is ignited and turned up again when it has burnt out. If you do not have the equipment for preparing the entire dessert at the table, preparations may be completed on the stove and the finished dessert ignited at the table.

BANANAS FLAMBÉ

6 *large bananas*
½ *cup butter*
12 *tablespoons honey*
¼ *cup lemon juice*
1 *cup canned black Bing cherries, drained*
½ *cup warm Jamaica rum*

Peel the bananas and cut them in half lengthwise. Melt the butter in a chafing dish. Arrange the bananas in the bottom of the dish and sprinkle with the honey and lemon juice. Cook over medium heat until bananas are tender and well browned. Add the drained cherries. *Do not stir.* Add the warm rum and ignite.

YIELD: 6 SERVINGS

STRAWBERRIES ROMANOFF

3 cups fresh ripe strawberries, hulled and cleaned
1/3 cup Curaçao
1/4 cup orange juice
1/3 cup granulated sugar
1 pint good commercial ice cream
1 1/2 cups whipped cream

Combine the strawberries, Curaçao, orange juice and sugar. Let soak in the refrigerator for approximately 1 hour. In the meantime, spoon out the ice cream into a chilled serving dish. When ready to serve, spoon the soaked strawberries over the ice cream and garnish with whipped cream.

YIELD: 5 TO 6 SERVINGS

STRAWBERRIES ROMANOFF FLAMBÉ

Place the soaked strawberries in a chafing dish. Sprinkle with 1/2 cup of warm Cognac and Curaçao liqueurs combined. Ignite at the table. Spoon the sauce quickly over the ice cream. Serve without whipped cream.

YIELD: 5 SERVINGS

CHERRIES JUBILEE

1 pint or can of black Bing cherries
1 teaspoon cornstarch
3 tablespoons cold water
2/3 cup warm kirsch
1 quart vanilla ice cream

Drain the cherries and reserve the juice. Dilute the cornstarch with the water. Place the cherry juice in a deep saucepan or chafing dish and bring to a boil for approximately 1 minute. Remove from heat, stir in the diluted cornstarch and blend well. Return to boil for 1 minute until the mixture thickens. Add the cherries and blend well. Sprinkle with warm kirsch. Ignite and spoon the flaming cherries with a large serving spoon over the vanilla ice cream. Serve immediately.

YIELD: 6 TO 8 SERVINGS

PLUM PUDDING FLAMBÉ

This delicious pudding can be prepared and cooked weeks in advance. Store well covered in a cool, dry place.

¼ cup butter
⅓ cup granulated sugar
3 eggs, separated
¼ pound ground suet
½ cup dark molasses
2½ cups sifted all-purpose flour
½ teaspoon ground cinnamon
¼ teaspoon allspice
½ teaspoon baking powder
1 teaspoon salt
1 cup diced prunes
1½ cups seedless raisins
1 cup diced candied fruits
¾ cup canned cranberry sauce
½ cup warm brandy

One 2-quart mold, greased

Cream the butter and sugar together until light. Add the egg yolks, one at a time, and blend thoroughly after each addition. Add the ground suet and molasses. Sift the flour, spices, salt and baking powder together twice and stir into the yolk mixture. Blend well. Add the diced prunes, raisins, diced candied fruits and cranberry sauce. Beat the egg whites stiff and fold gently into the fruit mixture. Pour into the prepared mold and cover tightly with the accompanying lid or with aluminum foil. Steam pudding for approximately 4 hours or until firm. When ready to serve, place the mold in a hot water bath for approximately 30 minutes or until warm; unmold onto a warm heat-proof serving tray. Pour brandy over the pudding and ignite.
YIELD: APPROXIMATELY 15 SERVINGS

This traditional pudding is often served with hard sauce.

HARD SAUCE

1 cup butter
1 cup confectioners sugar
¼ cup brandy
1 pinch nutmeg

Cream the butter and sugar together until fluffy. Gradually stir in the brandy. Add the nutmeg and chill until firm. Spoon over the warm pudding.

QUICK FLAMBÉ DESSERTS

Scoop out commercial ice cream (using the flavor of your choice) into chilled serving dishes, to form a pyramid, and place in the freezer to harden.

For the benefit of your guests at dessert time, prepare one of the following sauces in a chafing dish. Ignite it at the table where all can enjoy it and quickly spoon the hot sauce over the prepared ice cream.

PINEAPPLE SAUCE

½ cup diced fresh or canned pineapple
⅓ cup clear apricot jam or jelly
⅓ cup Jamaica rum

Combine and warm the diced pineapple and apricot jam. Stir in rum. Ignite and quickly spoon over the ice cream.
YIELD: 4 SERVINGS

APRICOT SAUCE

½ cup apricot purée
⅓ cup clear apricot preserves
⅓ cup good brandy

Use commercial apricot purée or blend drained canned apricots to a smooth purée in an electric blender or by passing the fruit through a sieve. Combine and warm the purée and apricot jam. Stir in brandy. Ignite and quickly spoon over the ice cream.
YIELD: 4 SERVINGS

BANANA SAUCE

3 ripe bananas blended into purée
⅓ cup granulated sugar
1 tablespoon lemon juice
¼ cup Jamaica rum
2 tablespoons Cointreau

Use commercial banana purée or blend ripe bananas to a smooth purée in an electric blender, or by passing them through a sieve. Combine the purée with the sugar and lemon juice and warm. Stir

in the rum and Cointreau. Ignite and quickly spoon over ice cream.
YIELD: 4 SERVINGS

BLUEBERRY SAUCE

1 jar raspberry jelly (approximately ½ cup)
2 tablespoons water
½ cup fresh, canned or frozen blueberries
⅓ cup kirsch

Warm the jelly and water together. Add the blueberries (if canned or frozen, drain off the juice). Stir in the kirsch. Ignite and quickly spoon over the ice cream.
YIELD: 4 SERVINGS

STRAWBERRY SAUCE

1 8-oz. package frozen strawberries, thawed
⅓ cup currant jelly
⅓ cup Grand Marnier

Warm the strawberries in their juice. Add the currant jelly and stir well to dissolve. Stir in the Grand Marnier. Ignite and quickly spoon over the prepared ice cream.
YIELD: 4 SERVINGS

CRÊPES
(French Pancakes)

⅔ cup sifted all-purpose flour
1½ tablespoons granulated sugar
2 whole eggs plus 2 egg yolks
1¾ cups milk
2 tablespoons melted butter
1 tablespoon kirsch
melted butter for frying

Sift the flour and sugar together. Beat the eggs and extra yolks lightly with a fork. Place the sifted flour in a bowl and gradually stir in the beaten eggs and the milk; blend well to obtain a smooth mixture without lumps. The batter should be of the same consistency as heavy cream. Add the melted butter and kirsch and let stand in the refrigerator for about 1 hour.

Heat a small frying pan (about 5 inches in diameter) and brush quickly with melted butter. Immediately pour approximately 1½ tablespoons of crêpe batter into the hot pan and, in a fast circular motion, spread the batter quickly and evenly over the bottom. (If batter is too thick and does not expand easily, add a little more milk to the ready mixture.) Brown on one side and quickly, with the help of a flexible spatula, turn the crêpe to brown on the other side. Remove the crêpe to a towel or waxed paper and continue until you have used up all the batter.

YIELD: 20 TO 24 CRÊPES

Note: Remember that crêpes have to be paper thin. They can be prepared well ahead of time, cooled, wrapped in a wet towel and stored in a cool place or in the freezer until needed.

The French have many different ways to prepare and serve these delicious pancakes. I have listed some of the most famous crêpes, the ones I found to be most appealing to the American palate.

CRÊPES SUZETTE
(The favorite French classic)

Always available in any first-class dining room, Crêpes Suzette are served from a chafing dish with the following sauce:

½ the recipe for Crêpe Batter (page 210)
4 lumps of sugar
grated rind of 1 orange
juice of 1 orange
1 tablespoon lemon juice
1 tablespoon butter
2 tablespoons Curaçao
3 tablespoons Grand Marnier
2 tablespoons hot Cognac

Prepare the crêpes as explained above. Combine the sugar, orange rind, orange juice, lemon juice and butter in a saucepan. Bring to a boil and reduce for 1 or 2 minutes. Add the Curaçao and Grand Marnier and bring back to a boil. Add the crêpes to the sauce one by one, turning them from time to time to saturate. Fold the crêpes in half, then in quarters, forming them into a triangle, and put them gently into a chafing dish. Repeat until all the crêpes have been saturated. Just before serving warm up the Cognac, pour it over the hot crêpes and ignite. Shuttle the pan back and forth gently to increase the flame. Serve immediately.

YIELD: ENOUGH SAUCE FOR 12 CRÊPES OR 4 SERVINGS

CRÊPES NORMANDES
(Apple Crêpes)

8 tart fresh apples
3 tablespoons butter
2 tablespoons granulated sugar
juice of 1 lemon
½ cup plus 2 tablespoons well-packed light brown sugar
1 recipe Crêpe Batter (page 210)

Peel, core and slice the apples. Place the butter in a frying pan and cook the apples until tender. Dust with granulated sugar and sprinkle the lemon juice over the cooked fruit and stir gently.

Make crêpes as previously explained on page 211. Pour the batter into the hot buttered pan and spread evenly and rapidly all over the bottom; drop a tablespoon of cooked apple mixture on the crêpe. Cover the apple with some more batter—just enough to hide the fruit, and brown the other side. Place crêpes side by side on a heatproof serving tray and dust with light brown sugar. Serve hot. If necessary, warm crêpes in a 425 degree F. oven.

YIELD: 16 CRÊPES OR ABOUT 5 SERVINGS

Note: Can also be sprinkled with Cognac and just before serving, ignite with a match. For detailed instructions on how to flambé desserts, see page 205.

CRÊPES CARIBBEAN
(Crêpes with Pineapple)

1 recipe for Crêpe Batter (page 210)
1 1-lb. can diced pineapple
½ cup clear apricot jam
2 tablespoons Jamaica rum
⅓ cup plus 1 tablespoon kirsch
⅓ cup light brown sugar

Prepare and cook the crêpes as previously explained (page 210).

Drain the pineapple and reserve half the syrup. Place the syrup in a saucepan and bring to a boil. Add the apricot jam and stir to dissolve. Remove from heat and add the drained pineapple, rum, 1 tablespoon each of kirsch and sugar. Spread approximately 1 tablespoon of pineapple mixture over each cooled crêpe and roll it like a jelly roll. Arrange the rolled crêpes on a heatproof serving tray. Dust with light brown sugar and put under the broiler briefly to caramelize the sugar. Sprinkle with ⅓ cup kirsch and ignite. Serve immediately.

YIELD: 16 CRÊPES OR 5 TO 6 SERVINGS

CRÊPES CRÉOLE

¼ the recipe for Crêpe Batter (page 210)
¾ cup Vanilla Pastry Cream (page 289)
1 *teaspoon Jamaica rum*
4 *egg whites*
⅔ cup granulated sugar
⅔ cup clear apricot jam
⅓ cup diced canned or fresh pineapple
1 *2-oz. glass Cognac to flame*

Set oven at 400 degrees F.

Prepare and cook 6 crêpes as explained previously (page 210). Spread each one with the pastry cream blended with rum. Roll each crêpe like a jelly roll and arrange them side by side on a large ovenproof serving tray.

Beat the egg whites stiff, adding the sugar gradually while beating. Cover the prepared crêpes entirely with the meringue and place in the oven for approximately 5 minutes or until golden brown.

Heat the clear apricot jam until dissolved and add the diced pineapple. Spread the hot sauce over the meringue. Flame with Cognac and serve.

YIELD: APPROXIMATELY 6 CRÊPES OR 3 SERVINGS

CRÊPES MONSEIGNEUR

⅓ the recipe for Crêpe Batter (page 210)
4 *bananas, ripe but firm*
⅓ cup sliced, roasted almonds
1 *tablespoon lemon juice*
2 *tablespoons kirsch*
confectioners sugar

Prepare and cook 8 crêpes as previously explained on page 210. Cut the bananas in half and place them under a hot broiler for about 3 minutes or until golden brown. Remove from heat and sprinkle with the roasted sliced almonds, lemon juice and kirsch. Ignite and spoon

the flaming bananas over the crêpes; when the fire dies out, roll the crêpes tight, dust with confectioners sugar and serve immediately.
YIELD: 8 CRÊPES OR 4 SERVINGS

CRÊPES CONFITURE
(Jam Crêpes)

Prepare and cook the crêpes as previously explained on page 210. Spread each crêpe with 1 tablespoon of the jelly or jam of your choice and roll up like jelly rolls. Arrange side by side on a heatproof tray. Dot with butter and dust with granulated sugar. Heat in 425 degree F. oven for approximately 10 minutes and serve hot.

CRÊPES LYONNAISE

Prepare and cook 12 crêpes as previously explained on page 210. Spread each crêpe with chestnut purée (take an 8-oz. jar of marrons glacés and pass them through a sieve). Roll them up like jelly rolls and arrange side by side on a heatproof tray. Dot each crêpe with 1 teaspoon clear apricot jam and place them under a hot broiler for about 3 minutes to warm.
YIELD: 1 DOZEN CRÊPES OR 6 SERVINGS

CRÊPES MAISON

Prepare and cook 16 crêpes as previously explained on page 210. Spread each crêpe with approximately 2 tablespoons of Vanilla Pastry Cream (page 289) and roll them up like a jelly roll. Arrange crêpes on a heatproof serving tray. Brush with Hot Currant Jelly and sprinkle with warm rum. Ignite and serve immediately. Two cups Vanilla Pastry Cream (page 289), ⅓ cup currant jelly and ¼ cup rum will fill and cover 16 crêpes for 8 servings.

COFFEE SPECIALTIES

CAFÉ AU LAIT

Many people not familiar with French eating habits wonder what is meant when a Frenchman speaks of "café au lait." If you are expecting some elaborate blending, I am sorry to disappoint you because, as the English translation indicates, it is simpling a blending of hot milk with fresh hot coffee. The proportions of the mixture are left up to each individual's taste. It is a typically French breakfast drink and is indulged in by the French people beginning at a very early age and carried through adult life. It is generally served as an accompaniment to fresh, hot brioches and croissants. These delicacies are baked daily in great quantities by every pastry shop in town and by 7:00 A.M., without fail, they are removed from the baker's oven and ready for his customers who are already waiting impatiently, come rain or shine.

During my school days, it was great fun going to our neighborhood pastry shop early in the morning and carrying back the paper bag with these warm and flavorful "goodies" for our family breakfast. However, I learned much later that preparing and baking them in the wee, dark hours of the morning held little of the same thrill for me.

VIENNA COFFEE

Two parts strong hot coffee blended with 1 part hot milk and garnished with a tablespoon of unsweetened whipped cream.

CAFÉ BRÛLOT

Prepare approximately 1 pint of strong coffee and pour it into a heated chafing dish:

the peel of 1/3 of a lemon, sliced thin
the peel of 1/3 of an orange, sliced thin
6 lumps sugar
1 broken stick cinnamon
1/3 cup good Cognac
6 cloves

Heat all ingredients over a strong flame, stirring constantly. Ignite the mixture and let it burn for 1 minute or so by shaking the dish back and forth. When the flame is about ready to die out, quickly pour it into the prepared hot coffee. Blend all ingredients well and *strain*. Pour into warm demitasse cups.

YIELD: 6 TO 8 SERVINGS

CAFÉ ROYALE

1 cup sugar soaked in good brandy

1 cup hot, fresh black coffee

Place the soaked sugar in a teaspoon and hold it over the hot coffee. Ignite the sugar and continue holding it until the flame is ready to die out; then quickly drop it into the coffee.

WINES, CHAMPAGNES AND LIQUEURS

CHAMPAGNE

Champagne is rightfully considered "king" of the wine family. It can be served proudly as an accompaniment to all types of food. Any part of the dinner course is considered the "proper" time for its serving. The sparkling bubbles and white foam of filled champagne glasses create an atmosphere of smiles and joy. A celebration of any importance is unheard of without a toast delivered with this enchanting beverage as the star attraction. Indeed, the French word "champagne" is universal and signifies to all who hear it an occasion for festivity and fun.

This wine has been cultivated and fabricated in the district of Champagne since time immemorial. It is made from a blend of red and white grapes grown in different vineyards. The great Champagne wineries ship under their famous brand names. Unlike other wine, champagne is bottled and corked at an early stage of fermentation to retain the carbonic acid gas in the bottle.

European vintage years are most important. Cultivation, along with climatic conditions, have a great bearing on the grapes. Like any other wine, champagne has its great, good and sometimes bad years. Nevertheless, it must be remembered that there are exceptions to every rule. You can expect some very good wines made even though the vintage does not carry the highest marks, just as there are some bad wines made in the very best vintage years. Unfortunately these hard facts become apparent only after the bottle is opened.

Serving Champagne

Always *chill* champagne before serving. If a champagne bucket is available, fill it ¾ full with crushed ice and set the bottle in the center for approximately 30 minutes prior to serving. If no bucket is available, simply chill the bottle in the refrigerator for at least 2 hours before serving time. To remove the cork safely without risk of spilling its precious contents, first remove the wire which secures the cork to the bottle, then wrap the bottle in a towel, hold tightly and at a slight angle and *gradually* work the cork free.

As with all wines, pour a small amount of chilled champagne into your own glass first; taste for approval and proceed to serve your guests.

Sizes of Champagne bottles

Champagne is generally served in ⅘-quart bottles. Other popular sizes are also available:

1. SPLIT: 6½ ounces (2 glasses)
2. HALF BOTTLE: approximately one pint or 13 ounces (4 glasses)
3. BOTTLE: ⅘ quart or 26 ounces (8 glasses)
4. MAGNUM: 2 bottles or approximately 52 ounces (17 glasses)
5. JEROBOAM: 4 bottles or approximately 104 ounces (34 glasses)

In Europe, for great festivity and rare occasions, much bigger sizes are also available but seldom seen. Their fabrication and distribution is rather limited as they are too impractical for shipping purposes. These unusual large sizes are:

1. REHOBOAM: 6 bottles or approximately 156 ounces (52 glasses)
2. METHUSELAH: 8 bottles or about 208 ounces (69 glasses)
3. SALMANASAR: 12 bottles or approximately 312 ounces (104 glasses)

LABELS

The labels on champagne bottles include one of the following terms:

BRUT Very dry, meaning wholly unsweetened Champagne. It may be served as an aperitif or at any time during the meal.

EXTRA DRY or EXTRA SEC Less dry than BRUT, with a small quantity of sugar added.

DEMI-SEC Meaning semi-sweet. Recommended for serving with fish, poultry, or any other white meat; with appetizers or as an aperitif.

DEMI-SWEET and DOUX Meaning distinctly sweet. Recommended for serving with cheeses, desserts and pastries.

BLANC DE BLANCS Made in small quantities, strictly with white grapes. A very fine and light Champagne, suitable with any food or sweet.

LIQUEURS

A selection of liqueurs, or fortified wines, adds an air of festivity to the conclusion of a meal. The French give credit to these colorful spirits as an aid to digestion. Though not supported by any medical authority, there is no doubt that lingering at the dinner table, sipping a liqueur and prolonging conversation do undoubtedly produce a feeling of well-being.

ABSINTHE A toxic green liqueur containing oils of wormwood, anise and other aromatics; 75 to 80 percent alcohol. Sale prohibited in most of Europe and the U.S.A. Pernod is most often substituted (see page 219).

ANISETTE French liqueur made with anise seeds.

APERITIFS French name for cocktails—a before-lunch or -dinner drink.

AQUAVIT Scandinavian liqueur flavored with caraway seeds, served ice cold.

ARMAGNAC A superior full-bodied brandy from southern France.

ARRACK A coarse brandy substitute obtained by allowing the sap of palms to ferment and adding rice wine and some sugar. A very strong, very particular flavor originally from Ceylon, India and the Dutch Indies.

BENEDICTINE Liqueur prepared by the Benedictine monks in the Monastery of Fécamp (France). Herbs, plants, peels and brandy are used for its preparation.

BRANDY Distilled wine, but also spirits made from other fruits, such as apples, pears, cherries, etc.

Calvados Brandy made from apple cider. Very strong; often mixed with coffee because of its potency.

Chartreuse A liqueur prepared by the Carthusian monks in the Monastery of the Grande Chartreuse, near Grenoble, France. Many herbs and plants are used in the secret preparation of this liqueur.

Cherry Brandy Sweet liqueur obtained by steeping cherries in brandy. Originally from Holland.

Cherry Heering Danish liqueur made from wild Danish cherries; sweet.

Cognac A brandy from the town of Cognac, region of Charente, France, which gave it its name. The best type of brandy.

Cointreau Colorless sweet liqueur made with orange peel and herbs.

Crème de Cacao Sweet liqueur made from cocoa beans, brandy and vanilla.

Crème de Menthe Green or white liqueur, strongly flavored with peppermint.

Curaçao Liqueur made from orange skins, sugar and brandies. Originally from Holland.

Drambuie Liqueur made of Scotch whisky, heather honey and herbs in Scotland.

Kirsch Also named *Kirschwasser*. Originally obtained by the distillation of black cherries. Mostly made in Switzerland, Alsace and Germany. Its appearance is like water but its taste is strong and unique.

Kümmel Liqueur flavored with caraway seeds. Originally from Riga, Lithuania.

Maraschino A strong bittersweet liqueur with a distinctive cherry taste, originally from Dalmatia.

Metaxa An excellent Greek brandy with a unique and pleasant flavor of its own.

Pernod Anise-flavored aperitif made in France by the Pernod firm.

Proof Measurement of alcoholic strength.

Rum A liqueur made from the fermentation and distillation of sugar cane.

Triple Sec A white liqueur with a pleasant orange flavor, original name used for Cointreau, but now used by manufacturers in many countries for this type of liqueur.

CHAMPAGNE PUNCH

½ cup granulated sugar
1 cup good Cognac
1 cup Cointreau
3 bottles chilled French Brut Champagne
4 cups ice cubes
1 orange, sliced
1 lemon, sliced
2 fresh mint leaves

Place the sugar in a punch bowl and add the Cognac and Cointreau. When ready to serve, add the remaining ingredients. Let stand for 10 minutes. Serve.

YIELD: APPROXIMATELY 24 SERVINGS

CHAMPAGNE STRAWBERRY PUNCH

2 cups fresh, ripe strawberries
¾ cup fine granulated sugar
2 tablespoons kirsch
juice of 1 lemon
1 pint imported champagne, chilled

Wash and dry the strawberries. Place them in a large bowl and add the sugar, kirsch and lemon juice. Refrigerate for at least 1 hour and just before serving, pour in the chilled champagne. This punch must be served *ice cold!*

YIELD: APPROXIMATELY 4 SERVINGS

Note: As yet, I have never seen wild strawberries in America; if they are available, try them and you will enjoy the greatest punch in the world. In France, we used to prepare this punch for special guests or occasions, and I still remember today the flavor of the wild woods' strawberries mixed with the glorious sweetness of the champagne!

HOLIDAY EGG NOG

8 egg yolks
¾ cup granulated sugar
¾ cup brandy
1 jigger Jamaica rum
1 quart milk
1 pint light cream
4 egg whites
⅓ cup sugar
1 teaspoon nutmeg

Beat the egg yolks with the sugar until light and fluffy. Stir in the brandy and rum. Add the milk and cream gradually and continue

beating at moderate speed. Beat the egg whites stiff but not dry, adding ⅓ cup of sugar gradually while beating. When ready to serve, pour into a punch bowl set over crushed ice. Dust with nutmeg.
YIELD: 2½ QUARTS OR APPROXIMATELY 12 SERVINGS

Note: If possible, allow the egg nog to remain in a cool place for at least 6 to 10 hours before serving.

Frozen Desserts

BOMBES

Although it may sound a complicated and time-consuming dessert to prepare, the Bombe is really only a simple mold lined with ice cream or sherbet and filled in the center with a flavored Bombe mixture. And yet it is an impressive dessert made known by the "haute cuisine." Any European chef can name the composition of dozens of the classic bombes originated many years ago according to the rules set forth by such famous international master chefs as Carême, Urbain Dubois and Escoffier.

PREPARATION OF BOMBES

Conventional Bombes should be molded in a cylindrical Bombe mold made out of strong galvanized tin, but any fancy or plain forms such as jelly dishes, or other shapes of your choice, can be used successfully.

The shell or outer covering of the Bombe is made from any good commercial ice cream whose flavor will harmonize with the inside filling or Bombe mixture. (See page 224.)

Liqueurs, candied fruits macerated in liqueur and nuts are often added to the Bombe mixture to enhance the distinctive flavor of this handsome frozen dessert.

TO COAT AND FILL BOMBE MOLDS

Set freezer to the coldest degree possible. Measure the approximate capacity of the mold by filling it with water and measuring the water in a cup. Bear in mind that ⅓ of this volume will be needed for the outer covering, or shell, and the remaining—or about ⅔ of the volume of the mold—will be required to fill the inside. Place mold in the freezer before attempting to cover the sides with ice cream. Then slightly brush the chilled mold with vegetable oil. Scoop out ice cream, using the flavor of your choice and quickly coat the sides and bottom of the mold to a thickness of approximately 1½ inches. Using a wooden spatula or other strong utensil, smooth out the ice cream, making it as even as possible. Return the mold to the freezer for about 45 minutes or until the ice cream has hardened. (During the hot summer months, I suggest you place the mold in crushed ice while filling to keep the ice cream from melting too quickly.)

Remove the mold from the freezer and pour flavored Bombe mixture into the cavity, being sure to fill it all the way to the top. Cover tightly with wax paper or foil and place in the freezer for at least 5 to 6 hours.

The preparation of this dessert a day in advance will produce better results and allow you more precious time for other meal arrangements.

TO UNMOLD BOMBES

Five minutes before serving, peel off paper. Dip mold quickly in warm water. Turn Bombe onto a serving tray or platter covered with a napkin. (This prevents dessert from sliding while cutting portions.) Garnish quickly with whipped cream, decorate handsomely with candied fruits or whole or sliced nuts. Cut Bombe with a sharp knife dipped in hot water. Bombes are traditionally served accompanied with sauces presented separately. See page 291 for special sauces to use for this purpose.

BASIC BOMBE MIXTURE

3 cups granulated sugar
1½ cups water
8 egg yolks (¾ cup)
desired flavor
1⅓ cups heavy cream, whipped stiff

Dissolve sugar and water over low heat, stirring from time to time to help dissolve. Cook syrup until sugar thermometer reaches 242 degrees F. (For detailed instructions on how to cook sugar properly, see page 12.) While sugar is cooking, beat egg yolks until light and fluffy with an electric mixer or wire whisk. When sugar has reached the desired temperature, pour slowly in a continuous stream over the beaten egg yolks; continue beating constantly while pouring hot syrup. Beat rapidly until cold and thick. Add desired flavor such as coffee, chocolate, liqueurs, etc. (See following formula.) Blend thoroughly. Chill in the refrigerator or over crushed ice until cold. Whip cream and fold into flavored yolk mixture. Pour into chilled Bombe mold already coated with ice cream and proceed as explained in "Preparation of Bombe." (Page 222.)

YIELD: ENOUGH MIXTURE TO FILL CENTER OF 2½-QUART MOLD OR 10 TO 12 SERVINGS. (Leftover Bombe can be stored in the freezer as you would do with ice cream.)

COFFEE BOMBE MIXTURE:
Coat chilled Bombe mold with vanilla or chocolate ice cream. Place in the freezer to harden as explained in "To Coat and Fill Bombe Molds," page 223. Add to egg yolk mixture: 3 packages or tablespoons instant coffee dissolved in ¼ cup boiling water. Chill as directed. Fold in whipped cream. Pour into prepared Bombe mold.

PRALINE BOMBE MIXTURE:
Coat chilled Bombe mold with coffee ice cream. Place in the freezer to harden as previously explained. Add to egg yolk mixture: 1 cup Praline Powder (see page 288). Chill. Fold in whipped cream. Pour into prepared Bombe mold.

STRAWBERRY BOMBE MIXTURE:
Coat chilled Bombe mold with strawberry ice cream. Place in the freezer to harden as previously explained. Add to egg yolk mixture: 1 cup fresh or thawed and drained frozen strawberries. Chill. Fold in whipped cream. Pour into prepared Bombe mold.

CHOCOLATE BOMBE MIXTURE:
Coat chilled Bombe mold with vanilla or coffee ice cream. Place in the freezer to harden as previously explained. Add to egg yolk mixture: 4 oz. melted sweet chocolate. Chill. Fold in whipped cream. Pour into prepared Bombe mold.

BOMBE MIXTURE AUX LIQUEURS:
Coat chilled Bombe mold with any desired flavor ice cream. Place in the freezer to harden as previously explained. Add to egg yolk mixture: ⅓ cup liqueur of your choice. Chill. Fold in whipped cream. Pour into prepared Bombe mold.

TUTTI FRUTTI BOMBE MIXTURE:
Coat chilled Bombe mold with vanilla ice cream. Place in the freezer to harden as previously explained. Add to egg yolk mixture: ⅓ cup small diced candied fruits soaked in ¼ cup of brandy or rum. Chill. Fold in whipped cream. Pour into prepared Bombe mold.

QUICK MOCHA BOMBE

If time does not permit you to go through all the preparations necessary for the making of a Bombe mixture, the following recipe will produce an excellent substitute. It is a Bombe prepared with two different flavors of ice cream.

Coat sides and bottom of a chilled 2-quart mold with 1½ quarts coffee ice cream. (To coat and fill Bombe molds, see page 223.) Return mold to the freezer for about 45 minutes, permitting ice cream to harden. Fill center of the mold with 2 cups softened chocolate ice cream or other ice cream of your choice. Cover with wax paper. Freeze for approximately 5 or 6 hours or until firm. Unmold as explained in "To Unmold Bombes," page 223. Garnish with whipped cream and dust with grated sweet chocolate. Serve with Hot Chocolate Sauce (page 291).
YIELD: 6 TO 8 SERVINGS

CLASSIC BOMBES

As I mentioned previously, many of the Bombes served in most dining rooms are creations of the French classic cuisine. On the following pages, along with some of the traditional Bombes, I have included some of my own creations which have proven to be extremely popular with many of my customers.

BOMBE STRAWBERRY:
Coat chilled mold with strawberry ice cream, fill with Basic Bombe mixture (page 224) combined with fresh orange sections. Serve with Melba Sauce (page 290).

BOMBE BORDALOU:
Coat chilled mold with vanilla ice cream, fill with Basic Bombe mixture (page 224) flavored with anisette. Serve with Custard Sauce, (page 293).

BOMBE COPPÉLIA:
Coat chilled mold with coffee ice cream, fill with Basic Bombe mixture (page 224) flavored with 8 oz. praline paste or powder. Serve with Hot Chocolate Sauce (page 291).

BOMBE DANITCHEFF:
Coat chilled mold with coffee ice cream, fill with Basic Bombe mixture (page 224) flavored with kirsch and maraschino cherry juice. Serve with Custard Sauce (page 293).

DUBARRY BOMBE:
Coat chilled mold with chocolate ice cream, fill with Basic Bombe mixture (page 224) flavored with instant coffee. Serve with Custard Sauce (page 293).

BOMBE EXCELSIOR:
Coat chilled mold with orange sherbet, fill with Basic Bombe mixture (page 224) flavored with Jamaica rum. Serve with hot or cold Sabayon Sauce (page 292).

BOMBE FROU-FROU:
Coat chilled mold with vanilla ice cream, fill with Basic Bombe mixture (page 224) flavored with Jamaica rum and canned and drained

diced pineapple. Serve with hot or cold Sabayon Sauce (page 292), or Custard Sauce (page 293).

BOMBE GABRIELLE:
Coat chilled mold with raspberry sherbet, fill with Basic Bombe mixture (page 224) flavored with vanilla extract and whole maraschino cherries. Serve with Custard Sauce (page 293).

BOMBE HUGO:
Coat chilled mold with coffee ice cream, fill with Basic Bombe mixture (page 224) combined with mixed diced candied fruits macerated with Grand Marnier.

BOMBE JEANNE D'ARC:
Coat chilled mold with vanilla ice cream, fill with praline-flavored Basic Bombe mixture (page 224). Serve with Hot Chocolate Sauce (page 291).

BOMBE MERCEDES:
Coat chilled mold with apricot sherbet and fill with Chartreuse-flavored Basic Bombe mixture (page 224). Serve with Hot Chocolate Sauce (page 291).

BOMBE SULTANE:
Coat chilled mold with chocolate ice cream, fill with praline-flavored Basic Bombe mixture (page 224). Serve with Hot Chocolate Sauce, (page 291).

BOMBE VENETIAN:
Coat chilled mold with a layer of vanilla and then a layer of strawberry ice cream, fill with Basic Bombe mixture (page 224) flavored with maraschino liqueur. Serve with Strawberry Sauce (page 293).

BOMBE ZAMORA:
Coat chilled mold with coffee ice cream, fill with Curaçao-flavored Basic Bombe mixture (page 224). Serve with Chocolate Sauce, hot or cold (pages 290 and 291).

NEGRESCO ICE CREAM BOMBE

Line the sides and bottom of a 2-quart melon or fancy mold with chocolate ice cream, approximately 1½ inches thick. Place in the freezer to harden for at least 45 minutes and proceed to prepare the following mixture:

1 teaspoon unflavored gelatin
⅓ cup warm water
4 egg yolks
⅓ cup granulated sugar
½ cup light cream, scalded
⅓ cup strong hot coffee
1 tablespoon instant coffee
1 tablespoon cream of cocoa
¾ pint heavy cream, whipped stiff

Soak gelatin in water. Beat egg yolks and sugar over hot water until thick and creamy; add scalded light cream, hot coffee, instant coffee and cream of cocoa. Stir all ingredients well. Remove from heat; add soaked gelatin. Chill in the refrigerator or place in a pan of cold water. When the mixture begins to set, fold in whipped cream and fill the center of the mold. Cover with oiled waxed paper. Freeze for at least 3 hours. Unmold and serve with Hot or Cold Chocolate Sauce (page 290).
YIELD: 8 TO 10 SERVINGS

ALASKA

BAKED ALASKA

Always impressive, Baked Alaska can be elegantly assembled ahead of time and stored in the freezer until needed.

1 sheet of Butter Cake (see page 21)
2 oz. of Grand Marnier or any other liqueur of your choice
1 quart brick, tricolored ice cream, very hard
5 egg whites at room temperature
⅛ teaspoon cream of tartar
¾ cup superfine granulated sugar
confectioners sugar

Place cooled sheet cake on a tray or a wooden board and sprinkle with Grand Marnier. Slice hard frozen ice cream and arrange on top leaving approximately 1-inch rim around the edge of the sheet cake. Store in the freezer. Then prepare meringue topping by beating egg whites and cream of tartar to medium peak, gradually add sugar and continue beating until stiff but not dry. When sugar is well dissolved and the meringue is stiff, remove ice cream from the freezer and cover it and cake entirely with stiff meringue. Dust with confectioners sugar and place under the broiler at *least 5 inches below the heat* for about 2 minutes to brown the meringue quickly. Serve immediately or return to the freezer until needed.

If desired, Baked Alaska can be browned for 3 or 4 minutes in a 475 degree F. oven. If you do not want to brown and then refreeze it, Baked Alaska can be assembled and frosted well ahead of time and browned just before serving. Meringue frosting will remain intact in the freezer for aproximately 48 hours or even longer.

YIELD: 5 TO 6 SERVINGS

STRAWBERRY ALASKA

Follow the basic recipe for Baked Alaska but eliminate Grand Marnier (see page 228) and use vanilla ice cream. Before spreading the meringue cover the top of the ice cream with a thick layer (approximately 1 cup) of sliced fresh strawberries. Sprinkle with 2 tablespoons kirsch liqueur.

YIELD: 6 SERVINGS

GRAPEFRUIT ALASKA SURPRISE

Scoop out the meat of a large half grapefruit. Fill ¾ full with small diced, fresh pineapple and fresh orange sections combined with chunks of fresh grapefruit. Sprinkle each fruit with 1 tablespoon rum or kirsch liqueur. Scoop a small portion of vanilla ice cream on top, and smooth evenly to obtain a flat surface. Using a pastry bag fitted with a star tube, cover the half grapefruit with French Meringue (page 282) in the shape of a pyramid. Dust with confectioners sugar and brown quickly in a 425 degree F. oven for about 3 to 4 minutes. Serve immediately.

YIELD: ONE-HALF GRAPEFRUIT PER SERVING

ORANGE ALASKA

Slice the top off a large orange; scoop out the contents carefully, leaving only a clean skin. Fill with orange sherbet. Using a pastry bag fitted with a star tube, cover the sherbet with French Meringue (page 282) in a pyramid shape. Dust with confectioners sugar and brown quickly in a 450 degree F. oven for 3 to 4 minutes. Serve immediately.

YIELD: ONE LARGE ORANGE PER SERVING

BAKED ALASKA FLAMBÉ

Make Baked Alaska according to directions (page 228). Place 2 empty egg shells over the meringue and space them evenly. Fill egg shells with warm brandy; light with a match and immediately carry to the table. (For detailed instructions on How to Flambé Desserts, see page 205.)

YIELD: 5 TO 6 SERVINGS

BUTTER CAKE FOR BAKED ALASKA

This cake can be made with the yolks of the eggs you will be using in the meringue mixture.

1/3 cup butter
2/3 cup granulated sugar
5 yolks, beaten with a fork
1 cup plus 3 tablespoons sifted cake flour
1 1/2 teaspoons baking powder
1/4 cup cold milk
1 teaspoon grated lemon rind
1 teaspoon vanilla or almond extract

Set oven at 350 degrees F.
One 8 x 8 x 2-inch baking pan, greased and lined with paper

Cream butter and sugar. Add beaten yolks gradually, approximately one at a time, beating well after each addition. Continue beating until mixture is light and fluffy. Sift flour and baking powder together. Stir sifted ingredients alternately with the cold milk into the batter mixture. Add lemon rind and flavoring. Pour cake batter into baking pan. Bake at 350 degrees F. for approximately 35 minutes.

Cool thoroughly on a wire rack before trimming for Baked Alaska. Cut and shape cake to fit tray or wooden board. For 1 quart brick ice cream, sheet should be approximately 5″ x 7″.

YIELD: ONE CAKE 8 x 8 x 2

ALASKA ICE CREAM PIE

½-inch-thick layer of sponge or white cake, large enough to fit a 9-inch pie tin
1 pint soft mocha ice cream
½ cup cold chocolate syrup
1 pint soft chocolate ice cream
5 egg whites
¼ teaspoon cream of tartar
1 cup granulated sugar
confectioners sugar, to dust

Set oven at 450 degrees F.

Fit the sponge cake, or white cake, into a 9-inch pie tin. Cover evenly with one 2-inch layer of mocha ice cream. Pour the cold chocolate syrup over it; spread chocolate ice cream on top. Even the top with a spoon or knife. Place in the freezer for approximately 20 minutes to harden. Beat egg whites with cream of tartar until foamy; continue beating while gradually adding sugar until they form stiff peaks. Remove prepared pie from freezer and spread the meringue over the top. Dust with confectioners sugar and brown for 5 minutes in a 450 degree F. oven or for 2 minutes under a hot broiler. The pie can be prepared well in advance. The meringue will hold up in the freezer after being browned for approximately 48 hours. Serve with Hot Chocolate Sauce (page 291).

YIELD: 8 SERVINGS

FROZEN SOUFFLÉS

COLD SOUFFLÉS

Cold soufflés can be prepared well in advance and stored in the freezer until needed. They are usually served with a hot or cold sauce according to the particular flavor used in their preparation.

PREPARATION OF SOUFFLÉ MOLDS FOR COLD SOUFFLÉS

Regular soufflé dishes should be used and a collar of paper, about 5 inches wide and long enough to go around the dish, must be secured all around the opening. Oil or grease the paper on both sides and press it to the inside of the mold so that paper will adhere properly. Fasten the ends together with a paper clip or Scotch tape, allowing the paper to extend at least 3 inches above the edge of the dish.

When soufflé is firm, peel the paper gently away. To facilitate removal of the paper in the event it sticks to the mixture, dip soufflé dish *quickly* in hot water and immediately proceed to remove the paper. Return the soufflé to the freezer or refrigerator until ready to serve.

Note: In the event soufflé dishes are not available, a deep mold with straight edges or a Pyrex dish can be substituted.

COOL UNTIL SET

This term, which will appear in every Frozen Soufflé recipe, means *chill until mixture mounds slightly when dropped from a spoon.* Do not attempt to fold whipped cream into a hot or warm mixture or the cream will immediately separate and spoil your valiant efforts.

FREEZING AND STORAGE OF FROZEN SOUFFLÉS

Your freezer must be in good working order if your results are to be successful; this is absolutely essential.

When ready for serving, frozen soufflés (or any frozen dessert, for that matter) must be the *same consistency as ice cream.* Depending upon the type and quality of your freezer, I suggest you check the consistency of your soufflé approximately 1 hour before serving time. If too hard, remove soufflé from freezer compartment and place it in the refrigerator until proper consistency is obtained.

FROZEN MOCHA SOUFFLÉ

1 envelope or 1 tablespoon of unflavored gelatin
¼ cup hot water
18 lady fingers (approximately)
5 egg yolks
1 tablespoon instant coffee dissolved in ⅓ cup boiling water
½ cup granulated sugar
1 cup heavy cream
1 tablespoon sugar
5 egg whites
¼ cup granulated sugar
1 teaspoon cocoa powder
1 teaspoon confectioners sugar

No paper collar is necessary for this delectable, frozen soufflé.

Soak gelatin in hot water. Line sides of a 2-quart greased soufflé dish with lady fingers. Blend yolks, dissolved coffee and sugar in a bowl. Cook over hot water, beating constantly until thick. Remove from heat; add soaked gelatin. Cool on ice or in the refrigerator until the mixture begins to set. Whip heavy cream with sugar until stiff. Beat egg whites, adding sugar gradually until they hold their shape and are rather stiff but not dry. Gently fold egg whites and whipped cream into the cooled yolk mixture. *Do not overmix.* Pour into prepared soufflé dish and freeze for at least 3 hours or until set. Just before serving, dust soufflé with 1 teaspoon cocoa powder mixed with same amount of confectioners sugar.
YIELD: 6 SERVINGS

Suggested sauce: Hot or Cold Americana Chocolate Sauce (page 290) or Custard Sauce (page 293).

FROZEN LEMON SOUFFLÉ

1 envelope or 1 tablespoon unflavored gelatin
¼ cup hot water
5 egg yolks
½ cup lemon juice
1 tablespoon Jamaica rum
grated rind of 1 lemon
½ cup granulated sugar
1 cup heavy cream
1 tablespoon sugar
5 egg whites
¼ cup sugar

Prepare a 1-quart soufflé dish with a paper collar as explained on page 232.

Sprinkle gelatin over hot water to dissolve. In a bowl, mix well: egg yolks, lemon juice, rum, grated lemon rind and granulated sugar. Cook over hot water, beating constantly until thick. Remove from heat and stir in gelatin. Cool on ice or in the refrigerator until the mixture begins to set. Beat heavy cream with sugar until stiff. Beat egg whites, adding sugar gradually until they hold their shape and are stiff but not dry. Gently fold egg whites and whipped cream into the cooled yolk mixture. Blend thoroughly but *do not overmix.*

Pour into prepared soufflé dish and freeze for at least 3 hours or until set. Peel off paper collar and serve.

YIELD: 6 SERVINGS

Suggested Sauce: Egg Nog Sauce (page 290).

CHOCOLATE FROZEN SOUFFLÉ

2 *cups heavy cream*
1 *tablespoon or 1 package of unflavored gelatin*
¼ *cup hot water*
8 *oz. melted sweet chocolate*
⅔ *cup confectioners sugar*
½ *cup light cream*
6 *egg yolks*
¼ *cup Cognac*
6 *egg whites*
2 *tablespoons granulated sugar*

Prepare a 1½-quart soufflé dish with a paper collar as previously explained on page 232.

Whip heavy cream until stiff. Let stand in the refrigerator while preparing the following:

Dissolve gelatin in hot water. Place chocolate (broken into small pieces) in a deep bowl and melt over hot water. Stir well to dissolve. Add confectioners sugar and light cream and remove from heat. Beat egg yolks until light and fluffy and gradually stir into the chocolate mixture. Then return mixture to heat and beat well over hot water with a wire whip, until mixture becomes thick enough to coat a spoon. Remove from heat, add softened gelatin, stir to dissolve. Add Cognac and cool over cold water or in the refrigerator until the mixture starts to set. Beat egg whites stiff, adding granulated sugar gradually. Fold into cooled chocolate mixture alternately with whipped cream. Mix gently and pour into the prepared mold. Place in the freezer and chill for at least 3 hours or until set. Peel off paper collar and serve in the same dish.

YIELD: 6 SERVINGS

Suggested Sauce: Hot or Cold Custard Sauce (page 293) or Americana Chocolate Sauce (page 291).

FROZEN LEMON RUM SOUFFLÉ

1½ tablespoons or 1½ envelopes unflavored gelatin
½ cup hot water
1 cup lemon juice
grated rind of 2 lemons
8 egg yolks
2 cups granulated sugar
⅔ cup Jamaica rum
2 cups heavy cream, whipped

Prepare a 1-quart soufflé dish with a paper collar extending approximately 4 inches above the rim as explained on page 232.

Sprinkle gelatin over hot water to dissolve. Combine lemon juice, lemon rind and egg yolks and beat for approximately 5 minutes. Add sugar and rum and continue beating until the sugar is well dissolved. Stir in the gelatin mixture and blend well. Cool over crushed ice or in the refrigerator until the mixture starts to set. Fold in the whipped cream.

Pour into prepared soufflé dish and place in the freezer for about 3 hours or until set. Peel off the paper collar and serve in the same dish.

YIELD: 6 SERVINGS

Suggested Sauce: Rum Sauce, page 292, or Custard Sauce, page 293.

FROZEN BANANA SOUFFLÉ

1 tablespoon or 1 envelope unflavored gelatin
½ cup hot water
5 egg yolks
½ cup powdered sugar
2⅓ cups mashed ripe bananas
1 tablespoon rum
1 teaspoon lemon juice
1 cup heavy cream
1 pinch ground nutmeg
5 egg whites
2 tablespoons sugar

Prepare a 1½-quart soufflé dish with a paper collar as explained on page 232.

Sprinkle gelatin over hot water to dissolve. In a deep bowl, place egg yolks and powdered sugar; cook over hot water, beating constantly until thick. Remove from heat, add gelatin and stir well to dissolve. Cool on ice or in the refrigerator until the mixture begins to set. In the meantime, mash bananas; add rum and lemon juice gradually to form a smooth purée without lumps. Add to yolk mixture and blend well. Beat heavy cream until stiff; stir in nutmeg. Whip egg whites, adding sugar gradually until they hold their shape and are stiff but not dry. Gently fold egg whites, whipped cream and nutmeg into the banana and yolk mixture. Blend well but *do not overmix.* Pour into prepared soufflé dish. Freeze for 3 hours or until set. Peel off paper collar and serve in the same dish.

YIELD: 6 SERVINGS

Suggested Sauce: Strawberry Sauce, page 293, or Melba Sauce, page 290.

FROZEN STRAWBERRY SOUFFLÉ

1 *8 oz. package frozen strawberries, thawed*
1 *envelope or 1 tablespoon unflavored gelatin*
¼ *cup hot water*
5 *egg yolks*
⅓ *cup sugar*
1 *tablespoon kirsch*
2 *drops red food coloring*
1 *cup heavy cream*
5 *egg whites*
2 *tablespoons granulated sugar*
8 *large fresh ripe strawberries, to garnish*
½ *cup hot currant jelly*

Prepare a 1-quart soufflé dish with a paper collar as explained on page 232.

Thaw strawberries and blend in an electric blender or mash well with a fork. Soak gelatin in hot water. Place egg yolks and sugar in a bowl and cook over hot water, beating constantly until thick. Remove from heat; add gelatin, kirsch, red food coloring and mashed strawberries; blend well. Cool on ice or in the refrigerator until the mixture starts to set. Whip cream until stiff. Beat egg whites, adding sugar gradually, until they hold their shape and are stiff but not dry. Fold into the cooled yolk mixture together with the whipped cream. Blend well. *Do not overmix.*

Pour into prepared soufflé dish. Freeze for at least 3 hours or until set. Remove paper collar and decorate with 8 large ripe strawberries dipped in hot currant jelly.

YIELD: 6 SERVINGS

Suggested Sauce: Melba Sauce, page 290, or Strawberry Sauce, page 293.

ICE CREAM AND SHERBETS

FREEZING INSTRUCTIONS FOR THE MAKING OF ICE CREAM OR SHERBET

ELECTRIC OR HAND FREEZER

Follow instructions packed with the freezer by the manufacturing company. They generally state that ice cream container should be packed with 5 parts of crushed ice to 1 part of rock salt.

REFRIGERATOR TRAY FREEZING

Set refrigerator at the lowest temperature possible. Place prepared and chilled mixture in a regular freezing tray. Allow cream to remain in the freezer compartment until mushy or not quite frozen. Remove from tray and pour into a round-bottomed bowl which has been previously chilled. Beat rapidly until smooth, using a wire whip or rotary beater. Return to freezing tray; cover with waxed or foil paper and finish freezing until firm.

Many recipes for homemade ice cream contain whipped cream. To whip cream properly, follow detailed instructions on page 10.

VANILLA ICE CREAM

½ *cup sugar*
1½ *teaspoons cornstarch*
1 *teaspoon vanilla extract*
4 *egg yolks*
1 *cup milk*
1 *cup heavy cream*

Combine sugar and cornstarch. In a deep bowl, beat vanilla and egg yolks lightly with a fork; add sugar mixture. Heat the milk until bubbles start to form around the edges of the pan, then gradually stir it into the egg yolk mixture and blend well. Cook over hot water, stirring constantly until mixture thickens and coats a spoon (approximately 15 minutes). *Do not boil.* Chill in refrigerator or over cold water, stirring from time to time to accelerate cooling. Beat heavy cream until thick but not stiff (until cream starts to hold its shape). Fold cream gently and thoroughly into the chilled mixture. Freeze according to directions previously given (page 237).

YIELD: APPROXIMATELY 1 QUART OR 5 SERVINGS

CHOCOLATE ICE CREAM

Same basic recipe and freezing instructions as for Vanilla Ice Cream (page 237). Stir 2 oz. unsweetened chocolate into the egg yolks at the same time the hot milk is added. Increase sugar to ¾ cup instead of ½.

COFFEE ICE CREAM

Same basic recipe and freezing instructions as for Vanilla Ice Cream (page 237). Stir 2 tablespoons instant coffee into the egg yolks at the same time the hot milk is added.

PISTACHIO ICE CREAM

Same basic recipe and freezing instructions as for Vanilla Ice Cream (page 237). Use almond extract instead of vanilla. To the chilled mixture, add ½ cup of finely sliced pistachio nuts and 1 teaspoon green food coloring at the same time the heavy cream is added.

TUTTI FRUTTI ICE CREAM

Same basic recipe and freezing instructions as for Vanilla Ice Cream (page 237). Soak ½ cup diced candied red cherries in 2 tablespoons Jamaica rum overnight; add to chilled mixture at the same time as heavy cream.

BANANA ICE CREAM

Same basic recipe and freezing instructions as for Vanilla Ice Cream (page 237). Add ½ cup mashed ripe bananas to the chilled mixture at the same time the heavy cream is added.

STRAWBERRY ICE CREAM

Same basic recipe and freezing instructions as for Vanilla Ice Cream (page 237). Omit vanilla; add 1⅓ cups of fresh crushed strawberries or 2 packages of frozen strawberries, drained and then mashed. Stir into the chilled mixture just before folding in the whipped cream.

FRENCH VANILLA ICE CREAM

4 *egg yolks*
½ *cup granulated sugar*
1 *cup light cream*
½ *cup milk*
1 *vanilla bean, split, or 3 drops vanilla extract*
½ *cup heavy cream*

Beat egg yolks and sugar until fluffy and pale in color. Heat light cream and milk just to boiling point. Add split vanilla bean or vanilla extract. Pour hot milk and cream gradually and in a slow stream over yolk mixture. Return to heat and cook until mixture becomes thick enough to coat a spoon. *Do not boil.* Strain, then cool in refrigerator or over cold water; stir from time to time to accelerate cooling. Beat heavy cream until thick but not stiff (until cream starts to hold its shape). Fold cream into chilled mixture. Freeze according to directions given on page 237.

YIELD: APPROXIMATELY 1½ PINTS OR 4 SERVINGS

For numerous other flavors, follow instructions for recipes following Vanilla Ice Cream, pages 238–239.

BISCUIT TORTONI

1 cup heavy cream
1/4 cup granulated sugar
1/2 teaspoon almond extract
1 tablespoon Jamaica rum
1/3 cup macaroon crumbs
1 egg white
2 tablespoons sliced, roasted almonds
4 maraschino cherries

Whip cream until almost stiff. Add the sugar and continue beating until stiff. Add almond extract and rum. Stir in macaroon crumbs. Place in a cool place while preparing the following:

Beat egg white until stiff but not dry. Fold egg white gently into cream mixture. Spoon out into individual dessert cups. Dust with sliced roasted almonds. Freeze for approximately 1 hour or until set.

Garnish each portion with a maraschino cherry just before serving.

YIELD: 4 SERVINGS

BANANA SHERBET

1 cup mashed, ripe bananas
3 tablespoons lemon juice
grated rind of 1 lemon
1/3 cup granulated sugar
1 egg white
1 cup milk

Force bananas through a fine sieve. Stir in lemon juice, lemon rind and sugar. Blend well. Beat egg white until stiff. Fold into banana mixture. Gradually add milk, while stirring constantly. Freeze according to the directions given on page 237.

YIELD: APPROXIMATELY 2 1/2 CUPS OR 4 SERVINGS

LEMON RUM SHERBET

3/4 cup lemon juice
grated rind of 1 lemon
1/2 cup superfine granulated sugar
1 1/2 cups milk
1/3 cup heavy cream
1 teaspoon rum

Combine lemon juice, lemon rind and sugar thoroughly. Stir in milk and heavy cream. Add rum. Freeze according to directions given on page 237.

YIELD: APPROXIMATELY 3 CUPS

OTHER FROZEN DESSERTS

FROZEN SABAYON FRANKIOLO

A perfect dessert for your husband's card game!

Many years ago, while I was working in Paris, a group of young pastry cooks used to gather in the evening at the home of a great pastry chef and true artist, Frankiolo, who also had a small boutique on Avenue Laumière.

We congregated there to learn the art of pastry decorating from this renowned master and generally we ended our enjoyable evening around a bowl of "Frozen Sabayon," while our teacher played his magic guitar. Happy memories indeed!!

With pleasure, I pass along the Frozen Sabayon recipe so that you too may experience this wonderful treat.

24 *lady fingers*
2 *tablespoons Jamaica rum or good Cognac*
8 *egg yolks*
⅓ *cup granulated sugar*
⅓ *cup Marsala wine*
½ *cup grated sweet chocolate*
⅓ *cup diced candied cherries*
1 *cup heavy cream*
2 *tablespoons sugar*
1 *pinch ground nutmeg*
2 *tablespoons rum or Cognac*

Arrange 12 of the lady fingers in the bottom of a 1½-quart soufflé dish or any other round container with straight sides. Sprinkle lady fingers with rum or Cognac. Chill in the refrigerator. Beat egg yolks with sugar over hot water until light and fluffy. Stir in Marsala, grated sweet chocolate and diced candied cherries. Blend thoroughly. Remove from heat. Place over cold water or in the refrigerator to chill. Stir from time to time to accelerate cooling. Beat heavy cream, adding sugar gradually until stiff. Fold cream gently into cooled yolk mixture, then pour into prepared chilled mold or dish. Dust with ground nutmeg. Cover entirely with the remaining lady fingers. Sprinkle with rum or Cognac. Place in the freezer for at least 2 hours or until set. This delicious and unusual dessert can be enjoyed to the fullest accompanied with a chilled glass of Marsala wine or good chilled French champagne.

YIELD: 4 TO 5 SERVINGS

ORANGES NORVEGIENNE

6 large oranges
⅓ cup drained crushed canned pineapple
1 tablespoon rum
¾ pint soft vanilla ice cream
3 egg whites
6 tablespoons sugar
confectioners sugar, to dust

Slice the top off the oranges. Scoop out the pulp. Place empty shells in the refrigerator for at least 1 hour. Combine drained crushed pineapple, rum and soft ice cream. Fill oranges to the top and place in the freezer to harden for at least 1 hour. Beat egg whites until they form stiff peaks, adding sugar gradually. Scoop meringue on top of the oranges using a large enough scoop to entirely cover the ice cream. Dust with confectioners sugar and place under the broiler to brown for approximately 3 to 4 minutes. Serve immediately.
YIELD: 6 SERVINGS

PEACHES IMPÉRATRICE

Something elegant and so different—a delectable surprise for sophisticated guests.

2 cups granulated sugar
3 cups water
6 large, fresh ripe peaches
1 cup vanilla ice cream
1 9-inch round layer of Light Sponge Cake (page 23)
2 oz. maraschino liqueur or Grand Marnier
¾ cup clear apricot jam
2 tablespoons sliced roasted almonds

Boil sugar and water for 1 minute in a deep saucepan. Remove from heat. Gently place the peaches in the hot syrup and allow to remain for at least 2 minutes. Drain and save the syrup. Peel the skin from the peaches with a sharp knife; cut each peach in half and remove the pit. Chill thoroughly. Sandwich the halves of each peach together with a small ball of vanilla ice cream. Arrange the peaches over a layer of sponge cake approximately 1½ inches thick. (The sponge cake can be baked the day before.) Sprinkle with maraschino or Grand Marnier liqueur or any other liqueur of your choice. Place in the freezer to chill. In the meantime, boil ¾ cup clear apricot jam diluted with ¼ cup of the sugar syrup you have left. Stir constantly to avoid burning. When apricot mixture is well dissolved, remove peaches from the freezer and brush entirely with the hot, clear jam. Sprinkle a few slices of roasted almonds over the top. Serve immediately.

YIELD: 6 SERVINGS

PEACHES SULTANE
(Pêches aux raisins)

6 *whole peaches or 12 ripe halves of peeled peaches*

SYRUP

2 *cups water*
2 *cups granulated sugar*
1 *tablespoon Cognac*

SAUCE

5 *egg yolks*
⅔ *cup sugar*
½ *cup white wine*
⅓ *cup seedless raisins*
1 *quart ice cream (any flavor)*

Peel peaches. Bring water and sugar just to a boil. Add the prepared peaches, reduce heat and simmer gently for about 10 to 15 minutes or until peaches are tender. Add Cognac. Remove from heat and let peaches cool in the syrup. Beat egg yolks and sugar over hot water until light and fluffy. Add wine and continue beating until thick. Remove from heat; add raisins and cool sauce in the refrigerator or over crushed ice. Arrange large scoops of ice cream on a chilled serving tray or platter. Place half a cooled peach over each scoop of ice cream. Cover entirely with sauce and serve immediately.

YIELD: 6 SERVINGS

Note: In the preparation of this classic dessert, good canned peaches or pears are an ideal substitute for fresh peaches.

FROZEN LIME PIE

1⅓ cups graham cracker crumbs
3 tablespoons melted butter
3 eggs, separated
1 8-oz. can sweetened condensed milk
grated rind of 1 lime
½ cup lime juice
1 pinch cream of tartar
¾ cup granulated sugar
1 cup heavy cream, whipped with
1 tablespoon sugar, to garnish

Blend graham cracker crumbs and melted butter. Press into a well-buttered 9-inch pie tin. Beat egg yolks with milk until pale in color; add lime rind and, gradually, the lime juice. Beat egg whites with cream of tartar until they form stiff peaks, adding sugar gradually. Pour the lime filling into the beaten egg whites and blend well. Pour into prepared pie shell and freeze for at least 1 hour, or until hard. Garnish with whipped cream just before serving.
YIELD: 6 TO 8 SERVINGS

Note: Lemon juice can be substituted for lime juice.

CHOCOLATE PROFITEROLLES

16 *Small Cream Puffs (page 163)*
16 *tablespoons Vanilla Ice Cream (page 237)*
1 *cup Hot Chocolate Sauce (page 291)*

Bake 16 small cream puffs, about the size of Ping-Pong balls. Cool; split in two. Fill each puff with 1 tablespoon Vanilla Ice Cream. Pile puffs on a serving dish or platter in the shape of a high pyramid. Set in the freezer to harden. Just before serving, coat entirely with Hot Chocolate Sauce.
YIELD: 4 SERVINGS

PARISIAN APRICOTS

24 *firm canned apricot halves, drained*
12 *tablespoons Vanilla Ice Cream (page 237)*
12 *large Almond Macaroons (page 136)*
1 *cup Melba Sauce (page 290) or hot or cold Sabayon Sauce (page 292)*
½ *pint heavy cream, whipped*

Sandwich drained apricot halves together with a tablespoon of Vanilla Ice Cream in the center. Place each filled apricot on a large Almond Macaroon. Arrange filled fruits and macaroons on a chilled serving tray or platter. Coat entirely with Melba Sauce or Sabayon Sauce. Decorate edges of the tray with whipped cream.
YIELD: 4 TO 6 SERVINGS

MARBLE MOUSSE

½ *teaspoon unflavored gelatin*
¼ *cup hot water*
1 *cup granulated sugar*
½ *cup water*
6 *egg yolks*
1 *pint heavy cream, beaten stiff*
⅓ *cup thick chocolate syrup*

Sprinkle gelatin over hot water and place over hot water to dissolve. Stir from time to time. Combine sugar and water and boil to 240 degrees F. on a candy thermometer. Place egg yolks in a bowl and beat with a fork. In a slow stream, while beating constantly, pour sugar mixture over egg yolks and continue beating with an electric mixer or rotary beater until the mixture thickens. Stir in dissolved gelatin. Remove from mixer or bowl and cool in refrigerator or over cold water. When the mixture starts to set, fold in the whipped cream and pour in the chocolate sauce in a thin stream, but *do not* blend completely. You should achieve a marbleized effect. Pour into chilled champagne glasses; freeze for about 2 hours or until firm.
YIELD: APPROXIMATELY 8 SERVINGS

STRAWBERRY ICE CREAM PIE

One 10-inch, baked and cooled pie shell made with graham cracker crust (page 51).
1/3 cup raspberry jam
6 fresh or drained canned peach halves
1 tablespoon Grand Marnier
1 3/4 pints strawberry ice cream
1 cup whipped cream
2 tablespoons grated sweet chocolate

Spread bottom of the pastry shell with raspberry jam to cover. Arrange well-drained peaches over the jam. Sprinkle with Grand Marnier. Cover with strawberry ice cream to fill the pie shell. Place in the freezer for approximately 1 hour to harden. Just before serving, garnish with whipped cream and dust with grated chocolate. Cut pie with a sharp knife dipped in hot water.
YIELD: 6 SERVINGS

Puddings, Custards & Mousses

RICE PUDDINGS

Rice pudding is most nourishing and a very palatable dessert.

To be truly successful in the making and final presentation of this popular dessert, I recommend the use of long grain rice.

PREPARING RICE FOR COOKING:
The rice must be thoroughly cleaned before cooking. The simplest and easiest method is to spread the rice on a large piece of white paper and eliminate any undesirable particles. Then wash the rice and boil it gently (1 part rice to 6 parts water) for approximately 10 minutes; this partial precooking accelerates the final cooking process of the rice. Drain thoroughly and proceed according to the directions given in the individual recipe. Rice triples in volume once cooked: i.e., 1 cup of raw rice equals approximately 3 cups of cooked rice.

HOW TO COOK RICE:
Properly cooked rice should be tender and fluffy but certainly not mushy. To help achieve proper results, never stir rice during the

cooking process with anything but a wooden spoon. Always cook rice in a pan made of heavy-weight metal such as cast iron or copper. Cook slowly and follow explicitly the instructions given in the recipe.

Because so much depends upon the quality of the rice and the type of utensils used, it is difficult to determine the correct baking time with complete accuracy. Check the rice from time to time by removing a few grains and squeezing them with your fingers to determine how near cooked it is. If yolks or eggs are to be added near the last stage of the cooking, it should be done when the rice is tender but not completely cooked. Bear in mind that when the rice is returned to the heat, it will continue cooking and soften further. Cooking rice properly requires some practice; constant and careful attention must be given, but the reward is well worth the effort.

AMERICANA RICE PUDDING

The ultimate in rice puddings!

½ cup long grain rice
1 quart milk (4 cups)
the peel of 1 orange
½ cup sugar
¾ teaspoon salt
1 cup light cream
2 egg yolks
½ teaspoon vanilla extract

to garnish:
4 teaspoons sugar mixed with
1 teaspoon cinnamon
½ cup whipped cream
8 glazed or maraschino cherries

Eight individual custard cups

Clean and boil the rice in hot water for approximately 10 minutes as explained in Rice Pudding (page 247).

Scald the milk. Pare the orange like an apple, going round and round so peel is in one long spiral. Stir the peel, boiled rice, sugar and salt into the scalded milk. Cook covered in a double boiler, or in a 360 degree F. oven, for approximately 1 hour or until the rice is tender but not well done. Stir occasionally during the first part of the cooking. Remove the orange peel. Mix the cream and egg yolks together and gradually stir in a small amount of the hot rice mixture. Blend this mixture into the remainder of the rice and mix thoroughly but gently. Continue cooking, covered, until the mixture thickens (about 10 minutes), stirring from time to time. Add the vanilla, pour into individual custard cups and let cool; chill if desired. Sprinkle with the cinnamon-sugar mixture. Garnish with whipped cream and decorate with glazed or maraschino cherries.

YIELD: 8 SERVINGS

CREAMY RICE PUDDING

½ cup long grain rice
3 cups boiling water
4⅓ cups milk, scalded
⅓ cup granulated sugar
1 teaspoon butter
1 teaspoon grated lemon rind
⅙ teaspoon salt
½ cup raisins
1 vanilla bean or 3 drops of vanilla extract
4 egg yolks or 2 eggs
⅓ cup milk

Set oven at 350 degrees F.
Eight individual custard cups

Stir the rice into the boiling water and continue to boil for approximately 10 minutes. Drain thoroughly. Pour the rice into the scalded milk and bring to a slow boil. Add the sugar, butter, lemon rind, salt, raisins and vanilla bean (or vanilla extract). Cover and place in a 350 degree F. oven for approximately 1 hour; stir from time to time with a wooden spoon. When the rice is tender to the touch but not well done, remove from the oven. Combine the egg yolks or eggs with the milk and gradually stir into the rice mixture. Blend well. Return to the oven for about 10 minutes. Pour into individual custard cups; serve warm or cold.

YIELD: 8 SERVINGS

RICE CONDÉ
(Rice for various French desserts)

¾ cup long grain rice
2 cups plus 2 tablespoons milk
1 vanilla bean
⅓ cup granulated sugar
4 egg yolks
1 tablespoon granulated sugar
½ cup diced glazed mixed fruits

1 1½-quart mold, oiled

Wash the rice in cold water. Place in a saucepan, cover entirely with hot water and boil for 3 minutes. Remove from heat and let soak for 10 minutes before draining. Boil the milk, vanilla bean and sugar together. Pour in the drained rice and simmer over medium heat until tender or approximately 35 minutes. Stir gently from time to time with a wooden spoon to avoid scorching. When the rice is thoroughly cooked, remove the vanilla bean and turn off the heat. (Rice should be rather thick in consistency if cooked correctly. For detailed instructions on how to cook rice properly, see page 247.) Beat the egg yolks with 1 tablespoon of sugar and the remaining 2 tablespoons of milk until light. Stir into the cooked rice, mixing rapidly but gently with a wooden spoon. Add the diced glazed fruits. Pour the hot rice mixture into the oiled mold, fancy ring-form or any other desired dish; let cool for 30 minutes or so and unmold over a large serving platter.

Rice Condé is used in the preparation of many classic desserts whose recipes are given on the following pages.

YIELD: APPROXIMATELY 6 TO 8 SERVINGS

PEARS OR PEACHES CONDÉ

Use fresh peeled, stewed or canned fruits. Mold Rice Condé (page 249) in a 10-inch round cake pan. Unmold on a round serving tray and cool. Arrange fruits in an artistic manner on top of the rice. Coat entirely with 1 cup cold Custard Sauce (page 293). Garnish with 1½ cups whipped cream flavored with 2 tablespoons liqueur of your choice. Use 1 pear or peach to each serving.

CHERRIES CONDÉ

Use fresh stewed and pitted cherries or canned black cherries. Mold Rice Condé (page 249) in an oval-shaped mold. Unmold on an oval serving tray. Arrange drained cherries in a pyramid shape around the rice and bind with some hot Currant Jelly Glaze for Tarts (page 80). Garnish with whipped cream flavored with kirsch. Use 6 cherries per serving.

APRICOTS CONDÉ

Drain one 8- or 10-oz. jar of firm apricot halves. Arrange them overlapping each other on a ring of cooked and cooled Rice Condé (page 249), placed on a serving tray. Decorate with candied fruits. Brush over with some hot Apricot Jam Glaze for Tarts (page 80). Cool and fill up the center of the ring with whipped cream. Use 4 apricot halves per serving.

PINEAPPLE CONDÉ

Drain one 8- or 10-oz. jar of sliced pineapple. Arrange on a ring of cooked and cooled Rice Condé (page 249) placed on a serving tray. Brush with hot Apricot Glaze for Tarts (page 80). Fill up center with whipped cream flavored with kirsch. Use 1 slice pineapple per serving.

RICE PUDDING IMPÉRATRICE

An outstanding dessert from the classic cuisine, named after the Empress Eugénie, wife of Napoleon III. It is considered one of the greatest European puddings. Spectacular and so delicious!

2/3 cup finely diced glazed fruits, such as cherries, pineapple, orange peel, melon, etc.
2 tablespoons kirsch
1 1/2 packages or 1 1/2 tablespoons unflavored gelatin
1 3-oz. package strawberry or raspberry Jell-O
1 cup boiling water
1/2 cup cold water
1 tablespoon vegetable oil, approximately
1/2 cup long grain rice
2 quarts boiling water
1 3/4 cups boiling milk
1 tablespoon butter
1 teaspoon vanilla extract
5 egg yolks
1 3/4 cups milk
2/3 cup granulated sugar
2 tablespoons clear apricot jam
3/4 cup heavy cream, whipped stiff
glazed cherries, to decorate
1 1/2 cups Sauce Liqueur (page 292), flavored to your taste

One 1 1/2-quart cylindrical mold or one 8-inch ring mold

Combine the glazed fruits and kirsch. Sprinkle the gelatin over the combined ingredients and let soak while preparing the following:

Combine the Jell-O with 1 cup of boiling water. Stir well to dissolve, then add ½ cup of cold water. Pour the prepared Jell-O mixture to a depth of approximately ½ inch in the bottom of the mold. Save remaining Jell-O to use as you wish. Brush the sides of the mold with vegetable oil and place in the refrigerator to allow the Jell-O to harden.

In the meantime, bring the 2 quarts of water to a boil. Clean the rice as directed on page 247. Add it to the water and continue to boil for 5 minutes or so. Drain thoroughly. Boil the milk; add the butter and vanilla. Stir in the rice; cook over a low flame until the rice is tender (for detailed instructions on How To Cook Rice, see page 247) and set aside. Beat the egg yolks with a fork. Blend with ¼ cup of the milk. Add the sugar gradually. Boil remaining 1½ cups of milk. Remove from heat and pour in a slow stream into the yolk mixture while beating rapidly with a wire whip. Continue beating to blend all ingredients well. Add the soaked diced fruits and stir to dissolve the gelatin properly. Add the apricot jam, stir in the cooked rice and mix gently with a wooden spoon to avoid breaking the rice. Cool in refrigerator or over cold water, stirring from time to time to accelerate cooling. Beat the heavy cream until stiff.

When the rice mixture is cold but not entirely set, fold in the whipped cream. Pour into the chilled mold on top of the Jell-O and refrigerate for approximately 4 hours or overnight if you wish. To unmold, dip the pan quickly in hot water. Run the point of a knife or a flexible spatula around the pudding. Reverse the mold onto a chilled serving tray. Decorate with red glazed cherries and serve with fruits or Sauce Liqueur flavored to your taste.

YIELD: APPROXIMATELY 8 SERVINGS

Note: Individual pudding cups can be used for the above recipe. Prepare the individual cups the same way as for large molds.

PEARS À L'IMPÉRATRICE

Slightly oil a ring mold 8 inches in diameter and fill with Rice Pudding Impératrice (page 251). Chill until set. Unmold rice on a round chilled serving tray. Fill in the center with 6 peeled, cored, poached and diced fresh Bartlett pears blended with ⅓ cup hot clear apricot jam and one tablespoon of Jamaica rum. Garnish with whipped cream over the pears and make a fancy border all around the base of the rice with whipped cream. Decorate with candied fruits.

YIELD: 6 SERVINGS

Serve with Liqueur Sauce of your choice (see sauces, page 292).

Note: Drained canned pears or any other fruits can be used instead of fresh pears, if you wish. If cherries, strawberries or blueberries are used, substitute hot currant jelly for hot apricot jam to blend the fruits.

CUSTARD PUDDINGS

Properly made custards are highly esteemed, nutritious, light desserts appreciated by both grown-ups and children. They are simple to prepare and can be made a day in advance.

When a custard of thin fragile consistency is desirable, 1 egg for each cup of liquid will be satisfactory. However, custard of this consistency will have to be served and eaten from the cup or dish in which it was baked.

PREPARATION AND BAKING:

When whole eggs are used, and unless otherwise specified in the recipe, the eggs should be beaten with a fork to break and blend the yolks and whites together, but not overmixed.

Custards are generally baked in individual earthenware cups or in a heatproof baking dish large enough to accommodate several servings. The container in which the custard is baked must be placed in a pan filled with approximately 1½ inches cold water before it is placed in the oven. Constant attention is necessary during the baking process to avoid overbaking the custard, which would result in a watery and curdled dessert. Near the end of the baking time, check custard with the point of a knife; if it comes out clean when inserted through the center of the custard, it is ready to be removed from the heat.

TO UNMOLD CUSTARD:

Chill the custard thoroughly before attempting to unmold it. Slip the point of a knife around the edges of the cups or baking dish. Place a serving plate or tray over the top of the dish and reverse, holding plate or tray tightly against the dish. Shake gently to loosen the edges and lift the mold carefully.

VANILLA CUSTARD PUDDING

1½ cups milk	*1 teaspoon vanilla extract*
*1 cup light cream**	*4 eggs*
1 small pinch salt	*¼ cup granulated sugar*

Set oven at 325 degrees F.
Six individual, oven-proof custard cups, brushed with soft butter and dusted with confectioners sugar
One baking pan, large enough to hold the cups

Brush 6 individual deep custard cups with soft butter and dust with confectioners sugar. Remove any excess sugar by turning the cup upside down and knocking it against a pastry board.

Scald the milk and combine with the light cream. Add the salt and vanilla extract. Break the eggs into a large round-bottomed bowl and beat just enough to blend the yolks and whites together. Add the sugar and beat for approximately 2 minutes. Add the milk and cream mixture and strain. Fill the prepared cups to the top. Set the filled cups in a baking pan filled with water to approximately ½-inch from the top of the cups. Bake at 325 degrees F. for about 50 minutes or until the point of a knife, when inserted through the custard, comes out clean. Cool or chill. To unmold and for detailed instructions concerning custard, see page 253.
YIELD: 6 SERVINGS

For larger quantities, bake the custard according to above directions in a 1-quart heatproof dish at 300 degrees F. for about 1 hour and 20 minutes, or until a knife, when inserted through the center, comes out clean.

* *Note:* For a custard not quite so rich, use additional milk instead of light cream.

CARAMEL CUSTARD PUDDING

½ cup granulated sugar
1 recipe for Vanilla Custard Pudding (page 254)

Six individual ovenproof custard cups, greased, or
one 1-quart ovenproof baking dish, greased

Melt the sugar over a low flame, stirring constantly until the syrup becomes liquefied and begins to brown. Quickly pour the caramel into the bottom of the prepared cups or dish. Cool until the caramel is firm. Meanwhile, prepare the pudding mixture. Pour over the caramel and bake as directed. When cool, unmold; the melted caramel syrup will run down the sides and form a tasty sauce. For instructions on how to unmold custard, see page 253.
YIELD: 6 SERVINGS

CHOCOLATE CUSTARD PUDDING

Follow the recipe for Vanilla Custard Pudding (page 254); add 2 squares or 2 oz. of melted semi-sweet chocolate to the scalded milk.

COFFEE CUSTARD

Follow recipe for Vanilla Custard Pudding (page 254); add 1 tablespoon instant coffee to the scalded milk.

CARAMEL CUSTARD RING

1 cup granulated sugar
4 whole eggs plus 2 egg yolks
3 cups milk
3 drops vanilla extract
1 pint fresh strawberries, sliced
2 tablespoons kirsch
1 cup whipped cream

Set oven at 360 degrees F.
One 9-inch ring mold
One baking pan large enough to hold the mold

Place ½ cup of the sugar in a deep saucepan and melt slowly over medium heat; stir constantly until golden brown. Pour immediately into the ring mold, coating the entire bottom and sides evenly. Set aside to cool. Beat the eggs, extra yolks and the remaining ½ cup sugar together until well blended. Scald the milk; add the vanilla and stir into the egg mixture. Blend all ingredients well. Let rest 5 minutes. Pour into the prepared ring mold. Set in a deep baking pan containing about 1½ inches water, and bake for approximately 45 to 50 minutes or until set. Cool for at least 1½ hours. Unmold onto a flat round serving tray. Fill the center with the sliced strawberries sprinkled with kirsch and garnish all around with whipped cream. Place in the refrigerator and serve cold.

YIELD: 6 SERVINGS

Note: To coat the mold properly, heat it in the oven while melting the sugar. Pour the syrup into the mold and, while holding with a pot holder or heavy towel, turn the mold constantly to spread the caramel syrup.

CARAMEL COCONUT CUSTARD

2 *cups less 2 tablespoons granulated sugar to melt*
4 *cups milk*
3 *whole eggs plus 3 egg yolks*
1 *teaspoon almond extract*
1 *cup flaked coconut*

Set oven at 360 degrees F.
One 1½-quart baking dish

Place 1⅓ cups of the sugar in a saucepan and melt over low or medium heat, stirring constantly to dissolve. When the sugar is liquefied and golden brown, pour it quickly into the baking dish, turning the dish rapidly to coat the bottom and sides evenly. Set aside. Scald the milk. Beat the eggs, extra yolks and remaining ½ cup sugar just enough to blend. Add the almond extract and gradually stir the milk into the egg mixture.

Brown the coconut in the oven at 360 degrees F. for about 10 minutes, stirring every 3 or 4 minutes to ensure even browning. (Coconut should be golden brown and not dark in color.) Blend the coconut into the custard and pour into the prepared mold. Place the mold in a pan of water, and bake at 360 degrees F. for approximately

1 hour and 35 minutes or until the point of a knife, when inserted through the center, comes out clean. Cool thoroughly. Unmold onto a chilled serving dish.

YIELD: APPROXIMATELY 6 SERVINGS

ORANGE CUSTARD

1 *cup light cream*
1 *cup fresh orange juice*
⅓ *cup granulated sugar*
4 *eggs plus* 2 *egg yolks*
1 *teaspoon grated orange rind*
1 *tablespoon Curaçao*

Set oven at 340 degrees F.
Five individual custard cups
One baking pan large enough to hold the cups

Scald the cream and blend with the orange juice. Beat in the sugar eggs and extra yolks and blend thoroughly. Add the orange rind and Curaçao. Pour the mixture into the custard cups. Set the cups in a pan filled with cold water and bake at 340 degrees F. for approximately 30 to 35 minutes or until a knife, when inserted into the center, comes out clean. Cool.

YIELD: 5 SERVINGS

SOUTHERN CUSTARD PUDDING

2 *cups milk*
4 *eggs*
¼ *cup molasses*
1 *pinch salt*
3 *drops vanilla extract*

Set oven at 350 degrees F.
Six individual custard cups, buttered and dusted with confectioners sugar
One baking pan large enough to hold the cups

Brush the custard cups with soft butter and dust with confectioners sugar, removing any excess by turning the cups upside down and knocking against a pastry board.

Heat the milk just to the boiling point. Beat the eggs, molasses, salt and vanilla together to blend. Remove the milk from the heat

and, in a slow stream, pour it gradually into the egg mixture, stirring rapidly. Blend all ingredients thoroughly. Strain and pour into the prepared custard cups. Place the cups in a deep pan filled with cold water and bake at 350 degrees F. for 35 minutes or until set. Cool before serving.
YIELD: 6 SERVINGS

MOCHA POTS DE CRÈME

2 cups light cream
1½ tablespoons instant coffee
6 egg yolks
½ cup granulated sugar
1 pinch salt

Set oven at 325 degrees F.
Six individual custard cups
One baking pan large enough to hold the cups

Scald the cream. Add the instant coffee and stir well to dissolve. In a deep bowl beat the egg yolks, sugar and salt together until light and fluffy. Gradually, while beating constantly, add cream mixture. Strain. Pour into the custard cups and cover with foil or the accompanying lids. Place the cups in a pan filled with water and bake at 325 degrees F. for approximately 15 to 18 minutes or until the point of a knife, when inserted through the center, comes out clean. Chill.
YIELD: 6 SERVINGS

VANILLA POTS DE CRÈME

2 cups light cream
1 vanilla bean or 1 teaspoon vanilla extract
½ cup granulated sugar
5 egg yolks
whipped cream, to garnish (optional)

Set oven at 325 degrees F.
Six individual custard cups
One baking pan large enough to hold the cups

Place the cream, vanilla bean or extract and ¼ cup of the sugar in saucepan and heat to the boiling point. Remove from heat. Beat the egg yolks with the remaining ¼ cup of sugar until fluffy. While stirring rapidly, add the hot cream in a slow stream to the yolks. Blend well. Strain. Pour into the custard cups and set in a deep pan filled with cold water. Cover each mold individually with its own lid or cover the entire pan with aluminum foil. Bake at 325 degrees F. for approximately 15 minutes or until the point of a knife, when inserted through the center, comes out clean. Cool and, if you wish, garnish with whipped cream.

YIELD: 6 SERVINGS

CHOCOLATE POTS DE CRÈME

A favorite of the French gourmet!

1 *cup milk*
1 *cup light cream*
1 *vanilla bean*
1½ *oz. sweet chocolate*
2 *whole eggs plus* 2 *egg yolks*
¼ *cup granulated sugar*
whipped cream to garnish (optional)

Set oven at 325 degrees F.
Six individual custard cups
One pan large enough to hold the cups

Place the milk, cream and vanilla bean in a saucepan and heat to the boiling point. Remove from heat; chop the chocolate into small pieces and add it to the hot mixture. Stir to dissolve. Remove the vanilla bean. Beat the eggs and extra yolks together with the sugar until fluffy. Gradually blend the hot chocolate mixture into the eggs. Fill the custard cups and place in a deep pan filled with cold water. Cover each mold individually with its own lid or cover the entire pan with aluminum foil. Bake at 325 degrees F. for 18 to 20 minutes or until the custard is set. Cool and, if desired, garnish with whipped cream before serving.

YIELD: 6 SERVINGS

Note: The greatest care should be taken for the proper baking of this delightful but very delicate dessert. See instructions for the preparation and baking of custard, page 253.

FLOATING ISLAND
(Oeufs à la neige)

5 eggs, separated
1 pinch salt
⅔ cup fine granulated sugar
1 cup milk
1 cup light cream
1 vanilla bean or 2 drops vanilla extract
2 tablespoons granulated sugar

Beat the egg whites and salt together until they form soft peaks. While beating constantly, gradually add the fine granulated sugar. Continue beating until stiff. Scald the milk and cream; then bring them to a slow boil. Add the vanilla bean or extract and the granulated sugar. Scoop out the meringue with a large wet spoon or ice cream scoop and drop it, in 5 or 6 individual portions, into the boiling milk. Cook for approximately 2 minutes, turning gently with a wooden spoon from time to time to insure even cooking. Remove and drain well. Strain the milk mixture and reserve. Beat the egg yolks in a deep bowl. Gradually add the hot milk mixture, beating rapidly with a wire whip to prevent curdling. Cook in a saucepan over low heat, stirring constantly. *Do not boil.* Chill. Just before serving, pour the sauce into a deep serving dish and drop the cooked meringues on top.

YIELD: 5 TO 6 SERVINGS

Note: The sauce may be flavored with chocolate or coffee. Stir either 2 squares grated sweet chocolate or 2 tablespoons instant coffee into the hot sauce.

CARAMEL FLOATING ISLAND

A spectacular and easy-to-prepare dessert. Poached meringue is sprinkled with golden caramel and floated on top of a rich custard cream. Sliced pistachio, dusted over the top, adds glamor and color to this ultra-tasty French classic.

MERINGUES

2 cups milk
1 vanilla bean or 2 drops of vanilla extract
4 egg whites
¾ cup granulated sugar
caramel sugar (see below)
rich custard cream (see below)
sliced pistachio nuts

Heat the milk and vanilla to the boiling point. Beat the egg whites until they form soft peaks. Add the sugar gradually and continue beating until stiff but not dry. Drop in 5 individual portions into the simmering milk, using a large wet spoon or an ice cream scoop. Cook over very low heat, turning gently and cooking for 2 minutes on each side or until the meringue is firm. Remove from the hot milk, and drain on a towel. Arrange the meringues side by side on a large *serving* tray and chill. Strain the milk and set it aside for the preparation of the sauce. In the meantime prepare the following:

CARAMEL SUGAR

⅔ cup granulated sugar *⅓ cup water*

Combine the sugar and water in a deep saucepan. Cook over medium heat until golden brown or approximately 330 degrees F. on a candy thermometer. Place the saucepan with the hot syrup over a pan filled with hot water.

CREAM FOR CARAMEL FLOATING ISLAND

leftover milk from the poached meringue
½ cup light cream
4 egg yolks
⅓ cup granulated sugar

Combine the leftover milk with the light cream and bring just to the boil over medium heat while stirring constantly. Beat the egg yolks and sugar together until light and fluffy. Stir the hot milk and cream gradually into the yolks. Beat rapidly to blend all ingredients thoroughly. Return to heat and cook the custard until it becomes thick enough to coat the spoon. *Do not boil.* Remove from the heat and chill in refrigerator or over cold water.

To finish and serve pour the cream into a deep serving dish. Place the meringues on top and sprinkle the caramel sugar over the poached meringues with a fork. Garnish with pistachio nuts. Serve immediately ice cold.

YIELD: 5 SERVINGS

CHOCOLATE SNOW EGGS

2½ cups milk
1 vanilla bean or 1 teaspoon vanilla flavoring
1 cup fine granulated sugar
4 egg whites
Chocolate Sauce for snow eggs (see below)

Heat the milk, vanilla and ¼ cup fine granulated sugar to the boiling point. In the meantime, beat the egg whites stiff but not dry, adding the remaining sugar gradually while beating. Drop the egg whites into the sugared milk in 4 or 5 individual portions, using a large wet spoon or ice cream scoop. Simmer over very low heat, turning gently, for approximately 2 minutes or until the meringue balls are firm. Remove from the milk and drain on a towel. Pile meringues onto a serving tray and chill. Strain the milk and reserve for the following sauce.

CHOCOLATE SAUCE FOR CHOCOLATE SNOW EGGS

¼ cup sugar
4 egg yolks
1 tablespoon brandy
2 cups sugared milk left over from the meringue
⅓ cup cocoa

Beat the sugar and egg yolks until light and fluffy. Add the brandy. Stir in the hot milk and cocoa and cook over a low heat, stirring constantly, until the mixture becomes thick enough to coat the spoon. *Do not boil.* Chill. Pour into a deep serving bowl. Arrange the chilled meringues on top and serve.
YIELD: 4 TO 5 SERVINGS

WINE CUSTARD

2 cups Sauterne wine
⅓ cup granulated sugar
pinch of ground nutmeg
6 egg yolks
whipped cream to garnish, optional

Set oven at 325 degrees F.
Six individual custard cups
One baking pan large enough to hold the cups

Place the wine, sugar and nutmeg in a saucepan and heat to the boiling point. Remove from heat and, while cooling, beat the egg yolks in a bowl over hot water until fluffy and pale in color. Pour the hot wine in a slow stream into the beaten yolks and continue beating for approximately 1 minute. *Do not boil.* Strain and pour into the baking cups. Set the cups in a pan filled with cold water and bake at 325 degrees F. for approximately 40 to 45 minutes or until a knife, when inserted through the center of the custard, comes out clean. Cool and, if desired, serve garnished with whipped cream.
YIELD: 6 SERVINGS

BREAD PUDDING

2 cups diced stale bread (about 4 slices)
½ cup melted butter
½ cup seedless raisins
3 eggs
½ cup plus 2 tablespoons granulated sugar
1 pinch salt
3 cups milk
1 pinch ground cinnamon
1 recipe for Custard Sauce (page 293)

Set oven at 325 degrees F.
One 1½-quart baking dish, greased
One baking pan large enough to hold the dish

Brush the bread slices with melted butter and dice. Blend the diced bread and raisins together and sprinkle in the bottom of the prepared baking dish. Beat the eggs, ½ cup sugar and salt together until light. Stir the milk into the beaten eggs. Blend all ingredients well and pour into the prepared dish. (Bread and raisins will come to the surface.) Place the dish in a pan filled with cold water and bake at 325 degrees F. for approximately 1 hour or until the point of a knife, when inserted in the center, comes out clean. Cool to lukewarm. Brush with the remaining melted butter. Mix the remaining sugar with the cinnamon and dust the top. Serve from the baking dish accompanied by Custard Sauce.
YIELD: APPROXIMATELY 6 SERVINGS

SNOW LIME PUDDING

2 tablespoons butter
2/3 cup granulated sugar
3 teaspoons grated lime rind
3 eggs, separated
1 cup creamed cottage cheese
2 tablespoons all-purpose flour
3 drops green food coloring
1/4 cup fresh strained lime juice

Set oven at 325 degrees F.
Six individual custard cups, buttered and dusted with confectioners sugar
One pan large enough to hold the cups

Cream the butter, sugar and lime rind together. Blend the egg yolks into the cottage cheese and beat well until fluffy and smooth. Stir in the flour, food coloring and lime juice and blend in the butter, sugar and lime rind mixture. Beat the egg whites until stiff but not dry and fold gently into the cheese mixture. Spoon into the prepared custard cups and place in a pan filled with cold water. Bake at 325 degrees F. for approximately 25 to 30 minutes or until firm. Cool before serving.
YIELD: 6 SERVINGS

GELATIN DESSERT PUDDINGS AND MOUSSES

UNFLAVORED GELATIN:
Unflavored gelatin is used in many of the following attractive and tasty pudding formulas. Gelatin should always be softened over hot water and allowed to stand for approximately 5 minutes. Too much gelatin will stiffen the pudding more than is necessary and alter the final taste. If an insufficient amount of gelatin is added, or if it is not sufficiently dissolved, the pudding will collapse and all your efforts will be fruitless.

Gelatin dessert puddings, like custard gelatin desserts, are simple to make and can be prepared successfully a day ahead.

FLAVORED GELATIN:
Gelatin is available in various flavors and colors at any grocery store.

TO UNMOLD GELATIN DESSERTS:
Quickly dip the mold into hot water. Loosen the sides by slipping a sharp knife all around the edges of the mold. Place a chilled serving dish on top of the mold and reverse while holding the dish tightly against the mold; carefully lift off the mold.

SETTING A GELATIN DESSERT:
Never fold whipped cream into a hot or warm mixture; this would cause the cream to separate and the mixture to curdle. "Cool the mixture until it starts to set" means to cool the ingredients until the liquid is becoming firm or until the mixture mounds slightly when dropped from a spoon. This is the precise time to fold in the whipped cream as outlined in the recipe.

Note: Curiously enough, gelatin desserts mixed with fresh pineapple will not become firm unless the pineapple is boiled in water first. This, however, does not apply to canned pineapple.

VANILLA BAVARIAN CREAM

1 *envelope or 1 tablespoon unflavored gelatin*
¼ *cup hot water*
4 *egg yolks*
½ *cup granulated sugar*
1½ *cups milk, scalded*
1 *pinch of salt*
3 *drops of vanilla extract*
1 *cup heavy cream, whipped stiff*
additional whipped cream, to garnish
fresh or frozen fruit, to garnish

One 1-quart bowl or 7 chilled champagne glasses

Soften the gelatin in hot water for approximately 5 minutes. Beat the egg yolks and sugar together until light and fluffy. Add the scalded milk and softened gelatin. Cook over hot water until the mixture becomes thick enough to coat the spoon. *Do not boil.* Stir constantly. Remove from heat and add the salt and vanilla extract. Cool in refrigerator or over cold water stirring from time to time to accelerate cooling. When the mixture starts to set fold in the whipped cream. Blend all ingredients thoroughly.

FOR LARGE SERVINGS:
Pour the mixture into a 1-quart bowl. Chill for about 3 hours or until firm. Unmold onto a large chilled serving tray. Decorate with additional whipped cream and serve. If desired, garnish with fresh or thawed and drained frozen fruits such as strawberries, blueberries or peaches, etc.
YIELD: 6 SERVINGS

FOR UNMOLDED INDIVIDUAL SERVINGS:
Place 1 tablespoon fresh or thawed and drained frozen fruits, such as strawberries, blueberries or peaches in the bottoms of 7 chilled champagne glasses. Pour the Bavarian mixture on top and chill in refrigerator for 2 hours or until set. Decorate each glass with a rosette of whipped cream.
YIELD: 7 INDIVIDUAL SERVINGS

CHOCOLATE BAVARIAN CREAM

1 *envelope or 1 tablespoon unflavored gelatin*
1/4 *cup hot water*
2 *cups milk, scalded*
3 *oz. or 3 squares sweet chocolate*
1 *oz. or 1 square unsweetened chocolate*
4 *egg yolks*
1/2 *cup granulated sugar*
1 *pinch salt*
1 *cup heavy cream, whipped stiff*

One 1-quart bowl or 7 individual dessert glasses

Soften the gelatin in hot water for approximately 5 minutes. Scald the milk and add the chocolates. Stir to dissolve. Beat the egg yolks and sugar together until light and fluffy. Add the chocolate mixture gradually into the beaten yolks while stirring rapidly. Place over hot water and cook until the mixture becomes thick enough to coat the spoon. *Do not boil.* Stir constantly. Remove from heat; stir in the soaked gelatin and salt and dissolve thoroughly. Strain into a deep bowl and cool in refrigerator or over cold water, stirring from time to time to accelerate cooling. When the mixture starts to set fold in the whipped cream and blend all ingredients thoroughly. Proceed as explained in Vanilla Bavarian Cream (page 265).
YIELD: ONE 1-QUART DISH OR 7 INDIVIDUAL SERVINGS

MOCHA BAVARIAN CREAM

Follow the recipe for Vanilla Bavarian Cream (page 265). Stir 2 tablespoons instant coffee into the scalded milk. Garnish with whipped cream and sprinkle with grated sweet chocolate.

YIELD: ONE 1-QUART DISH OR 7 INDIVIDUAL SERVINGS

STRAWBERRY BAVARIAN CREAM

1 *envelope or 1 tablespoon unflavored gelatin*
¼ *cup hot water*
1⅓ *cups crushed fresh ripe strawberries*
1 *teaspoon lemon juice*
3 *drops red food coloring*
⅓ *cup granulated sugar*
1 *cup heavy cream, whipped stiff*
additional whipped cream, to garnish
whole fresh strawberries, to garnish

One 1-quart bowl or 6 individual dessert or pudding cups

Soak the gelatin in hot water for approximately 5 minutes. Place over hot water and stir to dissolve. Crush the strawberries and add the lemon juice, food coloring and granulated sugar. Let soak for about 5 minutes; then stir in the dissolved gelatin. Blend well and chill until the mixture starts to set. Quickly fold in the whipped cream. Pour into a chilled 1-quart dish or 6 individual chilled pudding cups and chill in the refrigerator for 1 hour, or until set. Decorate with additional whipped cream and whole fresh strawberries.

YIELD: ONE 1-QUART DISH OR 6 INDIVIDUAL SERVINGS

WINE BAVARIAN PUDDING

2 *eggs, separated, plus 1 yolk*
⅓ *cup plus 2 tablespoons granulated sugar*
½ *cup Rhine wine*
⅓ *cup orange juice*
1 *tablespoon lemon juice*
1 *envelope or 1 tablespoon unflavored gelatin*
¼ *cup hot water*
½ *cup whipped cream*
additional whipped cream, to garnish (optional)
fresh or frozen fruit, to garnish

One 1-quart bowl, chilled, or 6 chilled champagne glasses

Beat the egg yolks and ⅓ cup of sugar together until light and fluffy. Stir in the wine, orange juice and lemon juice. Blend all ingredients well in a deep bowl and place over hot water, beating constantly until the custard thickens. Sprinkle the gelatin over hot water, stirring from time to time to help dissolve. Add the gelatin to the yolk mixture and blend thoroughly. Place in refrigerator or over cold water until the custard starts to set. Meanwhile beat the egg whites with the 2 tablespoons of sugar and whip the cream. Fold these quickly into the chilled custard and mix thoroughly. Pour into a 1-quart chilled bowl or 6 chilled champagne glasses. Cool in the refrigerator for 2 hours or until firm. Serve garnished with fresh or thawed and drained frozen fruits of your choice. Decorate with additional whipped cream if desired.

YIELD: 6 SERVINGS

SPANISH CREAM

2⅔ *cups milk*
1 *envelope or 1 tablespoon unflavored gelatin*
¼ *cup hot water*
3 *eggs, separated*
1 *teaspoon vanilla extract*
½ *cup granulated sugar*

One 1-quart bowl or 8 individual molds or custard cups

Scald the milk. Soak the gelatin in hot water and stir into the milk to dissolve. Beat the egg yolks, vanilla and ¼ cup of sugar in a deep bowl until light and fluffy. Gradually, and in a slow stream, pour the hot milk into the beaten egg yolks. Blend all ingredients well. Place over hot water and cook until the mixture becomes thick enough to coat the spoon. *Do not boil.* Remove from heat and cool in the refrigerator or over ice water until the mixture starts to set. Beat the egg whites stiff, adding the remaining ¼ cup of sugar gradually while beating. Fold into the gelatin mixture and pour into a 1-quart dish or 8 individual molds or custard cups. Chill until firm and serve with additional whipped cream, Strawberry Sauce or Custard Sauce (page 293).

YIELD: 8 SERVINGS

CHOCOLATE SPANISH CREAM

Follow the above recipe for Spanish cream, adding 2 oz. or 2 squares of grated unsweetened chocolate to the scalded milk. Stir to dissolve. Beat the egg yolks with ½ cup of sugar instead of ¼ cup.

APPLE DELIGHT PUDDING

1 envelope or 1 tablespoon unflavored gelatin
⅓ cup hot water
2 cups apple sauce
½ cup granulated sugar
juice of 1 lemon
grated rind of 1 lemon
½ teaspoon ground cinnamon
½ cup whipped cream
Melba Sauce (page 290)
whipped cream, to garnish

One 1-quart bowl or dish, lightly oiled

Soften the gelatin in hot water. Place the apple sauce, sugar, lemon juice, lemon rind and cinnamon in a saucepan and slowly bring to a boil, stirring from time to time to avoid burning. Add the softened gelatin to the apple sauce and cool in refrigerator or over cold water, stirring from time to time until the mixture starts to set. Fold in the whipped cream. Pour into the prepared bowl or dish and allow to set in refrigerator for approximately 3 hours or until firm. Dip quickly in hot water and unmold onto a chilled serving tray. Serve with Melba Sauce and garnish with whipped cream.
YIELD: 5 TO 6 SERVINGS

CHARLOTTE AUX FRAISES
(Strawberry Charlotte)

1½ pints fresh strawberries
⅓ cup granulated sugar
juice of 1 lemon
1 tablespoon or one envelope unflavored gelatin
¼ cup hot water
4 egg yolks, beaten with a fork
1 cup heavy cream

Line sides and bottom of a 1½-quart Charlotte mold, or any other deep mold of your choice, with 18 to 20 lady fingers (see page 110)

Wash, hull and drain the strawberries. Reserve several large whole ones to garnish. Force the rest through a sieve. Measure ⅔ cup of thick purée and combine purée with the sugar, lemon juice and softened gelatin. Cook over hot water, stirring constantly until the gelatin is well dissolved. Remove from heat and stir in the beaten egg yolks. Blend all ingredients well. Chill over cold water or in the refrigerator, stirring from time to time to accelerate the cooling process. Beat the cream until stiff. When the fruit mixture starts to set, fold in the whipped cream gently and pour into the prepared Charlotte mold. Chill in the refrigerator for 5 hours or until set. Reverse onto a large chilled serving tray. Decorate with fresh strawberries. Serve with Custard Sauce (page 293) or any other sauce of your choice.

YIELD: APPROXIMATELY 5 SERVINGS

CHARLOTTE RUSSE

approximately 26 lady fingers (see page 110)
1 recipe for Chocolate or Vanilla Bavarian Cream (pages 265, 266)
½ cup heavy cream, whipped

One 1½-quart soufflé dish, lined with paper

Cut the paper to fit the bottom of the soufflé dish. Cover entirely with approximately 8 lady fingers, attractively arranged. (They may have to be cut to fit properly.) Brush the sides of the mold with butter and line with approximately 18 lady fingers placed in an upright position and as close together as possible. Fill to the top with Vanilla or Chocolate Bavarian Cream. Place in the refrigerator or over cold water for approximately 2 hours or until set. Reverse onto a chilled serving tray. Garnish with whipped cream and serve.

YIELD: APPROXIMATELY 8 SERVINGS

FRESH APPLE MOUSSE

10 large cooking apples
½ cup sugar
¾ cup water
juice of 1 lemon
1 package or 1 tablespoon unflavored gelatin
⅓ cup hot water
2 cups whipped cream
2 tablespoons rum

Eight champagne glasses

Peel and core the apples and slice approximately ½-inch thick. Place in a saucepan with the sugar, ¾ cup of water and the lemon juice. Cook for 10 to 12 minutes or until the apples reach the consistency of a thick apple sauce; stir constantly to avoid burning.

Meanwhile, soften the gelatin in ⅓ cup hot water. Add it to the cooked apple mixture and beat well with a whip or electric mixer. Place in the refrigerator or over cold water, stirring from time to time to accelerate cooling. When the mixture starts to set, fold in the rum and the whipped cream. Pour into champagne glasses, chill for approximately 1 hour, or until set, and serve ice cold.
YIELD: 8 SERVINGS

CHOCOLATE MOUSSE

4 eggs, separated
¼ cup superfine granulated sugar
1 tablespoon Cognac
6 oz. semi-sweet grated chocolate
4 tablespoons good strong coffee
6 oz. or 6 tablespoons sweet butter, cut in small pieces
3 tablespoons granulated sugar
½ cup heavy cream whipped with
1 teaspoon granulated sugar
2 tablespoons roasted sliced almonds

One 1-quart mold or 8 individual dessert cups or
Eight champagne glasses

Beat the egg yolks and superfine sugar with a whisk or electric beater for approximately 3 minutes or until thick. Add the Cognac, set the

mixing bowl over hot water and continue beating for about 2 minutes, or until the mixture is hot. Remove from heat and place in the refrigerator for about 15 minutes or until cool. In a 1-quart saucepan, melt the chocolate in the hot coffee. Add the butter gradually and blend all ingredients well. Add the chocolate mixture to the yolk mixture and combine well. Beat the egg whites adding the granulated sugar gradually. Stir about ⅓ of the egg whites into the chocolate mixture, folding gently until they are well blended. Then fold in the remaining egg whites. Gently spoon the mousse into the mold, dessert cups or champagne glasses and refrigerate for about 1 hour or until cold. Whip the cream and granulated sugar until stiff. Decorate the mousse with whipped cream and roasted sliced almonds.
YIELD: 8 SERVINGS

CLASSIC CHOCOLATE MOUSSE

The original recipe for the French classic . . . so delightful!

4 *oz. or 4 squares sweet chocolate*
2 *tablespoons strong hot coffee*
4 *eggs, separated*
¼ *cup fine granulated sugar*
1 *teaspoon of Jamaica rum*
1 *cup of heavy cream whipped with one teaspoon of sugar*

Eight individual dessert cups or one 1½-quart soufflé dish

Grate the chocolate and melt over hot water, stirring constantly. Add hot coffee and blend well. Beat egg yolks and fine granulated sugar together with a whisk or electric beater for approximately 3 minutes or until they are thick and pale yellow in color. Stir in the chocolate mixture and rum. Whip the cream with the sugar then beat the egg whites stiff but not dry and *gently* fold into the chocolate mixture *alternately* with the whipped cream. Pour into chilled cups, champagne glasses or soufflé dish. Chill for approximately 1 hour or until set.
YIELD: APPROXIMATELY 8 SERVINGS

RUM EGG NOG MOUSSE

6 egg yolks
½ cup granulated sugar
⅓ cup Jamaica rum
½ teaspoon nutmeg
1½ cups heavy cream
6 to 8 maraschino cherries with stems
½ cup grated sweet chocolate

6 to 8 chilled champagne glasses

Beat the egg yolks and sugar together until light and fluffy. Stir in the rum and nutmeg. Beat the cream stiff and fold gently into the yolk mixture. Pour into chilled champagne glasses and decorate with a maraschino cherry. Chill in refrigerator for at least 2 hours. Just before serving, sprinkle with grated sweet chocolate.
YIELD: APPROXIMATELY 6 TO 8 SERVINGS

SABAYON MOUSSE

1 envelope or 1 tablespoon unflavored gelatin
⅓ cup hot water
1 cup boiling water
⅓ cup plus 3 tablespoons granulated sugar
½ cup Marsala wine
1 tablespoon kirsch
1 pinch ground nutmeg
4 egg whites
¾ cup heavy cream
ground nutmeg, to garnish (optional)

6 chilled champagne glasses

Sprinkle the gelatin over the hot water to soften. Stir in the boiling water and add ⅓ cup of the sugar, wine, kirsch and nutmeg. Beat for approximately 1 minute to dissolve all ingredients properly. Place in refrigerator or over cold water, stirring from time to time to accelerate cooling. When the mixture starts to set, beat egg whites stiff, adding 2 tablespoons of sugar gradually while beating and quickly fold into the gelatin mixture. Pour into chilled champagne glasses and refrigerate for approximately 1 hour, or until set. Before serving, garnish with ¾ cup cream whipped with 1 tablespoon of sugar. If desired, dust with a little ground nutmeg.
YIELD: 6 SERVINGS

STRAWBERRY MOUSSE

1 pint fresh strawberries plus 12 whole strawberries
1 teaspoon unflavored gelatin
¼ cup hot water
½ cup granulated sugar
¾ cup whipped cream
2 egg whites, beaten stiff
1 tablespoon kirsch or Cointreau

6 chilled champagne glasses or a 1-quart serving dish, chilled

Wash and clean 1 pint of strawberries. Crush and drain the strawberries and reserve the juice. Sprinkle the gelatin over the reserved strawberry juice and let stand for a few minutes to soften. Pour the juice and gelatin over the hot water and stir rapidly until the gelatin is well dissolved. Add the crushed strawberries and the sugar; mix all ingredients thoroughly and chill in the refrigerator for approximately 1 hour. Fold the whipped cream and beaten egg whites alternately into the cooled mixture. Pour into chilled champagne glasses or a 1-quart serving dish and cool in the refrigerator for at least 2 hours, or in the freezer for approximately 30 minutes, until firm.

Just before serving, sprinkle with a few drops of kirsch or Cointreau and decorate with the whole strawberries.

YIELD: 6 SERVINGS

BAVARIAN RASPBERRY MOUSSE
(made with fresh raspberries)

1½ tablespoons or 1½ pkgs. unflavored gelatin
¼ cup hot water
¾ cup granulated sugar
¾ cup boiling water
2½ cups fresh ripe raspberries
6 egg whites
1 cup heavy cream, whipped
24 whole raspberries

One 1½-quart ring mold, lightly oiled

Soften the gelatin in the hot water. Cook ½ cup of sugar and the boiling water in a saucepan for approximately 3 minutes. Add the raspberries and continue cooking until the fruits are soft and tender. Pass the raspberries and syrup through a fine strainer and stir in the gelatin. Cool in refrigerator or over cold water, stirring from time to time to accelerate cooling. When the mixture starts to set beat the egg whites with the remaining ¼ cup of sugar and fold into the cooled mixture alternately with the whipped cream. Blend all ingredients well. Pour into a lightly oiled ring mold and chill for at least 3 hours or until firm. Unmold and serve with whole fresh raspberries piled in the center of the ring.

YIELD: 6 SERVINGS

CHEESE DELIGHT
(Cheese with cream)

Quick and spectacular!

8 *oz. cream cheese*
3 *tablespoons confectioners sugar*
1 *tablespoon Grand Marnier*
¾ *cup whipped cream (slightly less than ½ cup heavy cream)*
¾ *cup sliced fresh or thawed and drained frozen strawberries*
¾ *cup diced fresh or canned pineapple, drained*
6 *maraschino cherries*
5 *tablespoons granulated sugar, optional*
1 *tablespoon cinnamon, optional*

6 chilled champagne or sherbet glasses

Cream the cheese until fluffy; add the confectioners sugar and Grand Marnier. Blend well. Fold in the whipped cream. Place the strawberries and pineapple in the bottom of 6 chilled champagne or sherbet glasses. Pour the cheese mixture over the fruits and chill for at least 3 hours or until firm. Decorate each serving with a maraschino cherry and, if desired, dust slightly with the granulated sugar and cinnamon, mixed together.

YIELD: 6 SERVINGS

Note: Other fresh, canned or frozen fruits can be substituted.

STEAMED PUDDING

INDIAN PUDDING

2 cups milk
2 cups light cream
½ cup yellow cornmeal
3 tablespoons melted butter
½ cup light molasses
1 tablespoon grated orange rind
¾ teaspoon salt
1 teaspoon ground cinnamon
1 pinch ground ginger
2 eggs, beaten with a fork
1 recipe for Custard Sauce (page 293) or 1 cup whipped cream

Set oven at 360 degrees F.
One 1½-quart soufflé dish
One pan large enough to hold the soufflé dish

Scald the milk and cream together in a deep saucepan. Gradually stir in the cornmeal and cook over medium heat, stirring constantly, for approximately 15 minutes or until the cornmeal is tender. Remove from heat. Combine the melted butter, molasses, orange rind, salt and spices. Beat the eggs and stir alternately with the molasses mixture into the cooked cornmeal. Pour into the soufflé or serving dish and place in a pan filled with water. Bake at 360 degrees F. for approximately 50 minutes or until set. Serve warm with Custard Sauce or whipped cream.
YIELD: 6 SERVINGS

Frostings, Sauces & Candies

WHIPPED CREAM TOPPINGS

CHOCOLATE WHIPPED CREAM

1 cup heavy cream
2 tablespoons cocoa
2½ tablespoons granulated sugar

Beat the heavy cream until it holds its shape. Combine the cocoa and granulated sugar and stir into the cream. Continue beating until stiff.
YIELD: APPROXIMATELY 2 CUPS

COFFEE-FLAVORED WHIPPED CREAM

1 tablespoon instant coffee
2 tablespoons boiling water
1 cup heavy cream, chilled
2 tablespoons sugar

Dissolve the instant coffee in the boiling water and chill over cold water or in the refrigerator. Meanwhile, beat the heavy cream and sugar together. When the cream begins to hold its shape, add the coffee mixture and continue whipping until stiff.

YIELD: APPROXIMATELY 2 CUPS

SPUN SUGAR

Spun sugar is undoubtedly a superb finish for many classic desserts. However, the making of spun sugar requires some experience and a very dry day. Dry weather must prevail in order for the sugar to hold its shape; dampness will rapidly melt it. Properly made, spun sugar is an attractive and magic-like garnishing for many frozen desserts. The fine threads of sugar resemble silk and can be quickly shaped into numerous forms such as nests, cups, etc., while still warm. Spun sugar will harden quickly and retain its shape. Do not store spun sugar in the refrigerator.

2½ *cups granulated sugar*
1 *cup water*
1 *teaspoon glucose*
1 *pinch cream of tartar*

Heat sugar and water stirring from time to time until the sugar is completely dissolved. (See detailed instructions on how to cook sugar properly, page 12.) Cook the syrup rapidly until the candy thermometer reaches 260 degrees F. Add the glucose and cream of tartar and continue cooking until the sugar reaches the hard crack stage or 312 degrees F. on a candy thermometer. Remove from heat and set the hot pan into water to prevent any further cooking of the sugar. Oil the handles of two long wooden spoons or broom handles and lay them, approximately 1½ feet apart, on a table with the ends projecting over the edges. Fasten each end with a weight to secure them on the table. Cover the floor underneath with paper or large baking sheet pans. Dip a wire whip, egg beater or several forks into the hot syrup and move the utensils rapidly back and forth over the handles. Repeat again and again until enough thread has accumulated. Shape quickly into desired forms.

YIELD: 2 CUPS OF SPUN SUGAR

Note: Any chosen food coloring can be added to cooked syrup.

FONDANT ICING

FONDANT ICING

3 *cups granulated sugar*
1 *cup water*
1 *pinch (or 1/8 teaspoon) cream of tartar*

Combine all ingredients in a deep saucepan and place over medium heat. Stir from time to time with a wooden spoon until the sugar is well melted. Increase the heat and cook rapidly until the temperature reaches 236 degrees F. on a candy thermometer. (For detailed instructions on how to cook sugar, see page 12.) Wash down the sides of the pan from time to time with a flat brush dipped in cold water to prevent any crystal formation. When the sugar has reached the desired temperature, remove from heat and transfer to the bowl of an electric mixer and cool to lukewarm or around 104 degrees F. Then work with a paddle at slow speed until the syrup becomes white and creamy. (If an electric mixer is not available, work the mixture back and forth with a wooden spoon until the syrup becomes creamy and pale in color. Then knead until smooth and creamy.) When the consistency of a rather solid paste is reached, stop the mixer and store the fondant in a jar with a tight cover. Fondant should remain in the refrigerator for at least 2 days before using. Pastry chefs have hundreds of uses for fondant. It should always be heated to *lukewarm* over hot water until creamy and of pouring consistency. Do not overheat the icing or it will lose its gloss. Fondant icing can be flavored and colored according to your need.

YIELD: 2 CUPS

CHOCOLATE FONDANT ICING is simply made by adding melted sweet chocolate and a small amount of hot water to fondant icing. A suitable proportion is: 3 oz. or 3 squares melted chocolate and 1 tablespoon hot water to 2 cups of fondant icing. Stir until well mixed.

COFFEE FONDANT ICING is made by stirring 1½ tablespoons instant coffee diluted with 1 tablespoon hot water into 2 cups of fondant icing. Stir until well mixed.

LIQUEUR FONDANT ICING is made by stirring 1 tablespoon of the liqueur of your choice into 1 cup of fondant icing.

DECORATOR ICING

HINTS FOR MAKING DECORATOR ICING

1. Always use egg whites at room temperature.
2. When making icing, all utensils must be free of grease and should be well rinsed in hot water before use.
3. Stainless steel or porcelain bowls are recommended for beating; tin or metal bowls might have some tiny rust spots that would cause the icing to become discolored.
4. Sifted confectioners sugar is always used for making this type of icing.
5. Always keep the icing bowl covered with a damp cloth to prevent any crust formation.
6. Do not allow the icing to harden inside your tools, tubes, bags or mixing bowls. When not using the utensils any longer, submerge them immediately in water to facilitate cleaning.

ROYAL ICING

Royal icing is the most widely used icing for decorating purposes.

1 *egg white at room temperature*
1½ *cups or 6 oz. sifted confectioners sugar*
1 *small pinch cream of tartar or*
2 *drops lemon juice*

Place the egg white in a mixing bowl with a paddle and beat for 2 minutes (or use a small bowl and electric mixer) gradually adding approximately 1 cup of the sifted confectioners sugar. Continue beating while adding the remaining sugar. Add the cream of tartar or lemon juice, and continue beating for approximately 10 minutes at moderate speed until the icing is stiff and holds its shape.*

* *Note:* If Royal Icing is to be used for spreading on top of pastries, such as Conversations, Allumettes, etc., do not beat icing too stiff, only thick enough to be spread over the prepared pastries.

To determine if decorator Royal Icing is ready to be used, withdraw the paddle from the batter; if the icing stands up in a sharp point and does not fall back, it is ready for piping.

The consistency of the icing is *most* important; therefore, depending upon the size of the egg used, a little more or less sugar may be necessary.

Coloring of your choice can be added after the beating process and as soon as the Royal Icing has reached the proper consistency.

MERINGUES

MERINGUE TOPPING FOR PIES, TARTS OR OTHER DESSERTS

½ cup egg whites at room temperature (3 or 4 whites)
½ teaspoon lemon juice
½ cup fine granulated sugar blended with
½ teaspoon cornstarch

Beat egg whites until foamy; add lemon juice. Gradually add sugar and cornstarch, a little at a time, and continue beating until stiff.

Pile, spread or squeeze meringue topping over a cooled and firm filling. Bake at 400 degrees F. for approximately 15 minutes or until golden brown. Remove from heat and let stand until cold before attempting to cut and serve.

ITALIAN MERINGUE

This meringue is an ideal filling, frosting or topping for pies, tarts, cakes or frozen desserts.

1 *cup fine granulated sugar*
⅓ *cup water*
1 *pinch cream of tartar or 3 drops lemon juice*
3 *egg whites, at room temperature*
1 *teaspoon vanilla extract*

Cook the sugar, water and cream of tartar or lemon juice together until the temperature reaches 245 degrees F. Beat the egg whites stiff and pour the cooked syrup slowly and in a continuous stream into the whites. Continue beating to ensure a proper blending and to prevent the egg whites from cooking while in contact with the hot syrup. Stir in the vanilla and beat at medium speed until cool. Use immediately while the meringue holds its shape.

YIELD: ENOUGH FROSTING FOR ONE 9-INCH LAYER OR ONE 9-INCH PIE

Note: Timing is an important factor in the preparation of this meringue. The egg whites should be stiff when the syrup is ready to pour. Undercooked syrup will result in frosting that is too soft; overcooked syrup will produce a frosting that is dark in color. Be sure to time yourself and keep an accurate watch for the proper temperature on your candy thermometer. Start beating the egg whites when the sugar has reached a temperature of approximately 230 degrees F. Increase or decrease the heat under the sugar according to the consistency of the egg whites.

CHOCOLATE ITALIAN MERINGUE

When the meringue has been beaten to the point where it holds its shape, add 3 squares or 3 oz. of melted unsweetened chocolate.

CARAMEL ITALIAN MERINGUE

Use brown sugar instead of fine granulated sugar.

FRENCH MERINGUE

For topping pies, tarts or any desserts that are browned or baked in the oven.

3 *egg whites*
1/8 *teaspoon cream of tartar or 3 drops lemon juice*
1 *cup fine granulated sugar*
1/2 *teaspoon vanilla extract*

Beat the egg whites and cream of tartar or lemon juice together until they form soft peaks. Gradually add the granulated sugar and vanilla extract and continue beating at full speed until all the sugar has been incorporated or until the meringue is of a very stiff consistency and holds its shape. The sugar should be thoroughly melted.

YIELD: SUFFICIENT TOPPING FOR ONE 9-INCH PIE OR CAKE

SWISS MERINGUE

An ideal quick frosting for cakes, tarts or pies.

1 *cup fine granulated sugar*
1 *pinch salt*
1/8 *teaspoon cream of tartar*
3 *egg whites*
2 *drops vanilla extract*

Combine all ingredients in a large deep bowl. Heat over hot water until hot (about 120 degrees F.), beating constantly to dissolve the sugar and to prevent coagulation of the eggs. Remove from heat and whip with an electric mixer or rotary beater for approximately 5 minutes or until the meringue holds its shape.

YIELD: ENOUGH FROSTING FOR ONE 9-INCH PIE OR CAKE

CHOCOLATE SWISS MERINGUE

When the meringue has been whipped to the stage where it holds its shape, add 3 squares or 3 oz. melted unsweetened chocolate.

CHOCOLATE MERINGUE TOPPING

An ideal topping for pies, tarts or custards.

3 *egg whites*
3/4 *cup granulated sugar*
1 *tablespoon dark cocoa, sifted*
1/2 *teaspoon vanilla*
confectioners sugar, to dust

Beat the egg whites; gradually add the sugar, then the sifted cocoa and continue beating until stiff. Stir in the vanilla. Dust with confectioners sugar and brown in a 375 degree F. oven.

YIELD: ENOUGH TOPPING FOR ONE 9-INCH PIE

BUTTERCREAMS

RICH BUTTERCREAM

¾ cup granulated sugar
¼ cup water
1 small pinch cream of tartar
5 egg yolks, beaten
1⅓ cups sweet butter at room temperature
3 drops vanilla extract

Combine the sugar, water and cream of tartar in a deep saucepan. Cook until hard ball stage or when the temperature on a candy thermometer reaches 245 degrees F. (For detailed instructions concerning cooking of sugar, see page 12.) Place the egg yolks in a deep bowl and beat with a wire whip, rotary beater or, better yet, an electric mixer. When the sugar has reached the correct temperature, pour the hot syrup gradually and in a continuous stream into the beaten yolks. Continue beating until the mixture is thick and cool. Add the butter gradually and whip all ingredients until creamy and light. Stir in the vanilla extract.

YIELD: ENOUGH FILLING AND FROSTING FOR ONE 9-INCH LAYER CAKE

Note: Buttercream filling will soften in a hot kitchen. Keep finished cakes in the refrigerator or in a cool place until serving time.

PRALINE BUTTERCREAM

Stir ¾ cup of Praline Powder (page 288) into the Rich Buttercream.

CHOCOLATE BUTTERCREAM

Melt 4 oz. or 4 squares semi-sweet chocolate over hot water, stirring constantly. Cool to lukewarm and stir into the Rich Buttercream. Blend thoroughly.

MOCHA BUTTERCREAM

Dissolve 3 tablespoons instant coffee in ¼ cup hot water. Cool to lukewarm. Stir the coffee mixture into the Rich Buttercream.

PISTACHIO BUTTERCREAM

Stir ⅓ cup finely chopped pistachio nuts into the Rich Buttercream. Add a few drops of red food coloring and 2 tablespoons of Grand Marnier.

LEMON OR ORANGE BUTTERCREAM
Stir 2 tablespoons of grated lemon or orange rind and 1 tablespoon of lemon or orange juice into the Rich Buttercream. Add a few drops of yellow food coloring and 2 tablespoons of Cointreau.

QUICK BUTTERCREAM

- ¾ *cup sweet butter at room temperature*
- 1½ *cups sifted confectioners sugar*
- 3 *egg yolks*
- *vanilla or any other desired extract, to taste*

Cream the butter until light and fluffy. Add the sifted sugar gradually. Stir in the egg yolks and beat until smooth. Add the flavor of your choice.

YIELD: ENOUGH FROSTING AND FILLING FOR ONE 9-INCH LAYER CAKE

Note: For flavoring Quick Buttercream, see instructions following the recipe for Rich Buttercream, page 284.

QUICK CHOCOLATE BUTTERCREAM

- 6 *oz. or 6 squares semi-sweet chocolate, melted*
- 5 *egg yolks*
- 1 *cup confectioners sugar*
- ½ *cup heavy cream*
- 1 *tablespoon instant coffee*
- 1¾ *cups soft butter*

Slowly melt the chocolate in a bowl over hot water while stirring constantly. Add the egg yolks, sugar and heavy cream to the melted chocolate and beat all ingredients vigorously over hot water for approximately 10 minutes. Add the instant coffee. Remove from heat and cool in refrigerator or over cold water, stirring from time to time to expedite cooling. When starting to set, add the softened butter and beat vigorously until smooth and fluffy.

YIELD: SUFFICIENT FILLING AND FROSTING FOR ONE 9- OR 10-INCH CAKE

Note: During the hot summer months, chill in the refrigerator before filling and icing cakes.

FROSTINGS, TOPPINGS AND FILLINGS

DELIGHT FROSTING

1½ cups granulated sugar
½ cup hot water
¼ teaspoon cream of tartar
4 egg whites, at room temperature (approximately ½ cup)
1 teaspoon vanilla extract
1 teaspoon grated lemon rind

Combine the sugar, water and cream of tartar in a deep saucepan and heat to 258 degrees F. or until a small amount of hot syrup, when dropped in cold water, forms a hard ball (for detailed instructions on how to cook sugar, see page 12). Beat the egg whites until stiff but not dry. Add the vanilla and lemon rind. Pour the hot syrup gradually into the egg whites while continuing to beat rapidly. Beat until lukewarm and thick.

YIELD: ENOUGH FROSTING FOR TWO 9-INCH LAYERS OF CAKE

CHOCOLATE DELIGHT FROSTING

Stir 3 oz. or 3 squares melted unsweetened chocolate into the Delight Frosting.

ORANGE DELIGHT FROSTING

Add 1 teaspoon orange extract to the Delight Frosting. Omit the grated lemon rind and substitute 2 teaspoons grated orange rind.

CHOCOLATE FROSTING

5 squares or 5 oz. unsweetened chocolate
2⅓ cups sifted confectioners sugar
¼ cup lukewarm water
2 egg yolks
6 tablespoons soft butter

Grate and melt the chocolate over hot water. Stir well to dissolve. Remove from heat and add the sugar and water. Beat rapidly. Add the egg yolks one at a time, beating well after each addition. Gradually stir in the butter, beating rapidly. Cool to lukewarm.

YIELD: SUFFICIENT FROSTING FOR TWO 9-INCH LAYERS

QUICK CHOCOLATE FROSTING

2 oz. or 2 squares unsweetened, grated chocolate
1 8-oz. can sweetened condensed milk
1 pinch salt
2 tablespoons whole milk
1 teaspoon instant coffee

Combine all ingredients in a saucepan. Place over hot water and cook until thick or for approximately 12 to 15 minutes, stirring constantly. Remove from the heat and cool to lukewarm.

YIELD: ENOUGH FROSTING AND FILLING FOR ONE 9-INCH CAKE

CARAMEL FROSTING

1¼ cups dark brown sugar
1½ cups granulated sugar
1⅓ cups milk
1 pinch salt
3 tablespoons butter

Combine the sugars and milk in a deep saucepan. Heat to 236 degrees F. or until the syrup forms a soft ball when dropped into cold water. Remove from heat. Add the butter and salt and cool to lukewarm. Beat vigorously until creamy and of spreading consistency.

YIELD: ENOUGH FILLING AND FROSTING FOR ONE 9-INCH LAYER CAKE

LEMON CREAM FILLING

¼ cup cornstarch
⅔ cup plus 1 tablespoon granulated sugar
1 teaspoon grated lemon rind
⅔ cup water
⅓ cup lemon juice
2 egg yolks
3 tablespoons melted butter

Combine the cornstarch, ⅔ cup of sugar, lemon rind, water and lemon juice in a deep saucepan. Place over medium heat and cook, stirring constantly, until the mixture thickens and almost reaches the boiling point. Remove from heat. Combine the egg yolks, remaining tablespoon of sugar and melted butter and blend gradually into the hot mixture while beating rapidly. Return to low heat and cook a little more until the mixture mounds slightly when dropped from a spoon. Remove from heat and cool.

YIELD: ENOUGH FILLING FOR TWO 9-INCH LAYERS

LIME FILLING

Follow the recipe for Lemon Cream Filling and substitute lime rind and juice for lemon.

PRALINE POWDER

1 *cup granulated sugar*
1 *cup whole almonds or hazelnuts*

One 10 x 10-inch baking sheet, oiled

Melt the sugar in a saucepan over a low flame; stir constantly until it turns a dark, golden color. Remove from heat and quickly stir in the almonds or hazelnuts. Immediately pour and spread the hot mixture onto the prepared baking sheet. Cool thoroughly. Crush the caramel and nut mixture into a very fine powder using a heavy rolling pin or an electric grinder. Store in a dry place in a tightly closed jar.
YIELD: APPROXIMATELY 1½ CUPS

Note: Praline Powder, also called Filbert Paste, can be bought from your retail bakery. You will need 1½ tablespoons of Praline Powder to flavor 1 cup of Vanilla Pastry Cream or Custard Sauce.

CREAMS

FRANGIPANE CREAM

¾ *cup almond paste*
1 *cup granulated sugar*
2 *whole eggs plus* 1 *egg yolk*
½ *cup butter at room temperature*
½ *cup sifted cake flour*
grated rind of 1 *lemon*
1 *teaspoon rum*

Blend the almond paste and granulated sugar together by kneading or mixing until a smooth paste is obtained. Add the egg yolk and mix thoroughly. Add the butter and continue mixing for approximately 1 minute longer. Add the 2 whole eggs, 1 at a time, creaming well after each addition. Scrape the sides and bottom of the bowl to obtain a cream free of lumps. Stir in the sifted flour, lemon and rum and blend all ingredients thoroughly to a smooth cream. Store in a cool place until ready for use.

YIELD: APPROXIMATELY 3 CUPS

Note: Almond paste can be purchased at any bakery or specialty food store. The unsweetened paste is sold in sealed cans or in bulk at retail bakeries.

VANILLA PASTRY CREAM
(Crème Patissière)

A rich cream filling used in numerous French and Continental desserts.

5 *egg yolks*
½ *cup sugar*
1 *teaspoon vanilla extract*
2 *cups milk*
6 *tablespoons flour*

Beat the egg yolks with ¼ cup of the sugar until fluffy and pale in color. Stir in the vanilla extract and ½ cup of the milk. Sift the flour and add to the egg mixture. Blend all ingredients thoroughly. In a deep saucepan, bring the remaining 1½ cups of milk and the remaining ¼ cup of sugar to a boil. Remove from heat and gradually pour the hot milk in a slow stream into the yolk mixture while beating rapidly. Blend well. Quickly return all ingredients to the saucepan and boil for approximately 2 minutes or until thick. *Stir constantly* and rapidly with a wire whip to avoid scorching. Remove from heat and pour into a bowl or dish.

If the pastry cream is not to be used immediately, brush the top of the cream with melted butter to prevent a hard skin from forming. Cool and cover with a piece of waxed paper. This cream will keep for several days in the refrigerator or it may be frozen. Store pastry cream in Pyrex glass, plastic or stainless steel dishes. Before using for filling, frosting, etc., always beat at moderate speed with a wire whip, egg beater or electric mixer until smooth.

YIELD: 3 CUPS

SAUCES

MELBA SAUCE

1 tablespoon cornstarch
¼ cup water
1½ cups fresh raspberries
⅔ cup currant jelly
3 drops red food coloring
juice of 1 lemon

Sift the cornstarch into a bowl and gradually stir in the water to obtain a mixture free of lumps. Heat the fresh raspberries and the jelly over a low flame until the jelly is completely melted. Add the diluted cornstarch. Continue cooking for approximately 10 minutes or until the mixture has boiled for 1 minute. Remove from heat. Pass through a fine sieve; add red food coloring and the lemon juice. Cool and store in a jar until needed.
YIELD: 2 CUPS

EGG NOG SAUCE

1 cup light cream
⅓ cup granulated sugar
3 egg yolks
2 teaspoons rum
2 teaspoons Cognac

Scald the cream and add the sugar. Beat the egg yolks with a fork. Pour the cream mixture in a slow stream over the beaten yolks. Blend all ingredients thoroughly. Place over hot water and stir constantly until the mixture becomes thick enough to coat a spoon. Remove from heat and stir in the liqueurs. Serve hot or cold.
YIELD: 1½ CUPS

CHOCOLATE SAUCE

4 squares or 4 oz. unsweetened chocolate
⅔ cup granulated sugar
⅔ cup water
⅛ teaspoon or 1 pinch ground cinnamon
1 teaspoon brandy
¾ cup heavy cream

Grate the chocolate and melt over hot water, stirring constantly. Blend the sugar and water in a deep saucepan and boil for 3 minutes.

Remove from heat and cool to lukewarm. Stir the melted chocolate, cinnamon and brandy into the warm syrup. Cool thoroughly. Stir in the heavy cream and blend well. Serve hot or cold.
YIELD: 2 CUPS

Note: To reheat, place the prepared sauce over hot water and stir well until the proper consistency is obtained. If the sauce is too thick, add a little more cream or milk.

HOT CHOCOLATE SAUCE

8 oz. or 8 squares grated sweet chocolate
¼ cup water
⅓ cup granulated sugar
⅓ cup light cream or ¼ cup milk

Grate the chocolate and melt over hot water, stirring constantly. Stir in the water and granulated sugar. Blend well until the sugar is completely dissolved. Add the cream or milk. Serve hot.
YIELD: 1 CUP

APRICOT SAUCE

2 cups clear apricot jam
¾ cup water
3 tablespoons granulated sugar
⅓ cup Curaçao

Combine the apricot jam and water and boil gently for 5 minutes, stirring constantly to avoid burning. Add the sugar and remove from heat. Cool to lukewarm and stir in the liqueur. Serve hot or cold.
YIELD: APPROXIMATELY 2 CUPS

SHERRY SAUCE

½ cup granulated sugar
3 egg yolks
⅔ cup sweet sherry
1 tablespoon good brandy

Beat the sugar and egg yolks over hot water until thick. Remove from heat and add the sherry. Continue cooking over hot water, beating constantly until light and fluffy. Stir in the brandy. Serve hot.
YIELD: APPROXIMATELY 1¼ CUPS

SAUCE LIQUEUR—NUMBER 1

Any liqueur (Curaçao, brandy, rum, Grand Marnier, Chartreuse, etc.) of your choice, can be used in the following recipe.

½ cup light cream
½ cup milk
3 egg yolks
3 tablespoons granulated sugar
2 tablespoons any liqueur of your choice

Scald cream and milk together. Beat the egg yolks and sugar with a fork until light. Pour hot milk and cream in a slow stream over the beaten yolks and blend well. Place all ingredients over hot water and beat constantly until the sauce becomes thick enough to coat a spoon. *Do not boil.* Remove from the heat and cool. Stir in the liqueur.
YIELD: 1½ CUPS

SAUCE LIQUEUR—NUMBER 2

3 egg yolks
⅓ cup fine granulated sugar
¼ cup liqueur of your choice
⅓ cup heavy cream

In a deep bowl, beat the egg yolks and sugar together until pale in color. Place over hot water and continue beating until fluffy and light. Stir in the liqueur and continue beating for approximately 2 minutes longer. Remove from heat and place over cold water or in the refrigerator to chill. Just before serving, beat the cream until it holds its shape and fold thoroughly but gently into the yolk mixture.
YIELD: 1 CUP

Note: Whipped cream should not be beaten stiff but only enough to hold its shape.

HOT SABAYON SAUCE

5 egg yolks
1 egg white
⅓ cup granulated sugar
1 cup Marsala wine
pinch of ground nutmeg, optional

Place the egg yolks, egg white and sugar in a bowl and whip over boiling water until thick and fluffy. Remove from heat and stir in the

wine. Return to the boiling water and beat for approximately 3 minutes longer. Pour into champagne glasses and serve immediately.
YIELD: 4 TO 5 SERVINGS

Note: A pinch of ground nutmeg may be added at the end to the above recipe.

COLD SABAYON SAUCE

5 egg yolks
1/3 cup granulated sugar
1 cup Marsala wine
1/3 cup heavy cream

Follow the recipe above; cool the sauce thoroughly in the refrigerator before stirring in the heavy cream.
YIELD: 4 SERVINGS

CUSTARD SAUCE

1/2 cup milk
1/2 cup light cream
1 vanilla bean or 1/2 teaspoon vanilla extract
3 egg yolks
1/4 cup granulated sugar

In a saucepan, scald the milk and light cream with the vanilla bean or extract. Beat the egg yolks and sugar together until thick and pale in color and stir gradually into the hot liquid. Blend well. Cook over hot water, stirring constantly, until the sauce thickens enough to coat a spoon. *Do not boil.* Strain the sauce and remove the vanilla bean. Serve hot or cold.
YIELD: 1 1/2 cups

STRAWBERRY SAUCE

1 tablespoon cornstarch
1/2 cup cold water
1 package (12 oz.) frozen sliced strawberries (thawed but not drained)
5 drops red food coloring
2 tablespoons kirsch

In a deep saucepan, blend the cornstarch and water well together until the mixture is free of lumps. Place over medium heat and boil for approximately 1 minute; remove from heat and stir in the thawed berries with their juice. Add red food coloring and cool thoroughly. Just before serving, stir in the 2 tablespoons of kirsch.
YIELD: 2 CUPS

CANDIES

CHOCOLATE CUPS

A fascinating French pastry—attractive and fun to prepare!

8 oz. or 8 squares semi-sweet chocolate
2 tablespoons soft butter

Six fluted paper cups
Six muffin tins

Melt the chocolate over hot water, stirring rapidly and constantly. Add the butter and blend thoroughly. Remove from heat and cool to lukewarm (approximately 85 degrees F.). Pour 1 large tablespoon of chocolate mixture into a strong fluted paper baking cup and quickly and evenly spread the chocolate around the sides and bottom until the cup is entirely coated. Place on a chilled tray or, if available, set the prepared cups into muffin tins (paper cups will hold their shape more readily). Continue until all the cups have been covered with chocolate mixture. Place in refrigerator to set for approximately 30 minutes. Very gently (*away from any heat*) peel the paper away, leaving only the chocolate crust. Fill with flavored whipped cream of your choice, ice cream or sherbet.
YIELD: 6 SERVINGS

SUGGESTED FILLING FOR CHOCOLATE CUPS

½ cup heavy cream
2 tablespoons granulated sugar
2 tablespoons green Crème de Menthe
6 maraschino cherries, with stems

Whip the cream until thick. Add the sugar and Crème de Menthe and continue whipping until stiff. Fill the chocolate cups and garnish each cup with a stemmed maraschino cherry.

CHOCOLATE FUDGE

2 squares unsweetened chocolate
¾ cup light cream
1¾ cups granulated sugar
2 tablespoons butter
1 teaspoon vanilla extract

One baking pan, 6 x 5 x 1 inches, oiled

Place the chocolate, broken in small pieces, in a deep saucepan. Add the cream and stir over a low heat until dissolved and well blended. Add the sugar and bring to a boil. Continue cooking until the syrup forms a soft ball when dropped in ice water or until it reaches a temperature of approximately 235 degrees F. on a candy thermometer. Remove from heat and add the butter and vanilla. Cool over cold water until lukewarm. Beat the cooled mixture until it thickens. Pour into the prepared pan and chill thoroughly. Cut into squares.

YIELD: APPROXIMATELY 12 PIECES

PARISIAN CHOCOLATE BONBONS

¾ lb. sweet chocolate
½ cup light cream
¼ lb. or one stick butter
2 egg yolks, beaten with a fork
1 teaspoon Jamaica rum
¾ cup grated semi-sweet chocolate

One large baking sheet, lined with waxed paper

Break the sweet chocolate into small pieces. Boil the cream and combine with the chocolate. Place over hot water and stir constantly until the chocolate is well melted. Cool to lukewarm. Stir in the butter and beat rapidly until the butter is well incorporated into the chocolate mixture. Stir in the beaten yolks and rum. Spread approximately 1 inch thick on the prepared baking sheet. Chill in the refrigerator for at least 1 hour or until firm. Shape into small balls not bigger than walnuts and roll in the finely grated semi-sweet chocolate. Store in a cool place.

YIELD: APPROXIMATELY 3 DOZEN PIECES

NUT CARAMEL CANDY

1¼ *cups granulated sugar*
¾ *cup white corn syrup*
¼ *cup butter*
1 *cup light cream*
⅓ *cup finely diced nuts*
1 *teaspoon vanilla extract*

One baking pan, 8 x 6 x 3 inches, greased

Combine the sugar, corn syrup, butter and cream in a deep saucepan and cook until the temperature reaches 252 degrees F. on candy thermometer. Remove from heat; add the diced nuts and vanilla. Blend all ingredients well. Pour into the prepared pan and cool in the refrigerator for about 2 hours or until firm. Cut into 1-inch squares with a knife dipped in hot water. Wrap each candy in cellophane paper.

YIELD: APPROXIMATELY 18 1-OUNCE CANDIES

CHOCOLATE NUT CARAMEL:
Follow the recipe for Nut Caramel and add 1½ squares or 1½ oz. unsweetened chocolate at the end. Cook to 250 degrees F.

PEANUT BRITTLE

1 *cup granulated sugar*
⅓ *cup corn syrup*
½ *cup water*
¾ *cup peanuts, blanched*
1½ *teaspoons butter*
½ *teaspoon vanilla extract*
1 *teaspoon baking soda*

One large baking sheet, oiled

Place the sugar, corn syrup and water in a deep saucepan and cook until a candy thermometer registers 240 degrees F. Stir in the blanched peanuts and continue cooking, stirring from time to time, until the sugar thermometer reaches 310 degrees F. Remove from heat. Add the butter, vanilla and baking soda. Blend all ingredients well. Pour and spread over the prepared baking sheet. Cool to lukewarm. Stretch the candy by pulling it as thin as desired. Cool for another 15 minutes and break into small pieces.

YIELD: APPROXIMATELY 3 DOZEN PIECES

DIVINITY CANDY

3 *cups granulated sugar*
⅔ *cup corn syrup*
¾ *cup water*
3 *egg whites, beaten stiff*
1 *cup nuts*
½ *teaspoon vanilla extract*

One large baking sheet, oiled

Combine the sugar and corn syrup in a deep saucepan and cook until the temperature reaches 265 degrees F. on a candy thermometer. Pour in a slow stream over the stiffly beaten egg whites and continue beating until the mixture becomes stiff. Stir in the nuts and vanilla. Drop by the teaspoonful onto the prepared baking sheet and cool.

YIELD: APPROXIMATELY 2 DOZEN PIECES

CHOCOLATE ORANGE PEEL

4 *large oranges*
water
2 *cups granulated sugar*
1 *cup (8 oz.) sweet chocolate*

Remove the peel from the oranges in sections. Boil the water in a deep saucepan. Drop the orange skins into the boiling water and simmer for approximately 25 minutes or until the orange skins are tender to the touch. Drain and cool the peels. With a sharp knife, remove as much of the white skin as possible. Cut the orange peel in narrow strips approximately ⅙-inch thick. Combine the sugar and remaining cup of water and cook rapidly until the temperature reaches 240 degrees F. on a candy thermometer. When this syrup has reached the proper temperature, drop in the orange peels and simmer over a low flame for about 10 more minutes. Remove from the heat and allow the oranges to macerate for two days in the thick syrup.

Drain the syrup thoroughly from the peels and melt the sweet chocolate over hot water. Do not overheat. Proper dipping temperature is approximately 85 degrees F. Dip each strip of peel into the melted chocolate and spread on aluminum foil to harden. Chill. Remove from the foil and store in a cool place until needed.
YIELD: APPROXIMATELY 48 CANDIES

HONEY CANDIED GRAPEFRUIT PEEL

1 *grapefruit*
1½ *quarts water combined with 1 teaspoon salt*
⅔ *cup honey*
2 *cups hot water*

Divide the grapefruit into 8 sections and peel. Soak the grapefruit peel in the salted water overnight. Drain, cover the peel entirely with cold water and bring to boil. Drain again, replace the water, return to the fire and finish cooking until the peel is tender to the touch. Drain and cool. Remove as much as possible of the white part of the rind. Slice the peel on a wooden board to desired shape. Combine the honey and hot water and bring to a boil. Put the cooked peel into the hot syrup and continue to boil slowly for approximately 5 minutes. Cool and pour into a jar. Cover and let soak for at least 48 hours.

Note: Orange peel can be prepared in the same manner.

CHOCOLATE FRENCH TRUFFLES

These delicious chocolate candies are by far the best sellers in any French pastry shop.

1 *lb. milk chocolate chopped in small pieces*
½ *cup heavy cream, scalded*
1 *teaspoon vanilla extract*
8 *squares (1 oz. each) sweet chocolate, melted*
½ *cup cocoa powder*

One 6-inch square baking pan, lined with aluminum foil

Melt the chopped chocolate in a deep bowl over hot water and stir well to blend properly. Add the scalded cream. Pour into a mixing bowl, add the vanilla and whip at moderate speed until smooth and beginning to set. Pour immediately into the prepared pan and chill in the refrigerator for approximately 1 hour, or until firm. Cut into small squares and roll each square into a ball no larger than a small walnut. Dip each ball quickly in the melted sweet chocolate and roll in cocoa powder. Store in a cool place.

YIELD: APPROXIMATELY 50 TRUFFLES

Variations: Roll in chopped nuts, chocolate chips or chopped toasted shredded coconut.

Various Fruit Desserts

PEARS ANDALOUSE

4 whole Bartlett pears
2 cups currant jelly
2 cups water

Peel the pears, leaving the stem. Combine the jelly and water and bring to a boil. Add the pears to the hot syrup, cover and simmer until the fruit is tender, about 10 to 15 minutes, depending upon the size of the pears being used. Remove from heat; cool and chill in the refrigerator. Remove from syrup. Arrange the pears on a serving tray or platter and serve with the following sauce:

2 egg yolks
¼ cup granulated sugar
1 teaspoon kirsch
⅓ cup heavy cream
1 teaspoon sugar

In a deep bowl, mix the egg yolks and sugar. Place over hot water and beat until thick. Stir in the kirsch and continue beating for 1 minute or so. Remove from heat and place over cold water or let stand in refrigerator to chill. Just before serving, beat the cream and sugar together until stiff and fold into the yolk mixture. Coat the prepared pears with the chilled sauce.

YIELD: 4 SERVINGS

PEARS GRAND DUC
(Poires Glacées à la Duc)

2 cups granulated sugar
2 cups water
the peel of 1 orange
6 whole fresh pears
1/4 pint vanilla ice cream

Boil the sugar, water and orange peel together for 2 minutes. Remove peel. Peel the pears, add them to the hot syrup and poach until tender but firm. Core each fruit carefully; avoid breaking the pulp. Cool in the refrigerator. When cooled, fill each pear cavity with soft vanilla ice cream and place in the freezer while preparing the following:

6 egg yolks
1 cup granulated sugar
1 1/2 cups heavy cream
1/3 cup Grand Marnier
1 cup warm, clear apricot jam

Beat the egg yolks and sugar together over hot water until thick and pale in color. Remove from the hot water and continue beating until cool. Beat the cream until stiff. Fold the whipped cream and Grand Marnier gently into the cooled yolk mixture. Place in a large serving dish and chill thoroughly in the refrigerator. When ready to serve, heat the apricot jam. Arrange the prepared pears on top of the cream mixture and quickly brush each fruit with warm, clear apricot jam.

YIELD: 6 SERVINGS

Note: Drained canned pears, peaches or apricots can be used instead of fresh pears.

STRAWBERRIES HUGO

1 quart fresh, ripe strawberries
1 cup thick sour cream
1 tablespoon kirsch
1/3 cup light brown sugar

Wash and hull the strawberries. Pour into a chilled serving dish. Just before serving, stir in the cream, kirsch and light brown sugar.

YIELD: 5 TO 6 SERVINGS

BANANA POMPADOUR

6 bananas, halved lengthwise
¼ pound butter
⅓ cup light brown sugar
grated rind of 1 lemon
grated rind of 1 orange
⅓ cup fresh orange juice
1 tablespoon lemon juice
¼ cup Curaçao
1 tablespoon Grand Marnier
12 lady fingers (*see page 110*)

Arrange the bananas in a shallow flameproof dish. Melt the butter in a large saucepan. Add the sugar, rinds, orange and lemon juice and boil for approximately 2 minutes. Remove from heat and add the Curaçao and Grand Marnier; stir well. Pour over the bananas. Heat all ingredients over medium heat until the bananas become tender. Place the lady fingers in the bottom of a heatproof serving dish and spoon the banana mixture gently over the lady fingers.

YIELD: 6 SERVINGS

BROILED GRAPEFRUIT

4 large grapefruit halves
4 teaspoons brown sugar
4 tablespoons honey
4 teaspoons Cointreau
1 tablespoon soft butter

Preheat broiler

Score the grapefruit halves to loosen each section. Arrange the fruit on a baking sheet and sprinkle each half with 1 teaspoon of brown sugar; pour 1 tablespoon honey over each grapefruit half. Sprinkle each half with 1 teaspoon of Cointreau and brush with soft butter. Place under a very hot broiler until brown. Serve immediately.

YIELD: 4 SERVINGS

JAMAICAN BROILED GRAPEFRUIT

2 large, ripe grapefruits
4 tablespoons Jamaica rum
4 tablespoons brown sugar

Preheat broiler

Halve, remove seeds and loosen segments of the grapefruits. Pour a tablespoon of rum into the center of each half. Dust evenly with brown sugar. Place under the hot broiler for approximately 5 minutes to caramelize the sugar. Serve immediately.
YIELD: 4 SERVINGS

HONEY BAKED APPLES

6 large baking apples
⅔ cup honey
2 teaspoons grated orange rind
½ teaspoon ground nutmeg

Set oven at 375 degrees F.
One 10 x 10 x 3-inch baking pan

Core the apples and starting at the stem end, pare them ⅓ of the way down. Place in a deep baking dish. Fill each cavity with honey and orange rind and sprinkle with nutmeg. Cover with aluminum foil and place in a 375 degree F. oven for approximately 40 minutes. Remove the paper and bake for 15 minutes longer or until tender when pricked with a fork. Serve warm or cold.
YIELD: 6 SERVINGS

SOUTHERN BAKED APPLES
(Baked apples with pecans)

8 large baking apples
⅔ cup chopped pecans
10 tablespoons dark brown sugar
2 teaspoons melted butter
2 tablespoons honey

Set oven at 350 degrees F.
One 10 x 10 x 3-inch baking pan

Core the apples from the top without cutting through the bottom. Peel the top third of each apple and stand them side by side in a deep baking dish. Mix all remaining ingredients well and spoon some into the center of each apple. Fill the bottom of the baking dish approximately ⅓ full of water and bake the apples at 350 degrees F. for about 40 minutes or until tender.
YIELD: 8 SERVINGS

BRANDIED PEACHES

6 large, ripe peaches
3 cups water
1 lb. granulated sugar
1 cup brandy per cup of sugar syrup

Dip the peaches in boiling water for 1 minute or so. Drain and cool. Peel the peaches carefully with a sharp knife. Boil 3 cups of water and 1 pound of sugar for 1 or 2 minutes. Drop 3 peaches at a time into the boiling syrup and simmer for 5 minutes or until the fruit is tender. Remove and repeat with the remaining peaches.

Place the cooked peaches in a large sterilized glass jar. Heat the syrup to 230 degrees F. on candy thermometer and cool thoroughly. To each cup of syrup add 1 cup of good French brandy. Fill the jar to the top, covering the fruit entirely. Seal tightly.

YIELD: 6 SERVINGS

Note: Unpitted fruit will be more tasty and will keep their shape better during the maceration period, which should be at least 2 weeks. Peaches prepared this way will keep for many months and are always a pleasure to have on hand for unscheduled guests. Serve with ice cream or garnished with whipped cream. In any case, brandied peaches will taste better if served chilled.

ALMINA ORANGES

4 oranges
2 cups Vanilla Bavarian Cream (page 265)
12 lady fingers (see page 110)
4 teaspoons Curaçao

Slice the tops of large oranges, scoop out the contents carefully, leaving only a clean skin. Fill in with Vanilla Bavarian Cream blended with lady fingers soaked in Curaçao. Cool in the refrigerator until set. Replace the tops. Arrange on serving dishes and serve.

YIELD: 4 SERVINGS

ORANGES RUBANNÉES

4 *oranges*
1 *cup fruit Jell-O*
1 *cup Vanilla Bavarian Cream (page 265)*
1 *cup whipped cream*
16 *orange sections*

Slice the top of each orange and scoop out the contents carefully, leaving only a clean skin. Fill the empty orange with alternate layers of fruit Jell-O and Vanilla Bavarian Cream. Chill until set before pouring the next layer. When firm, arrange on a serving tray; garnish with whipped cream and fresh orange sections. Serve immediately.

YIELD: 4 SERVINGS

Low-Calorie Gourmet Desserts

My sincere thanks to Sara Hervey Watts, Home Economics Consultant for Abbott Laboratories. Her valuable contributions to the low-calorie dessert chapter are deeply appreciated.

CAKES AND PANCAKES

LOW-CALORIE APPLE-CHEESE CAKE

Here's a spicily fragrant, deliciously smooth Apple-Cheese Cake that also boasts of being low in calories! Easy to make, too!

3 *oz. cream cheese*
1 *cup skim milk*
3 *eggs*
1 *tablespoon non-nutritive liquid sweetener*
½ *cup all-purpose flour*
¼ *teaspoon salt*
1 *1-lb. can water-packed applesauce (or unsweetened applesauce)*
1 *tablespoon lemon juice*
1 *tablespoon cinnamon*
chopped nuts, to garnish (optional)

Set oven at 375 degrees F.
One 9-inch round cake pan, well greased

Combine the cream cheese, milk and eggs in an electric blender. Blend well for 30 seconds or until smooth. Add the sweetener and blend a few seconds longer. Combine the flour and salt; add to the cheese mixture and blend for 30 seconds. Combine the applesauce, lemon juice and cinnamon, mixing well. Pour the batter over the applesauce, folding just enough to mix. Pour into the prepared cake pan and bake in a moderate oven for 35 minutes. Let cool before serving.

YIELD: 8 SERVINGS
Each serving contains 128 calories

LOW-CALORIE GOLDEN SPICE CAKE

Here's a delicious pumpkin-chiffon cake especially designed for dieters. Rich with the flavor of pumpkin, fragrant with spices, moist and tender, this cake saves you one-third of the total calories normally found in the recipe.

- 1¾ *cups sifted cake flour*
- 1½ *teaspoons baking powder*
- 1½ *teaspoons cinnamon*
- ¾ *teaspoon cloves*
- ¾ *teaspoon nutmeg*
- ¼ *teaspoon salt*
- 7 *eggs, separated*
- 3 *tablespoons non-nutritive liquid sweetener*
- 1 *cup fresh cooked or canned pumpkin*
- ½ *cup salad oil*
- ¼ *cup water*
- ½ *teaspoon cream of tartar*

Set oven at 350 degrees F.
One 8-inch tube pan, ungreased

Combine the flour, baking powder, spices and salt in large bowl. Add the egg yolks, sweetener, pumpkin, salad oil and water and beat until smooth. Beat the egg whites until foamy; add the cream of tartar and continue beating until stiff but not dry. Gently fold the beaten egg whites into the pumpkin mixture. Spoon the batter into the prepared pan and bake in a moderate oven for 45 minutes. Remove from oven and invert until cool, or for approximately 1 hour.

YIELD: 20 SERVINGS
Each serving contains 111 calories

LOW-CALORIE BREAKFAST COFFEE CAKE

¼ cup skim milk
⅓ cup butter or margarine
1 teaspoon salt
1½ teaspoons non-nutritive liquid sweetener
2 packages active dry yeast
½ cup lukewarm water
2 eggs, beaten
3 cups sifted all-purpose flour
⅓ cup chopped walnuts
ground cinnamon
1 tablespoon powdered sweetener

Set oven at 400 degrees F.
One 9-inch square cake pan, greased

Scald the milk; add the butter, salt and liquid sweetener and stir until the butter is melted. Cool to lukewarm (70 degrees F.). Dissolve the yeast in warm water and add to the milk mixture. Add the beaten eggs and sifted flour and mix well. Spoon into the prepared cake pan. Cover and allow to rise in a warm place until doubled in bulk. Scatter the chopped walnuts, mixed with a light sprinkling of powdered sweetener and ground cinnamon, over the top and bake at 400 degrees F. for 20 minutes.
YIELD: 9 SERVINGS
Each serving contains 246 calories

LOW-CALORIE CHOCOLATE SPONGE ROLL

5 eggs, at room temperature, separated
5 teaspoons non-nutritive liquid sweetener
1 tablespoon lemon juice
2 teaspoons vanilla extract
¼ teaspoon red food coloring
¾ cup sifted cake flour
¼ cup sifted cocoa
¼ teaspoon salt
¼ teaspoon baking soda
1 tablespoon cornstarch

Set oven at 300 degrees F.
One jellyroll pan (15½ x 10½ x 1-inch), lined with well-oiled waxed paper

Beat the egg yolks in a large bowl at high speed for approximately 5 minutes or until light. Add the sweetener, lemon juice, vanilla, and food coloring to the yolks and continue beating until thick and fluffy. Beat the egg whites until stiff but not dry and fold carefully into the yolk mixture. Sift the flour, cocoa, salt, and baking soda together 3 times and blend gradually into the egg mixture, beating at low speed for approximately 2 minutes. Pour the batter into the prepared pan and smooth the top. Bake at 300 degrees F. for 20 minutes, or until the top springs back when pressed lightly. Turn the cake out onto a sheet of waxed paper, sprinkled with 1 tablespoon cornstarch, and peel paper off the bottom of cake. Trim off the crisp edges and roll the cake up with the waxed paper until cool. Unwrap and spread with filling; then rewrap and chill in the refrigerator for at least 2 hours before serving.

YIELD: 12 SERVINGS

Each serving of filled cake contains 95 calories

CREAM FILLING FOR LOW-CALORIE CHOCOLATE SPONGE ROLL

2 tablespoons cornstarch
¼ teaspoon salt
1 cup water
1 tablespoon cream
1½ teaspoons non-nutritive liquid sweetener
1 egg yolk, lightly beaten
¼ teaspoon vanilla

Put cornstarch and salt in a saucepan; add the water and stir until smooth. Add the cream and sweetener and cook, stirring constantly, over a medium heat until the mixture comes to a boil and is medium thick. Mix a small amount of the sauce with the egg yolk and then blend the yolk mixture into the remaining sauce. Cook about 3 minutes longer or until well thickened. Stir in the vanilla and cool. Spread on the cooled sponge roll.

LOW-CALORIE SPONGE CAKE

7 eggs at room temperature, separated
½ cup cold water
3 tablespoons non-nutritive liquid sweetener
½ teaspoon vanilla extract
2 tablespoons lemon juice
¾ teaspoon cream of tartar
1½ cups sifted cake flour
¼ teaspoon salt

Set oven at 325 degrees F.
One 9- or 10-inch tube pan, ungreased

Beat the egg yolks for approximately 5 minutes or until thick and lemon-colored. Combine the water, sweetener, vanilla and lemon juice and add to the egg yolks; beat for approximately 10 minutes or until thick and fluffy. Beat the egg whites until foamy; add the cream of tartar and continue beating until stiff but not dry. Fold the egg whites carefully into the yolk mixture. Combine the sifted flour and salt; sift a little at a time over the egg mixture, folding in gently. Pour the batter into the pan and bake for 1 hour and 15 minutes.

YIELD: 12 SERVINGS
Each serving contains 91 calories

LOW-CALORIE STRAWBERRY CHEESE CAKE

2 *tablespoons unflavored gelatin*
1/4 *cup hot water*
2 *eggs, separated*
1/4 *teaspoon salt*
1 *cup skim milk*
3 *tablespoons non-nutritive liquid sweetener*
1 *teaspoon grated lemon rind*
2 *tablespoons lemon juice*
1 *teaspoon vanilla extract*
3 *cups creamed cottage cheese*
1/3 *cup non-fat dry milk*
1/3 *cup ice water*
2 *tablespoons crushed cornflakes*
3 *cups whole strawberries*

One 9-inch round cake pan, lightly oiled

Soften the gelatin in hot water. Combine the egg yolks, salt, milk, and 1 tablespoon of sweetener in top of a double boiler. Stir constantly over hot water until thickened. Remove from the heat and add the softened gelatin, lemon rind, lemon juice and vanilla. Let stand at room temperature until the mixture begins to set. Force the cottage cheese through a sieve and fold into the thickened gelatin. Beat the egg whites until stiff but not dry and fold into the gelatin mixture. Combine the dry milk and ice water and beat until the consistency of heavy cream; fold into the gelatin mixture. Sprinkle cornflake crumbs on sides only of the prepared cake pan and spoon the cheesecake mixture into the pan. Refrigerate for about 1½ hours, or until firm. Sweeten the strawberries with the remaining 2 tablespoons of sweetener and arrange on top of the cheesecake.

YIELD: 10 SERVINGS
Each serving contains 243 calories

LOW-CALORIE CINNAMON COFFEE CAKE

This handsome coffee cake with its cinnamon crumb topping looks just as irresistible and tastes just as delicious as any you've ever eaten. Yet there's one important difference. Calories have been reduced by well over 100 for every serving!

TOPPING

1 *tablespoon melted butter*
½ *teaspoon cinnamon*
½ *teaspoon non-nutritive liquid sweetener*
¼ *cup toasted dry bread crumbs*

CAKE

2 *cups sifted cake flour*
3 *teaspoons baking powder*
¼ *teaspoon salt*
3 *tablespoons soft butter*
¾ *cup skim milk*
1 *tablespoon non-nutritive liquid sweetener*
4 *drops yellow food coloring*
1 *egg*

Set oven at 375 degrees F.
One 8-inch round cake pan, greased

Combine the topping ingredients, stirring until blended, and set aside.

Sift the flour, baking powder and salt together into a small bowl. With an electric beater, cut in the butter on low, then medium speed, for 3 to 5 minutes, until mixture is completely blended and looks like fine corn meal. (This assures a fine grain.) Mix ½ cup of the milk with the sweetener and food coloring and add to the flour mixture. Beat ½ minute on medium speed. (The batter will be stiff.) Add the remaining milk and beat 1 minute longer. Add the egg and beat 1 minute more. Pour into the prepared pan, sprinkle with the topping mixture and bake for 20 minutes or until the cake springs back when pressed lightly.

YIELD: 8 SERVINGS
Each serving contains 169 calories

LOW-CALORIE APPLESAUCE NUT BREAD

2 cups sifted flour
1½ teaspoons baking powder
½ teaspoon cinnamon
½ teaspoon salt
½ teaspoon baking soda
¼ cup chopped walnuts
1 egg, well beaten
1 cup unsweetened applesauce
1 tablespoon non-nutritive liquid sweetener
2 tablespoons melted butter

Set oven at 350 degrees F.
Two loaf pans (5 x 3 x 2 inches), greased

Combine the flour, baking powder, cinnamon, salt, baking soda and chopped nuts. In a large bowl, combine the remaining ingredients and mix well. Add the flour mixture all at once, stirring only until all the flour is dampened. Spoon into the prepared pans and bake for 1 hour and 15 minutes.

YIELD: 24 SERVINGS
Each serving contains 57 calories

LOW-CALORIE REFRIGERATOR BANANA CHEESE CAKE

This handsome cake boasts of a rich-tasting, luscious filling in a chilled cornflake-crumb crust.

CRUST:

3 tablespoons melted butter
1 cup crushed cornflakes
1½ tablespoons non-fat dry milk
1½ teaspoons non-nutritive liquid sweetener

One 9-inch spring form pan

Combine all ingredients. Press the crumbs along the bottom and sides of the pan. Chill for about 2 hours, then fill.

FILLING:

1 pound cottage cheese
3 medium bananas
2 tablespoons or 2 envelopes unflavored gelatin
½ cup hot water
3 eggs, separated
1 tablespoon non-nutritive liquid sweetener
½ cup water
¼ teaspoon salt

Mash the bananas and blend with the cottage cheese. Soften the gelatin in hot water. Combine the egg yolks, sweetener, water and salt and cook over low heat, stirring constantly, until the mixture becomes thick enough to coat a spoon. Add the softened gelatin and dissolve. Blend the yolks into the cottage cheese–banana mixture and cool until it starts to congeal. Beat the egg whites until they form soft peaks, then fold into the gelatin mixture. Pour into the crust-lined pan and chill for about 1 hour or until firm.

YIELD: 12 SERVINGS
Each serving contains 119 calories

LOW-CALORIE APPLESAUCE CAKE

This is a low-calorie version of an old-fashioned favorite. But only calories have been sacrificed. It's still rich-tasting, moist, tender and delicately spiced. So delicious when served warm!

½ cup butter or margarine
1 tablespoon non-nutritive liquid sweetener
2 eggs
2 teaspoons vanilla extract
2½ cups sifted all-purpose flour
3 teaspoons baking powder
1 teaspoon baking soda
2 teaspoons cinnamon
1 teaspoon ground cloves
½ teaspoon salt
1½ cups unsweetened applesauce

Set oven at 350 degrees F.
One 1½-quart ring mold, oiled

Cream the butter or margarine in a large bowl with an electric mixer on high speed until well softened. Add the sweetener, eggs and vanilla and continue beating until thoroughly blended. Sift the dry ingredients together and add alternately with the applesauce to the butter and eggs. Pour the batter into the prepared mold and bake for 50 to 60 minutes. Cool 10 minutes before removing from the mold.

YIELD: 25 ½-INCH SLICES
Each slice contains 84 calories

LOW-CALORIE FEATHER PANCAKES WITH ORANGE SAUCE

Something new and exciting, something that tastes utterly scrumptious, and something light and easy on the calories. Here's just the answer . . . tiny, featherweight rolled pancakes topped with a luscious, golden orange sauce. The combination is pure ambrosia, one that nobody could possibly resist.

FEATHER PANCAKES

¾ cup skim-milk cottage cheese
¼ teaspoon salt
¼ cup all-purpose flour
⅓ cup non-fat dry milk
¼ cup water
3 eggs, separated
1 teaspoon butter (for griddle)

Force the cottage cheese through a sieve and combine it with the salt, flour, dry milk and water. Add the egg yolks and beat until smooth. Beat the egg whites until stiff but not dry and fold into the cheese mixture. Drop by spoonfuls onto a hot, lightly greased griddle and cook until golden. Roll each pancake before serving with orange sauce.

YIELD: 20 3-INCH PANCAKES
Each pancake contains 33 calories

ORANGE SAUCE

1½ cups orange juice
½ teaspoon grated orange rind
2 tablespoons cornstarch
1 teaspoon non-nutritive liquid sweetener
few grains salt
1 large orange, sectioned

Combine all ingredients except the orange sections in a small saucepan and cook over medium heat, stirring constantly, until the mixture thickens. Add the orange sections and cool. Serve with Feather Pancakes, above.

YIELD: 1½ CUPS SAUCE, OR 6 SERVINGS
Each serving contains 54 calories

PIES AND TARTS

LOW-CALORIE LEMON-BLUEBERRY CHIFFON PIE

Luscious, cool-tasting filling in a crisp and crunchy pie shell makes this pie just right for hot-weather appetites.

CRUST:

- 2 *tablespoons melted butter*
- ⅔ *cup crushed cornflakes*
- 1 *tablespoon non-fat dry milk*
- ¾ *teaspoon non-nutritive liquid sweetener*

Set oven at 350 degrees F.
One 8-inch pie plate

Combine all ingredients and press into the bottom of the pie plate. Bake for 10 to 12 minutes. Cool.

FILLING:

- 1 *tablespoon or 1 envelope unflavored gelatin*
- ¼ *cup hot water*
- 4 *eggs, separated*
- 2 *tablespoons non-nutritive liquid sweetener*
- ½ *cup lemon juice*
- 1 *teaspoon grated lemon rind*
- ½ *teaspoon salt*
- 1 *cup fresh blueberries*

Soften the gelatin in hot water. Combine the egg yolks, sweetener, lemon juice, lemon rind and salt in the top of a double boiler and cook, stirring, until thick. Add the softened gelatin and chill for about 15 minutes or until partially set. Beat the egg whites to stiff

peaks and fold into the chilled mixture along with the blueberries. Spoon into the baked crust and chill for about 1 hour or until firm.
YIELD: 6 SERVINGS
Each serving contains 124 calories

LOW-CALORIE RUM AND COFFEE CHIFFON PIE

PASTRY:

1 cup sifted all-purpose flour
1/8 teaspoon salt
1/3 cup shortening
2 tablespoons water

Set oven at 450 degrees F.
One 9-inch pie plate, greased

Combine the flour and salt. Blend in the shortening and water. Roll out on a floured board and arrange in the prepared pie plate. Bake for 12 minutes. Cool.

FILLING:

1 tablespoon or 1 envelope unflavored gelatin
1/4 cup hot water
3 eggs, separated
2 tablespoons non-nutritive liquid sweetener
1/4 teaspoon salt
1/2 teaspoon cinnamon
1/8 teaspoon cloves
1/2 cup skim milk
3/4 cup strong coffee
2 tablespoons rum

Soften the gelatin in hot water. Combine the egg yolks, sweetener, salt, spices, milk and coffee in the top of a double boiler and cook, stirring, until thick. Remove from heat and stir in the softened gelatin until dissolved. Chill for approximately 15 minutes or until the mixture begins to thicken. Add the rum. Beat the egg whites to stiff peaks and fold into the chilled mixture. Pour into the baked pastry shell and chill for about 1 hour, or until set. Garnish, if desired, with Topping for low-calorie Lemon Chiffon Pie (page 319) and shaved chocolate.
YIELD: 8 SERVINGS
Each serving with topping contains 167 calories

LOW-CALORIE PUMPKIN CHIFFON PIE

Bake this very special Pumpkin Chiffon Pie on Thanksgiving morning, and the whole family will cheer. It's tantalizingly fragrant with spices, rich-tasting yet delectably light; the perfect ending for a festive dinner.

CRUST:

3/4 cup crushed cornflakes
2 tablespoons melted butter
1 teaspoon non-nutritive liquid sweetener
1 tablespoon non-fat dry milk

Set oven at 375 degrees F.
One 9-inch pie plate

Combine all ingredients and press onto the sides and bottom of the pie plate. Bake for 10 to 12 minutes. Cool.

FILLING:

1 envelope gelatin
1/2 teaspoon salt
1/2 teaspoon nutmeg
1/2 teaspoon cinnamon
1/2 teaspoon ginger
1/4 teaspoon cloves
2 eggs, separated
1 cup evaporated milk
1/2 cup cold water
1 1/4 cups canned pumpkin
4 teaspoons non-nutritive liquid sweetener

Combine the gelatin, salt and spices. Beat the egg yolks in the top of a double boiler. Stir in the milk, water, pumpkin and sweetener; then add the gelatin-spice mixture. Cook over boiling water for 10 minutes. Cool, then refrigerate for about 1 hour, or until thick and syrupy. Beat the egg whites until stiff but not dry and fold into the thickened pumpkin mixture. Spoon into the prepared crust and chill for about 1 hour, or until set. If desired, top with Maple Whipped Topping (below) and stud with toasted almonds.

YIELD: 8 SERVINGS

Each serving contains 116 calories without topping or nuts

MAPLE WHIPPED TOPPING FOR PUMPKIN CHIFFON PIE

½ cup non-fat dry milk
½ cup ice water
1 teaspoon non-nutritive liquid sweetener
½ teaspoon maple flavoring

Combine all ingredients and beat in mixer at high speed until consistency of whipped cream.
YIELD: 2 CUPS OR 8 SERVINGS
Each serving contains 27 calories

LOW-CALORIE LEMON CHIFFON PIE

1 envelope unflavored gelatin
¼ cup lemon juice
2 teaspoons grated lemon rind
4 egg whites
2 egg yolks
¼ cup water
¼ teaspoon salt
5 teaspoons non-nutritive liquid sweetener
¼ cup cake flour
¾ cup boiling water
½ cup non-fat dry milk
½ cup ice water
⅛ teaspoon yellow food coloring
¼ cup fine toasted bread crumbs

One 9-inch pie plate, oiled

Mix the gelatin with the lemon juice and rind. Beat the egg whites until soft peaks form. Beat the egg yolks with the water, salt, sweetener and flour until blended. Add the boiling water. Pour the mixture into a saucepan and bring to a rapid boil. Stir vigorously for approximately 1 minute as the mixture thickens. Remove from heat and add the softened gelatin immediately, stirring until blended. Fold the beaten egg whites into the lemon mixture. In a small bowl, whip the dry milk with the ice water and food coloring and fold into the lemon mixture. Sprinkle the sides and bottom of the prepared pie plate with the crumbs. Pour in the lemon mixture and chill for about 1½ hours, or until firm.

TOPPING FOR LOW-CALORIE LEMON CHIFFON PIE

½ cup non-fat dry milk
½ cup ice water
1 teaspoon non-nutritive liquid sweetener

Combine all ingredients and beat on high speed of mixer until consistency of whipped cream. Spread on pie and sprinkle with grated lemon rind.

YIELD: 8 SERVINGS
Each serving contains 102 calories

LOW-CALORIE BANANA CREAM PIE

Look what happened to this Banana Cream Pie! Without sacrificing even a little bit of its rich-tasting goodness, we've lopped off nearly half the calories.

¼ cup toasted dry bread crumbs
1 tablespoon unflavored gelatin
¾ cup hot water
2 eggs
1½ cups skim milk
1 tablespoon non-nutritive liquid sweetener
¼ teaspoon salt
4 drops yellow food coloring
½ teaspoon banana or almond extract
1 cup sliced (2 small) bananas

One 8-inch pie plate, oiled

Sprinkle the prepared pie plate with half the crumbs, coating the sides and bottom evenly. Add the gelatin to the hot water and set aside. Combine the eggs, milk, sweetener, salt and food coloring in the top of a double boiler and beat just enough to blend. Slowly cook over barely simmering water for 12 to 15 minutes, or until the mixture becomes thick enough to coat a spoon lightly. Remove from heat and add the gelatin and vanilla; stir until dissolved. Cool over ice water for about 10 minutes or until the mixture starts to mound. Stir occasionally. Put half the mixture into the prepared pie plate. Add half the banana slices and cover with the remaining cream mixture. Arrange the remaining banana slices, dusted with bread crumbs,

around the edge of the plate. Top with additional banana slices, if desired, and chill for approximately 1 hour before serving.
YIELD: 6 SERVINGS
Each serving contains 89 calories

LOW-CALORIE CAFÉ-AU-LAIT PIE

This exciting dessert gets its sophisticated flavor from the subtle blending of coffee, vanilla and nutmeg. Its crumb crust has almost a nut-like flavor, and is a perfect complement to the delicately smooth filling.

CRUST:

- 3 *tablespoons melted butter*
- 1½ *tablespoons non-fat dry milk*
- 1 *cup crushed cornflakes*
- 1 *teaspoon non-nutritive liquid sweetener*

Set oven at 375 degrees F.
One 9-inch pie plate

Combine all ingredients and press firmly into the pie plate, reserving some crumbs for topping. Bake for 12 minutes; cool.

FILLING:

- 1 *tablespoon gelatin*
- ¼ *cup hot water*
- ½ *cup non-fat dry milk*
- 4 *teaspoons non-nutritive liquid sweetener*
- ⅛ *teaspoon salt*
- 1½ *cups water*
- 3 *eggs, separated*
- 1 *tablespoon instant coffee*
- 1 *teaspoon vanilla extract*
- ¼ *teaspoon nutmeg*

Soften the gelatin in the hot water. Combine the dry milk, sweetener, salt and water in the top of a double boiler and blend until smooth. Add the egg yolks and cook over hot water until the mixture becomes thick enough to coat a spoon. Add the softened gelatin and stir until dissolved. Cool for approximately 15 minutes or until the mixture jells slightly. Combine the egg whites, coffee, vanilla and nutmeg and beat until stiff but not dry. Fold the egg whites into the thickened gelatin mixture and spoon into the cooled pie shell. Chill slightly; then sprinkle with the remaining crumbs.

YIELD: 6 SERVINGS
Each serving contains 153 calories

LOW-CALORIE SPICY PEACH PIE

Just another dessert sometimes isn't good enough when you're entertaining. But here's one that's quite a different matter. The Spicy Peach Pie deserves compliments on several scores. It's a beauty to behold . . . it's deliciously sweet and spicy . . . and what's more, it's low in calories!

pastry for a 2-crust pie (page 54)
2 1-lb. cans dietetic peach slices
2 tablespoons cornstarch
½ teaspoon salt
½ teaspoon nutmeg
½ teaspoon mace
1 teaspoon non-nutritive liquid sweetener
2 tablespoons lemon juice
1 tablespoon butter

Set oven at 425 degrees F.
One 8-inch pie plate, greased

Drain the peaches, reserving 1⅓ cups of juice. (Add water, if necessary, to obtain the 1⅓-cup measure.) Combine the cornstarch, salt, nutmeg, mace, sweetener and peach juice and cook over low heat until thickened. Remove from heat and add the lemon juice and butter. Roll out half the pastry dough and arrange in the bottom of the prepared pie plate. (For detailed instructions on the preparation of fruit pie, see page 55.) Arrange the peach slices in the pie shell and cover with the thickened juice. Roll out the top dough and arrange in a lattice pattern over the fruit. Bake for 30 to 40 minutes, or until the crust is a golden brown.

YIELD: 6 SERVINGS
Each serving of filling (not including the pastry) contains 74 calories

LOW-CALORIE BANANA GLACÉ PIE

Banana Glacé Pie doesn't look or sound like a dieter's dessert, but that's just what it is!

CRUST:

3 tablespoons melted butter
1 cup crushed cornflakes
1½ tablespoons non-fat dry milk
1 teaspoon non-nutritive liquid sweetener

Set oven at 375 degrees F.
One 9-inch pie plate

Combine all ingredients and press firmly onto the bottom and sides of the pie plate. Bake for about 12 minutes. Cool.

FILLING:

3 tablespoons cornstarch
4 teaspoons non-nutritive liquid sweetener
¼ teaspoon salt
2 cups skim milk
3 eggs
1 teaspoon vanilla extract
2 bananas
1 tablespoon lemon juice
3 tablespoons dietetic cherry jelly
1 tablespoon water

Combine the cornstarch, sweetener and salt in the top of a double boiler. Add 1¾ cups of the milk and cook over hot water, stirring constantly, until the mixture thickens. Beat the eggs lightly and stir in the remaining milk. Add to the thickened mixture and continue cooking until very thick. Remove from heat, add the vanilla and chill. Mash 1 banana, add the lemon juice and fold into the chilled mixture. Spoon into the prepared crust. Heat the jelly with the water to soften and spoon it over the filling to glaze. Slice the remaining banana and use to garnish the top of the pie. Chill for 1 hour.
YIELD: 8 SERVINGS
Each serving contains 141 calories

LOW-CALORIE FLUFFY COCONUT PIE

PASTRY:

1 cup sifted all-purpose flour
⅛ teaspoon salt
⅓ cup shortening
2 tablespoons water

Set oven at 450 degrees F.
One 9-inch pie plate, greased

Combine the flour and salt. Blend in the shortening and add the water. Roll out on a floured board and arrange in the pie plate. Bake for 12 minutes. Cool.

FILLING:

1 tablespoon or 1 envelope unflavored gelatin
½ cup hot water
3 eggs, separated
2 tablespoons non-nutritive liquid sweetener
½ cup skim milk
1 teaspoon vanilla extract
¾ cup shredded coconut

Soften the gelatin in hot water. Combine the egg yolks, sweetener and milk in the top of a double boiler and cook, stirring, until thick. Remove from heat and stir in the softened gelatin. Chill for approximately 15 minutes or until the mixture begins to thicken. Beat the egg whites to stiff peaks and fold into the chilled gelatin mixture along with the vanilla and coconut. Pour into the baked pastry shell. Garnish, if desired, with extra coconut. Chill for 1 hour, or until firm.
YIELD: 8 SERVINGS
Each serving contains 189 calories

LOW-CALORIE WALNUT TORTE

Count your calories if you must, but don't deny yourself this heavenly bit of good eating in a nutshell.

3 eggs, separated
½ teaspoon orange extract
3½ teaspoons non-nutritive liquid sweetener
⅛ teaspoon salt
1 teaspoon lemon juice
1 cup walnuts, ground

Set oven at 350 degrees F.
One 8-inch-square baking pan, well greased

Combine the egg yolks, orange extract, 1½ teaspoons of sweetener and the salt in a bowl and beat until the yolks are very light and fluffy. Beat the egg whites until they form soft peaks; add the lemon juice and the remaining 2 teaspoons of sweetener and beat until stiff but not dry. Fold the egg whites and ground nuts into yolk mixture. Pour into the prepared baking pan and bake for about 35 minutes.

YIELD: 10 SERVINGS
Each serving contains 88 calories

LOW-CALORIE BLUEBERRY TARTS

If you're a calorie counter, and you love blueberries, do try this recipe for Low-Calorie Blueberry Tarts. They're delicious!

PASTRY:

1 *cup sifted cake flour*
½ *teaspoon salt*
⅓ *cup shortening*
1 *to* 2 *tablespoons ice water*

Set oven at 450 degrees F.
Seven individual tart pans

Combine the flour and salt; add the shortening until the mixture takes on the consistency of cornmeal; blend in the water. Roll out to ⅛ inch thick on a floured board and cut into 7 circles to fit the individual tart pans. Bake for 10 to 12 minutes, or until golden. Cool.

FILLING:

2 *cups* fresh *blueberries*
⅓ *cup water*
1 *tablespoon non-nutritive liquid sweetener or* 24 *tablets, crushed*
1 *teaspoon cornstarch*

Combine the blueberries, water and sweetener. Bring to a boil and cook for one minute. Drain and reserve the juice. Thicken the juice with the cornstarch and cook for about 2 minutes until clear and smooth. Gently combine with the berries; cool slightly and spoon into the tart shells.

YIELD: 7 TARTS
Each tart contains 160 calories

COOKIES

LOW-CALORIE LEMON COOKIES

½ cup shortening
1 tablespoon non-nutritive liquid sweetener
1 egg
1 tablespoon water
1 tablespoon lemon juice
½ teaspoon grated lemon peel
1 tablespoon vanilla extract
½ cup shredded dry coconut
2 cups sifted all-purpose flour
1 teaspoon baking powder
½ teaspoon salt

Set oven at 400 degrees F.
One large baking sheet, ungreased

Cream the shortening in a small mixer bowl at high speed. Add the sweetener, egg, water, lemon juice, lemon peel and vanilla. Beat until thoroughly blended. Mix in the coconut. Sift the flour, baking powder and salt together and add to the creamed ingredients, mixing thoroughly. Form the dough into a roll, 2 inches in diameter; wrap in waxed paper and chill for approximately 1 hour or until firm. Cut into thin slices and bake for 10 to 15 minutes.
YIELD: APPROXIMATELY 4½ DOZEN COOKIES
Each cookie contains approximately 35 calories

LOW-CALORIE APPLESAUCE COOKIES

1¾ cups cake flour
½ teaspoon salt
1 teaspoon cinnamon
½ teaspoon nutmeg
½ teaspoon cloves
1 teaspoon baking soda
½ cup butter
1 tablespoon non-nutritive liquid sweetener
1 egg
1 cup unsweetened applesauce
⅓ cup raisins
1 cup all-bran

Set oven at 375 degrees F.
One large baking sheet, greased

Sift the flour, salt, cinnamon, nutmeg, cloves and baking soda together. Beat the butter, sweetener and egg together until light and fluffy. Then add flour mixture and applesauce alternately, mixing

well after each addition. Fold in the raisins and all-bran. Drop by level tablespoonfuls spaced about 1-inch apart onto the prepared baking sheet and bake for 20 minutes, or until golden brown.
YIELD: APPROXIMATELY 4 DOZEN COOKIES
Each cookie contains approximately 39 calories

LOW-CALORIE CHOCOLATE BANANA DROP COOKIES

The best thing about these cookies (in addition to the fact that they're just plain good to eat) is that they're really low in calories.

2¼ cups sifted flour
2 teaspoons baking powder
¾ teaspoon salt
¼ teaspoon baking soda
⅔ cup butter
1 teaspoon vanilla extract
2 tablespoons water
2 eggs
1 tablespoon non-nutritive liquid sweetener or 24 tablets, crushed
2 medium bananas, mashed
1 square unsweetened chocolate, melted

Set oven at 400 degrees F.
One large baking sheet, greased

Sift the flour, baking powder, salt and baking soda together. Cream the butter, vanilla, water, eggs and sweetener together until creamy and smooth. Add the sifted flour mixture and mashed bananas alternately to the egg mixture and blend well but do not overmix. Stir in the melted chocolate and drop by rounded teaspoonfuls onto the prepared baking sheet. Bake at 400 degrees F. for 12 to 15 minutes.
YIELD: APPROXIMATELY 6 DOZEN COOKIES
Each cookie contains approximately 34 calories

LOW-CALORIE PEANUT BUTTER COOKIES

Dieters won't have to pass by this cookie jar empty-handed. It's filled with wonderfully good Peanut Butter Cookies, calorie-streamlined for weight-watchers.

¼ cup butter
½ cup peanut butter
5 teaspoons non-nutritive liquid sweetener
⅓ cup skim milk
1 egg
1 teaspoon vanilla extract
1 cup sifted all-purpose flour
1 teaspoon baking powder
½ teaspoon salt

Set oven at 375 degrees F.
One large baking sheet, greased

Combine the butter, peanut butter and sweetener and blend well. Combine the milk, egg and vanilla and add to the peanut butter mixture. Sift the flour, baking powder and salt together and add to the other ingredients, blending well. Drop by rounded teaspoonfuls onto the prepared baking sheet and bake at 375 degrees F. for about 15 minutes.

YIELD: APPROXIMATELY 52 COOKIES
Each cookie contains approximately 31 calories

LOW-CALORIE CHOCOLATE NUT BROWNIES

1 square unsweetened chocolate
⅓ cup butter
2 tablespoons non-nutritive liquid sweetener
2 teaspoons vanilla
2 eggs, beaten
1 cup sifted cake flour
½ teaspoon salt
½ teaspoon baking soda
¾ cup chopped walnuts

Set oven at 325 degrees F.
One 8-inch-square cake pan, greased

Melt the unsweetened chocolate and butter in a saucepan over a low flame. Remove from the heat and add the sweetener, vanilla and the beaten eggs. Stir until well blended. Add the sifted cake flour, salt and baking soda, and mix well. Stir in the chopped walnuts and pour into the prepared pan, making sure that the batter is evenly distributed. Bake at 325 degrees F. for 20 minutes. Cool and cut into bars.

YIELD: 32 BROWNIES
Each brownie contains 55 calories

PUDDING, SOUFFLÉS AND FROZEN DESSERT

LOW-CALORIE BAKED LEMON PUDDING

3 eggs, separated
¼ teaspoon salt
1 tablespoon non-nutritive liquid sweetener
⅓ cup lemon juice
2 tablespoons melted butter
5 tablespoons all-purpose flour
1½ cups skim milk

Set oven at 350 degrees F.
One 1-quart casserole, greased
One pan large enough to hold the casserole

Combine the egg whites, salt and sweetener and beat until stiff but not dry. Combine the egg yolks with all remaining ingredients and beat until smooth. Fold the egg yolk mixture gradually into the whites. Pour into the prepared casserole; set in a pan of hot water and bake at 350 degrees F. for 1 hour. Let the casserole cool in the pan of water to keep the pudding from shrinking.
YIELD: 6 SERVINGS
Each serving contains 117 calories

LOW-CALORIE BAKED LEMON SOUFFLÉ

2 tablespoons butter
2 tablespoons all-purpose flour
¼ teaspoon salt
1 tablespoon lemon juice
⅓ cup water
4 eggs, separated
grated rind of 1 lemon
2 tablespoons non-nutritive liquid sweetener

Set oven at 325 degrees F.
One 1-quart soufflé dish or straight-sided casserole, greased on the bottom only
One pan, large enough to hold the casserole

Melt the butter and blend in the flour and salt. Add lemon juice and water and cook until thick, stirring constantly. Cool. Beat the egg yolks and stir into the cooked ingredients along with the lemon rind.

Whip the egg whites and sweetener together until stiff but not dry and fold into the lemon mixture. Pour into the prepared casserole or soufflé dish and place in a pan of hot water. Bake at 325 degrees F. for 1 hour and 10 minutes, or until puffy and light and firm on top. Serve immediately.

YIELD: 6 SERVINGS
Each serving contains 96 calories

LOW-CALORIE ORANGE SOUFFLÉ

"The daintiest last, to make the end most sweet." Shakespeare surely would have approved our choice for a sweet ending to a perfect meal. For what could be more delectable than a light and golden Orange Soufflé? It's a heavenly bit of frou-frou, this classic dessert, and surprisingly easy to make.

4 *tablespoons butter*
5 *tablespoons flour*
¼ *teaspoon salt*
1 *cup skim milk*
3 *eggs, separated*
3 *tablespoons orange juice*
1 *tablespoon lemon juice*
1 *tablespoon grated orange rind*
1 *tablespoon non-nutritive liquid sweetener or 24 tablets, crushed*
½ *teaspoon vanilla extract*
⅛ *teaspoon almond extract*

Set oven at 325 degrees F.
One 1-quart casserole, greased on the bottom only
One pan large enough to hold the casserole

Melt the butter in the top of a double boiler. Blend in the flour and salt, followed by the milk. Cook, stirring constantly, until thick. Cool. Beat the egg yolks and add the juices and rind to the beaten egg yolks and blend well; then add to the cooled sauce. Beat the egg whites until stiff but not dry. Add the sweetener and flavorings and fold into the sauce. Spoon into the prepared casserole. Place in a pan of hot water and bake at 325 degrees F. for 1 hour, or until the point of a knife, inserted into the center, comes out clean. Serve at once.

YIELD: 6 SERVINGS
Each serving contains 144 calories

LOW-CALORIE VANILLA FROZEN DESSERT

1¼ cups skim milk
½ cup evaporated milk
2 teaspoons unflavored gelatin
½ cup hot water
1 tablespoon non-nutritive liquid sweetener
2 teaspoons vanilla extract
½ cup non-fat dry milk
½ cup ice water

Combine the skim milk and evaporated milk and scald. Soften the gelatin in hot water; add the sweetener and vanilla and blend into the scalded milk. Pour into a freezer tray and let cool at room temperature. When cooled, place in the freezer for approximately 30 minutes or until frozen around the edges and thick in the center. Remove from the freezer and beat in a chilled bowl until smooth. Combine the dry milk and ice water and beat until the consistency of whipped cream; fold into the gelatin mixture. Pour into 2 freezer trays and freeze until firm.

YIELD: 1 QUART OR 8 SERVINGS
Each serving contains 65 calories

SHERBET AND FRUIT DESSERTS

LOW-CALORIE ORANGE-PINEAPPLE SHERBET

1 6-oz. can frozen unsweetened orange juice concentrate
1 6-oz. can frozen unsweetened pineapple juice concentrate
3½ cups cold water
2 tablespoons non-nutritive liquid sweetener
1 cup non-fat dry milk

Set the refrigerator control at its coldest setting. Combine all ingredients, in the order listed, in a 2-quart mixing bowl. Beat just enough to blend. Pour into 2 ice cube trays and freeze for 1 or 2 hours, or until half-frozen. Remove from the freezer and beat at low speed in a chilled mixing bowl until softened; then beat at high speed for 3 to 5 minutes longer, or until creamy but not liquid. Pour into freezer containers or 2 ice cube trays and freeze.
YIELD: 20 SERVINGS (½ CUP EACH)
Each serving contains 58 calories

LOW-CALORIE STRAWBERRY SPONGE

1 envelope unflavored gelatin
½ cup hot water
1 tablespoon non-nutritive liquid sweetener
1½ tablespoons lemon juice
1 pint fresh strawberries, crushed
2 egg whites

One 3-cup dessert mold or 6 individual molds, lightly oiled

Put the gelatin and hot water in the top of a double boiler to soften. Add the sweetener and lemon juice and heat, stirring, until the gelatin dissolves. Remove from the heat and add the crushed strawberries. Let stand at room temperature until the mixture begins to thicken; then beat until light and fluffy. Beat the egg whites until stiff but not dry, and fold into the gelatin mixture. Spoon into the mold or molds and chill for about 1 hour, or until firm.
YIELD: 6 SERVINGS (½ CUP EACH)
Each serving contains 29 calories

LOW-CALORIE PRUNE WHIP

½ pound dried, pitted prunes
1 cup plus 1 tablespoon water
1 teaspoon unflavored gelatin
4 egg whites
2 teaspoons lemon juice
2 teaspoons non-nutritive liquid sweetener

Simmer the prunes in one cup of water until soft. Force them through a food mill with the juice they are cooked in. Soften the gelatin in the remaining 1 tablespoon of water and dissolve over a pan of hot water. Beat the egg whites until foamy. Gradually beat in the dissolved gelatin, lemon juice and sweetener. Then fold in the prune pulp and chill.
YIELD: 6 SERVINGS
Each serving contains 98 calories

LOW-CALORIE CHERRIES FLAMBÉ

1 tablespoon cornstarch
1 tablespoon non-nutritive liquid sweetener
¼ teaspoon salt
½ cup water
¼ teaspoon red food coloring
*2 ounces (4 tablespoons) brandy**
1 1-pound can water-packed sour cherries, drained (reserve liquid)

In chafing dish, table skillet or in a saucepan on the stove, combine the liquid from the cherries with the cornstarch to make a smooth paste. Add the sweetener, salt, water and red food coloring and cook, stirring constantly, until the mixture thickens. Stir in 1 ounce (2 tablespoons) of the brandy. Add the cherries, stirring until heated through. When ready to serve, warm the remaining ounce (2 tablespoons) of brandy in a large spoon or ladle over a candle or flame. Ignite the brandy and toss the flames over the cherries. Serve at once, alone or over dietetic ice cream or fruit. *(If desired, ½ oz. of lemon or orange extract may be used in place of the brandy to flame the dessert.)

YIELD: 4 SERVINGS
Each serving contains 99 calories

SAUCES

LOW-CALORIE CHOCOLATE SAUCE

1 tablespoon butter
2 tablespoons cocoa
1 tablespoon cornstarch
few grains salt
1 cup skim milk
2 teaspoons non-nutritive liquid sweetener
½ teaspoon vanilla extract

Melt the butter. Combine the cocoa, cornstarch and salt and blend into the melted butter until smooth. Add the milk and sweetener and cook over moderate heat, stirring constantly, until slightly thickened. Remove from heat and stir in the vanilla. Set pan in ice water and stir for approximately 5 minutes or until completely cold. The sauce will thicken as it cools.

YIELD: 1 CUP (16 TABLESPOONS)
Each tablespoon contains 16 calories

LOW-CALORIE LEMON SAUCE

- 1 *tablespoon cornstarch*
- 1/8 *teaspoon salt*
- 1 *cup water*
- 2 *teaspoons non-nutritive liquid sweetener*
- 1 *drop yellow food coloring*
- 1 *tablespoon grated lemon rind*
- 3 *tablespoons lemon juice*
- 2 *tablespoons butter*

Combine the cornstarch and salt. Gradually blend in the water and sweetener and cook over medium heat, stirring constantly, until thickened. Remove from heat and blend in the food coloring, lemon rind, lemon juice and butter. Cool.

YIELD: 1 1/4 CUPS SAUCE

Each 1/4 cup serving contains 48 calories

Index

Born in Lyons, France, Dominique D'Ermo came to this country after serving as head pastry chef in hotels and restaurants in both Paris and London; his positions included head pastry chef at the Père Bise in Talloires at age twenty and, subsequently, head pastry chef at Brown's Hotel in London.

In America, M. D'Ermo was the executive pastry chef at the Americana Hotel in Bal Harbour, Florida, from 1956 to 1962.

Participating in international pastry competitions all over the United States, he has been the recipient of the most distinguished culinary honors in this country, including twenty-three gold medals, as well as the gold medal for culinary achievement awarded by the French government in 1962. In 1974, the French Minister of Agriculture awarded M. D'Ermo the most coveted medal and title of Chevalier de l'Ordre du Mérite Agricole.

Formerly vice president of the Shoreham Hotel in Washington, D.C., and vice president of Princess Hotels International, M. D'Ermo is now the proprietor of Dominique's restaurant located close to the White House, in the heart of Washington, D.C.

Much praised by the press, food artists, and critics, Dominique's offers the best in classic French cuisine and is considered one of the top restaurants in Washington, D.C.